The Art of Selling and Organizational Productivity: Why Experienced and Talented Salespeople are a Dying Breed

Adrian Davieson, PhD

ISBN: 1537583220
ISBN-13: 978-1537583228

Published in the United States of America by Literary Focus Publishing Inc., in association with Createspace Publishing, an Amazon affiliate.

DEDICATION

My children: Adriana, Diana, Brett and Chelsea, who continue to inspire me to do more. To the unsung heroes of labor whose voices are often unheard; but who continue to work with dignity, pride and dedication to assuage a worthy cause. To the progress of mankind so that a lasting peace can reign in the global political landscape to benefit productivity and growth.

CONTENTS

"The Romantic Hero was no longer the knight, the wandering poet, the cowpuncher, the aviator, nor the brave young district attorney, but the great sales-manager, who had an Analysis of Merchandizing Problems on his glass-topped desk, whose title of nobility was "go-getter."

-Sinclair Lewis, Babbitt

Preface

Selling is an art, that once mastered, becomes personified and embedded in one's DNA, a sage once wrote. But to sell and be successful at it, one must first be willing to sell self in a way that the buyer would have no hesitation in making an offer. Selling and impression are interwoven, and intertwined in a unique way that one does not go without the other. Without that initial first impression, a sale can often not be made - at least that is how it works in automobile sales. Unlike selling insurance, stocks, shoes, clothes, houses, jewelries, pharmaceuticals, etcetera, where choices are often limited, automobiles abound in a ubiquitous way that the buyer can simply walk away and find a better and similar choice elsewhere, within a nearby radius or proximity. The irony is that the buyer may find a better bargain elsewhere! Automobiles, especially new ones, come, a dime a dozen, as dealerships dot every street, road and highway. The reason is not farfetched; automobiles of different and often similar brands are everywhere you turn!

Successful salespeople are often born with the talent to sell, a renowned social psychologist once said. But the sphere of deciphering the innate skills of salespeople is hardly within the domain of a social psychologist but when the phenomena of selling is closely discerned, one begins to see that not everyone can be successful at selling. The uniqueness of selling is a phenomenon by itself and, in a way, uncharacteristic, if not abysmal. The pro fession is almost non-noble, encompassed with indignity, and in many cases, saddled with scorn and disrespect from all and sundry. But the gifted and talented salesperson often ignores the obvious to achieve his laurels and plentitude – and there is abundance of monetary rewards for the gifted salesperson if he is willing to endure the ridicule of his chosen age-old, ignoble profession. Despite the often perceived baseness, lowness and meanness of the profession, by buyers, patrons and observers, the sales profession can be rewarding, gratifying, and prideful.

In the automobile retail industry, a salesperson is not just the person standing in front of the dealership, in the parking lot, dressed in shirt and tie, or in suit and tie, khaki pant and polo shirt, waiting for a customer. Merriam Webster defined a salesperson as "a person whose job is to sell things," which means that a salesperson can be the finance contractor (often referred to as finance manager), who sells finance products like extended warranty, gap insurance, credit life insurance, etcetera, in finance. A salesperson can also be the General Manager of the dealership who has the onerous responsibility of promoting, and fostering sales and profits at the dealership. In the dealership business, everyone is involved in selling; from service advisors to service technicians, and sales managers. Everyone is a salesperson. But the real selling is unarguably done by the frontline salespeople who have to do whatever it takes to sell the vehicles sold by the dealership. Frontline salespeople often receive commissions for every automobile sold. Unlike the other group of salespeople mentioned above, frontline salespeople have to make a sale for any modicum of livelihood. The other group of salespeople feed off the sweat of the frontline salespeople. Yet, the frontline salespeople are often the most marginalized group in the selling hierarchy, according to studies. Studies have shown that marginalization is one of the reasons experienced and talented salespeople are gradually becoming a dying breed in the profession.

A 2011 study published in ProQuest database found that marginalization accounts for 50% reason for voluntary turnover among salespeople in the automobile retail industry. The other reasons were low morale (30%), followed by lack of incentives (20%).

If salespeople are often perceived with contempt and scorn, why do people still enter the profession of selling? Having been in sales for over 25 years, I can give you a lot of reasons why people continue to enter the profession and why talented and experienced salespeople continue to leave.

As you read each chapter of this book, you will see the mystery, if not enigma, of automobile sales unraveled, in a way you have never seen it explained, decrypted, decoded, or deciphered before. Each chapter of this book will introduce, and indoctrinate you, into the arcane world of automobile sales, and on how a chosen few made it a lifelong, and almost noble profession that they have yet regretted.

Many talented and experienced salespeople have moved on to other more dignifying, and fulfilling careers, occupations and professions because, according to one veteran, "the business has become corrosive, and inundated with immaturity, amateurism, ignorance and dissatisfaction." But many newcomers do not agree that the profession is less noble than other professions. There is a reason for this belief. One of the most obvious is that many of the newcomers are only too glad to be in a profession where there is no standard decorum and where being ungainly dressed up is allowed, to flourish. Some of these newcomers had been in other forms of sales, selling shoes, insurance, jewelries, and are only too glad to belong to a more lucrative profession, where there is less decorum. But with time, the newcomers who are lucky to weather the storm of the rollercoaster business would find their dissatisfactions when the dust of newness settles down. That often happens with salespeople who have paid their dues, found their niches, or thought they did, and have paved their place in the profession, in a near-successful fashion!

The basic belief in the automobile retail business, as far as frontline salespeople are concerned, is that many are called but few will remain, meaning that only a few will choose to stay after they have suffered the blows and buffets of unpredictability that the art of selling is infamous for.

This book also covers the different characteristics and traits of leaderships and the role they have played in enhancing morale, positive behavior and motivation in the sales-force. The transactional leadership behavior, along with transformational and situational leaderships are examined to see what impact, if any, they have made in the behaviors and attitudes of salespeople in the automobile retail industry. As you go into the depth, and essence of this book, you will also come across feasible and effective factors that organizations can adopt to improve their processes such as quality control, Six Sigma, ISO 9000, and management by objective (MBO).

Chapter 1

The Salesman

There is an element of selling in every human endeavor. As humans we go about our daily routines craving that ultimate goal that we hope will elevate us to the pinnacle of success. Many often do not get to meet the preset objective, or achieve success at first attempts, even with subsequent attempts. But the diehards will often keep trying until success is achieved. To achieve any modicum of success we have to sell ourselves to our own objectives, beliefs and ambition. It is when we are convinced that we are on the right path that we go on to sell our ideas or plans to others. Now, selling our ideas or plans to others can come in different fashions, designs and dimensions. When we apply for a job, we sell our skills to potential employers. We often convince potential employers of our ability to succeed and accomplish given tasks and goals. Though the employer may not already know our ability to excel or accomplish a task, our words, body language and demeanor often create the impression, and deliver the message that we can. In essence we sell our skills to the highest bidder when we apply for jobs, or engage in a business transaction. Whether we fail or succeed depends on how we are able to convince others. It sometimes helps to know how to convince others; whether we are conversant and properly informed or not, it is all in the words and how the words are conveyed.

The most successful pastors and preachers today know how to use words to convince skeptics among worshippers to accept and believe in their sermons. A fast talking and convincing preacher will often end up with a sizable proportion of congregations because he has the gift to use words to convey religious beliefs and messages. Like a successful preacher, a successful salesperson has to be convincing, and able to exude confidence and self assurance. This is a gift many do not have, or have, but do not know how to explore and use. To use the gift of eloquence and, oratory, you have to recognize that you have it in you, and that you can effectively use it to convey your message. To do this, you do not necessarily have to be super eloquent; but you need to be effective in conveying the message with as much eloquence as you can muster. To be effective, you first want to avoid irrelevant topics that do not relate to the subject at hand. A good salesperson knows to stay on the subject and not deviate. Self timing is important in selling. You have to recognize when you are losing the customer in the process of over-talking. You want to avoid talking too much! This is where too much eloquence can be a disadvantage. Loose lips can cause you to sink your own sales!

The attributes of a good salesperson can almost be traced to a hundredfold of sterling qualities that are almost innate, that often come from within than without. These innate qualities are what make a successful salesperson what he is, or can be. These cadres of successful salespeople do not portray a desperate demeanor to prospects or potential customers; they simply present themselves as down-to-earth as possible, and almost trustworthy. Studies after studies have shown that salespeople are not trustworthy but it doesn't hurt to try to portray trustworthiness. The waterloo can only come when you try to oversell or overdo it! The public is already sold on the perception that salespeople are not trustworthy, that they will do whatever it takes to sell a product; so trying to present trustworthiness will only hurt your chances at selling, not aid it.

"If you are not going to be great in sales, go get another career, because it's too hard to do if you're not going to succeed," Grant Cardone, the author of *Sell or Be Sold: How to Get Your Way in Business and in Life*, wrote. In a way, Cardone made a valid point that selling can be hard, *if you make it hard*! In the over 25 successful years I have been selling, I have never considered selling to be a hard career. With hard work and serious effort, success can be achieved. Like most careers, you can do well if you choose to; it is all mental, and in determination. In Julius Caesar, William Shakespeare wrote that *the fault is not in our stars but in ourselves*, so in selling, our ability to achieve greatness is in our determination to succeed. To not succeed is not ingrained in our DNA but in ourselves. But like everything else in life, you have to be *called* and *talented*, to make it in sales! Unless you work extra hard to make up for the missing talent!

In the automobile retail industry, salespeople are the lifeblood of the business, even though they are often the least respected and recognized, for their productivity. Good salespeople are the engine that drives sustainability in the automobile industry, and are often the unsung heroes who immensely contribute to the growth of the industry; but are often not adequately rewarded for their efforts. In a 2011 doctoral research study where salespeople selling different brands of automobiles were surveyed, it was found that lack of incentives, disrespect, and lack of morale were some of the reasons salespeople do not enjoy job satisfaction as their peers in other professions.

To be successful in sales, a salesperson must know how to use time to his advantage by not wasting it. Closing a deal as fast as time permits is paramount, and crucial. But the salesperson has to be mindful not to be seen as being pushy and overbearing. Many customers do not like being pushed and rushed. They want to take their time as this is a crucial investment for them. They want to make sure they are making the right decisions. A good salesperson must learn to understand the customer's psyche and how to mildly encourage him to make the deal without appearing to be pushy. This can be tricky but allowing a breathing space to the customer, while gently pushing the process, can be the key to the successful closing of a sale.

A superb and successful salesperson maintains a strong presence of optimism, and believes in his craft. My basic philosophy when I was a rookie, and later a seasoned veteran was that if the owner of the dealership believes that he will sell his products to pay his overheads and make profits, why shouldn't I believe in myself that I will do well. This core belief has been a source of inspiration and optimism, in addition to my strong ambition to succeed. And in sales, to succeed you have to believe you will, or you will *not.* There is no room for negativity or pessimism in sales, as a downer will only take you to the ruins on a fast race to the bottom.

In sales, it is not uncommon to have a bad day or even a bad week but being able to persevere and weather the storm of unpredictability, and wade through the rough times, is part of the art of selling. The saying *that when the going gets tough the tough gets going,* is a valid philosophy in sales, because in sales there will be moments that may seem like a doomsday; but surviving those moments often takes iron determination and the willingness to beat all odds and succeed. A true salesperson will not allow a bad day or week to discourage and becloud him or her. To succumb to defeat and failure is a weakness by itself. One cannot, and should not, accept defeat in sales. Like in boxing for example, just because you are knocked down does not mean you will lose the fight! Many great and successful boxers have turned knockdowns to their advantage by fighting harder and prevailing at the end. There are boxers though that will succumb to one knockdown and become a punching bag for the opponent to prevail and win the fight. Such boxers often become failures in boxing because they did not have the will and determination to turn a disadvantage into an advantage. A true fighter will see a blessing in a disadvantage. For such fighters, a knockdown becomes a wake up call that defeat is imminent.

Like a successful boxer, a talented and skilled salesperson will not let a bad day ruin his month. A bad day is an opportunity to reexamine what is not being done right and to make adjustments and improvements for a better tomorrow! And there will be a better tomorrow for the determined salesperson who is willing to work harder to succeed. The saying that every dog has its day may be true sometimes for salespeople who count on luck for a good payday. But such *manna* may not always occur if you rely on luck to make a paycheck. You may have your dog-day sometimes, but such dog-days will be seldom or even nonexistent in the future. Just because the first customer that you approached at the dealership's parking lot bought a vehicle without giving you a hassle, and a hard time by test-driving half of the vehicles on the lot before telling you he was looking to buy in the near future, does not mean it will always be rosy. There will be customers that will take you through the wringer by making you test-drive several cars with them, and then negotiate each vehicle, and afterward tell you, hours later that they are in the first stage of shopping! Yes, there will be such customers. If you are not strong-hearted and determined, a window-shopping customer can hurt your spirit and weaken your resolve to make money.

To make it in sales, you have to learn how to handle customers who come to the dealership to test-drive and negotiate a vehicle they are not ready to buy. It is easy to spot a customer who is not in the market but wanting to test-drive cars and test your product knowledge. Whenever a customer starts to ask you ridiculous customers about a vehicle such as the length and width of the vehicle, size of the battery, torque, and the type of brake pads on the vehicle, it means the customer may not be a serious customer. The first thing you want to do is to test such a customer to see if he or she is ready to buy before wasting your precious time. The most effective test is to tell the customer that the dealership is having a special promotion for that day with zero down and zero interest, and *up to* 50% off, with approved credit. The catch will be the phrase *up-to* 50% off. Wait a few seconds to see how the customer reacts to the comment. If the customer ignores it, then try another, but be careful not to appear pushy or overzealous. Ask the customer when he or she plans to buy, and if he or she is buying anytime soon. Usually a sincere customer will tell you upfront that he or she is not ready to buy but in the first stage of shopping. If they tell you they are in the first stage of shopping, gently probe for more understanding and clarification. If they are sincere enough to tell you they are shopping, they might just buy that very day or the next day, depending on how you impress them. There are insincere customers that will say they are buying soon, depending on the deal. Such customers can make you try harder in vain; especially if they give you false hope that they are going to buy. With those types of customers, you are likely to waste your entire day, hoping they will buy, only to be disappointed, hours later. A good salesperson will quickly improvise by quickly and gently getting the customer to reveal his or her intentions, or falsity. Knowing how to improvise and to do-away with time-wasting customers takes natural talent and skill in understanding the psyche of human minds, which according to psychologists often have multiple dimensions.

The first obvious dimensions of human minds are the hidden intentions that are seldom revealed during interactions. Understanding the ulterior motive of human intentions is to first unmask that hidden intention without creating a suspicion, experts say. Usually, in-depth but subtle approach can be effective in unraveling a customer that is out to burn and waste your time. Some customers do not realize that you are on commission, that without a sale you will not get paid. Some however know but do not care about wasting your time. The latter types of customers are the ones you want to watch out for. They are the ones that will stop by a dealership to kill time by test-driving vehicles they have no intention of buying. Some of these customers will even go to the extent of negotiating prices, and even making you go through the trouble of preparing the vehicle for delivery! Sometimes though, a flaky customer can become a true and *real* customer; that is why it is imperative to carefully understand the motive of a customer before dismissing him or her as a flake. The *flake* might turn out to be a real buyer!

Tact and diplomacy can be an effective way of unmasking a real customer. Sometimes, it may help to do a little selling, by being a true salesperson. The way to do that is to talk as little as possible about the vehicle, by concentrating on the safety features, gas mileage, resale value, and technology package that came with the vehicle. Spend as little time as possible to cover all these basic areas, without being too in-depth. You can tell when a customer is impressed with your sales tactics. The customer will naturally ask a few questions, which you will do your best to answer. If you do not know the answers, change the subject as gently, and as abruptly as possible, and talk about unrelated subjects such as the finance specials available on the vehicle. Doing this takes tact, and subtlety.

The salesman has insurmountable odds stacked against him at any given situation. In an attempt to make a sale, he must do everything possible to overcome some of the oddities against him. The first is to be as friendly, and as firm as necessary when meeting a potential buyer for the first time. The impression created at that first encounter will either result in a sale or failure to make a sale. First impression counts and goes a long way in sales. The way and manner you impress a customer at first encounter will either kill your sale, or enhance your opportunity to make a sale. To do this, the salesperson must shed away the negative perceptions that have become part and parcel of the sales profession. Some of the public perceptions about salespeople are that (1) salespeople are untrustworthy; (2) that they lie unconscionably; (3) that they are thieves that will steal a customer's down payment; (5) that they will cheat to make a sale; (6) that they are lowlifes; (7) that they are crooks; and (8) that they have no integrity.

To overcome these negative perceptions, the first impression a salesperson must make at first encounter is to first show civility, and a subtle superiority in personality and in demeanor over the customer. Excessive display of superiority can be interpreted as being pompous which can instantly be a turn-off, and loss of sale. One of the most effective ways to impress a customer is how you dress and talk. If your clothes look like they have been slept on, and dirty, with a three-day stubble on your chin and face, you are presenting a poor image that a potential customer will quickly distrust. This can be worsened if you reek of cigarette smoke or worse still, if your breath ranks with alcohol and cigarette! That can be gross and coarse! It is equally bad if you approach a customer with a cigarette smoldering between your fingers! Your chances of a sale can die a sudden death if the customer is not a smoker. Since secondhand smoking is as dangerous as direct smoking, nonsmokers often avoid smokers. Customers who really want to buy from you will tell you to put out the cigarette while others will simply tell you in an unfriendly manner that they are just shopping, and want to be left alone to look around. What they are indirectly telling you is that they are looking for a *real* salesperson that will not poison their lungs with cigarette smokes!

Competition in the automobile retail industry is cutthroat, and to earn a customer's business, one must be adroit in customer relations, and in understanding human psyche. According to experts, humans only respond to impression and positive personality traits. Confidence in approach and speech can create lasting impression that will subconsciously create a subtle control in people, experts say. When you have cultivated, and earned a customer's respect, you can control the sale from that point onward. It can be counterproductive to mistake a customer's acquiescence, for foolishness. Many a salespeople have made this mistake only to regret it afterwards. Don't think you are in control because a customer is agreeing, or appearing to do so, to everything you say. Some customers have a habit of listening, and reaching instant judgment about you on the spot, without you knowing. The best approach is to always never to try to underestimate a customer. When you underestimate a customer, you are likely to lose! Many customers are wary about salespeople, and when you try to entrap them into a sale, they will quickly spot it! Such insidious approach will only harm your chances of making a sale!

When selling, you don't want to be too much of a salesman as excessive sales techniques can ruin a sale. You can talk about the product without overdoing it. Some salespeople believe that displaying substantive and excessive product knowledge will impress the customer. This is not necessarily true. While knowledge about the product can be helpful, it will not help your sale if you spend too much time talking about the product! Only a small proportion of customers that buy vehicles actually care about product knowledge. At a time when technology is ubiquitous, the average customer has already done his homework before coming to the dealership. What a customer is mostly interested in is the deal, and not lectures about the vehicle! Though product knowledge is good in sales, it can also be a disadvantage if you cannot impress the customer with a deal. The essence of selling is to be able to make a deal with as little hassles as possible so that the customer will have a pleasant buying experience.

Chapter 2

Why Some Salespeople Fail and Others Succeed

Steve Job, the founder of Apple, once said that "you can never give up if you want to succeed." In sales, to give up is to not want to succeed. A successful salesperson must be dogged, astute, and subliminally aggressive, if he must succeed. In the sales profession, aggression is an integral part of success while hard-work is a must-have attribute. Laziness and the ineffectual habit of watching the clock can be a debilitating factor that can limit and weaken the chances of success.

Successful salespeople do not care about time and how fast or slow it is going; all they care about is trying to make a sale and beat the clock! A true and successful salesperson will stay as long as it takes at the dealership to make a sale, without accepting defeat and going home. "He wants to justify the day's productivity and output and there will be no going home until a deal is made," an expert wrote about the iron mindset of a successful salesperson. It is not just hunger and the willingness to assuage a hunger that drives a successful salesperson; it is the uncanny willingness to succeed. He believes he has to succeed, rain or shine and that nothing will, and should stop him. Without these core beliefs, a salesperson is unlikely to succeed. He has to believe in his ability to persevere and withstand the torture of a tough day. And it is only when he exercises patience that he will earn the day's blessing of a sale, at dusk, near sunset. While the early prime hours of the day may defeat him, he will not give up, even when it seems it is hopeless and undoable, to the bystander and onlooker. But with iron determination, and utmost optimism, he has little left outside these domains. He cannot see a life outside the realms of success. He forces himself to stay within the confines of success as his last bastion. He knows no other way. He cannot succumb to what seems too obvious but hopeful.

Sales are generally not a profession for the lazy but for the diehard and persistent ironclad person who wants to succeed and make a decent living out of the profession. Selling is only worth it, if it is profitable to the seller, Michael Dell, the founder of Dell Computers reportedly said. Selling requires a great deal of patience and persistence, if one intends to succeed at it. In sales, there will always be the danger of a looming failure but being able to recognize the possibility of failure is often what spurs the extra effort to do well. The possibility of failure can be an inspiration to succeed, experts said. But it is not just recognizing the prospect of failure that spurs success it is actually making serious efforts that heralds success.

When faced with challenges to survive, humans often excel by exceeding expectations in achievements. The light bulb, airplane, computer, cell phone, and many innovative products wer e created due to the obstacles and challenges that their absence in our existence presented. An ancient Greek philosopher, Plato, once said that "necessity is the mother of invention." The implication is that problem often inspires, and motivates the need for a solution or creativity. That is also true in every endeavor. When we are faced with needs, we do our best to satisfy such needs. When obstacles occur, innovative minds look for solutions, and then, ultimately success beckons. But trying to achieve success is not enough; one must be willing and ready to set a goal, a form of objective for success. To do this, you must have a roadmap for success, of what you want to do and how you plan to accomplish it. You have to be true to yourself, and be specific as to the purpose of the set goals. The challenges often encountered by those that seek success are not having enough motivation to create the zeal to succeed. The motivation should be beyond trying to making a living; it should be trying to get *rich* in the process. Now, that is a motivation. When the prospects of wealth are in the offing, the sky can become the limit!

There is an old cliché that he who asks for direction will never get lost. That is true with success. Successful salespeople often seek answers from those who have succeeded in the field. While that can help, it is the inner drive of the seeker that matters most in the quest for the Holy Grail of success. Asking questions on how to succeed as a salesperson from those who have succeeded in the business is a crucial part of learning the pathway to becoming successful. It is okay to ask questions but the questions that matter the most are quality questions that pattern to the business of selling. A renowned social psychologist once wrote that the best way to succeed in any endeavor is to emulate those who have done well in the business. Emulating successful people can also include asking quality questions on how to succeed. A salesperson can also learn from customers by gently probing for details about their interests and the reason they chose a particular product. Whether you know it or not, there is a great deal to learn from customers. While learning from a customer can be a good resource, it can also be a disadvantage if you make yourself look like a novice or a rookie who is learning the ropes. Some customers will help you by answering your questions as you go through the sales process. But some will ask for a more experienced salesperson to help and guide them through the purchase process. Many customers prefer experienced salespeople, especially customers who have credit problems and are strapped for cash. They know that an experienced salesperson will know how to cut corners and find the right financing for them.

Another reason some salespeople don't do well in sales is that many often neglect, and ignore the obvious. When meeting a potential customer, it is often imperative to know the needs and goals of the customer. Make sure you understand the customer's objective and concerns. Making an effort to understand these crucial things about a potential customer will enable you to decipher the customer's hesitation, when it comes. You can quickly figure out why a customer will hesitate about making a decision immediately, if you understand the customer's goals and concerns. If the customer's goal is to save more money, and you understand that money is an issue in his/her decision to buy, you can quickly solve the problem by offering a zero down option, that will allow the customer to make the purchase without a down-payment. When you understand a customer's needs, you can almost certainly handle any objection and hesitation that he/she may come up with. But to do this, you have to gently probe the customer for details about his/her objectives, goals and concerns.

A crucial aspect about becoming a successful salesperson is the ability to listen to a customer's requests. Most salespeople do not listen. They are often too busy doing the talking that they don't bother to listen to the customer. To successfully make a sale, you have to *listen* to the customer. Many customers come to the dealership ready to make a purchase but as soon as they run into the wrong salesperson they can get confused and change their minds. A bad salesperson can create confusion in the mind of a customer by either talking too much about the product, or showing too many products. Many customers often do their homework before coming to the dealership, by surfing the internet for the type of vehicle and color they want. If you are lucky to meet such a customer, you want to listen to the customer by not trying to change what they came for. Don't try to suggest a different option as that can lead to confusion, and postponement of the purchase.

The only reason you should ever make a suggestion to the customer is when the customer picks a color that you don't have or a vehicle that is clearly beyond his/her means. But before you make this premature decision as to what a customer can afford, you want to ask questions about the customer's budget and if he/she is paying cash or seeking financing. Don't ask these questions unless you have created an ample discussion that gradually leads to budgets and payments. You don't want to presuppose what a customer can afford! Some customers get offended when you start to ask about their finances before showing them the vehicle or product they came for. You want to show them the vehicle first, and then when you are sure it is safe to ask, then you can ask if they are paying cash or financing. Even to ask that, you will need to be very careful as you can send the wrong message. Tell the customer about the finance specials the dealership is currently offering. At that point, the customer will lead you to your next question. Some customers will bluntly tell you that they don't want to spend too much money or that they don't have good credit. At that point, you have to ask questions that relate to their comments. Again, do not presuppose anything, until the customer gives you the clue or hint!

The problem that many unsuccessful salespeople have is that they often answer their own questions without allowing the customer to answer! Many customers see a garrulous salesperson as rude, if not obnoxious. The ideal way to handle a customer is to listen and answer his/her questions as briefly as possible, without adding unnecessary personal anecdotes. In truth, the customer is not there to listen to your personal story; he/she is there to make a purchase! Save your personal stories for your coworkers! A good salesperson knows that a customer will tell him what he wants if he handles the customer properly, with respect. Respect is another thing that customers crave and love. The average customer is somewhat sensitive, experts have said. And when you show respect at first encounter, you unmask an aspect of the customer that he/she may not know is being unmasked! A famous psychologist once said that humans love being respected, and that respect breaks down human barriers. With customers, a display of respect can break down the initial barrier, and will also create a first positive impression about your skill as a salesperson. Showing respect will portray you as polished and well mannered which many customers appreciate.

Given the right opportunity, a true and successful salesperson can learn all he needs to know about a customer without making the customer feel the pressure. When you can successfully make a customer feel comfortable with you to earnestly talk without inhibitions, you have half sold that customer. The next step in the sales process will be easy if the salesperson says the right things, and behaves appropriately. Don't try to give unwanted compliments as that can be interpreted as patronizing and unsavory. You want to be as polite, firm, and as mildly friendly as possible without appearing to be too anxious to please. Just as you can lose a sale for being rude, you can also lose a sale for being too nice!

Words are silver while silence is golden, and it is widely known that loose lips can sink ships, and in the sales profession, it can sink sales. While it helps to introduce yourself, and explain the product you are selling, it does not help your sales to be too *in-depth.* A quick summary and less talk is pivotal in every sales transaction.

It will surprise you to know that most successful salespeople do not have in-depth knowledge about the vehicles they sell. They know enough to present the vehicles to customers but when it comes to fully knowing the vehicle, from traction controls to the major technical explanations about the vehicles, they wouldn't know. But the best part is that they create enough rapport with the customers that product knowledge becomes a nonissue. Just as it will surprise you to know that the best salesperson at the dealership may not have in-depth knowledge about the vehicles he sells, so it will surprise you to know that the person that knows the vehicle in-depth at the dealership is often the most unproductive salesperson in the dealership! The product knowledge wiz is hardly a successful salesperson! The successful salesperson does not have the time or inclination to be learning the details about the vehicles he sells! He feels all he needs to know is the size of the engine, the gas mileage, cruise control, and the name of the vehicle! He believes his personality will sell the vehicle, and he is often right! Personality sells!

One of the reasons most salespeople fail is that they do not know how to inculcate passion in their game. When selling, the passion you display about the product can make the customer like the product more. When talking about the products or vehicles you sell, you have to apply as much passion as you can without overdoing it. Let the customer see that you believe in your products. It will be incongruous to a customer for a salesperson that sells a Honda to drive a Toyota product. The impression that you create is that you do not like the product you sell. If you are passionate about your product, the customer can get the impression that you also use the product, or drive the same brand of vehicles you sell. Sometimes your passion about what you sell can make a customer assume you also drive the same vehicle! Passion tends to get a customer's full attention and it helps when they know you are passionate about your wares!

Another reason passion is a good indicator of success is that when a salesperson is passionate about his/her job, the chances for success is greater, because of the enthusiasm that will be brought to every task. That enthusiasm can stem from love for your career and your willingness to succeed at it. Most successful people love what they do, and because they love their job, they put in more efforts than those who hate what they do. In life, everyone needs motivation to succeed. For some, that motivation can come from the love they have for the job, while monetary incentives can serve as an inspiration for others. The love one has for what he/she does can also lead to commitment and job satisfaction. Experts believe that monetary incentive can also produce commitment and dedication, which in turn can lead to job satisfaction. But the strongest predictor of success is when an employee is passionate about the job. In terms of greater zeal to succeed, monetary incentive becomes the sole predictor of success in the sales profession.

Experts believe that when a salesperson is passionate about the vehicles he/she sells that the enthusiasm therein will reflect in every sales transaction, and in every discussion. While the act of being passionate can create love for career, which can translate into greater sales, it can also lead to what psychologists call subconscious overindulgence of love for the products one sells. Too much love can lead to overselling which can be a turn-off and a counterproductive factor that can have a diminishing return! Excessive love and enthusiasm for the product one sells can limit the ability to negotiate and cut a deal. If a salesperson believes that his/her product is too good, he/she will create inflexibility which can result in lack of sales.

A successful salesperson can be passionate to some extent and still be able to control the enthusiasm that ensues from the love for the product. Rather than let the love for the products he sells overflow, the successful salesperson will be cognitive of the obvious, that he/she is not the only one with the product, that the nearest competitor may have a better and cheaper selection. Recognizing that once a sale is lost it is gone forever the successful salesperson will quickly negotiate an attractive deal that will entice the customer to make a quick decision to purchase. Some salespeople or even sales managers will often say a vehicle is too nice and therefore if a set amount of profit is not realized that all offers will be rejected. This is a wrong way of generating sales and profits. You cannot turn away customers because you feel a vehicle or product is too nice to sell at a certain price, especially when your competitor is selling a similar product, *probably for less!* Whenever you come across a salesperson or sales manager with such an excessive enthusiasm for a product, you are likely to find a failed salesperson or an unsuccessful sales manager. Sometimes it is better to make a $1500 profit and satisfy a customer who may bring in more referrals than to try to make $4500 profit and turn away customers. Always remember that there is another seller a mile away selling the same product, at possibly a cheaper price. Don't think your product is too good that you have to make *all the money* on it. Thinking so can make your product stay longer on your lot than necessary.

A smart way of selling is to sell as many vehicles as possible even if they yield small profits for each unit. Every little drop of water can create a mighty ocean; so it is with profits. There is a greater profit advantage in higher numbers than in bigger profits in smaller numbers. Always remember that the more customers you sell the greater your chances of generating repeat customers and referrals. If you limit your customer base to excessive-profit-oriented base, you will have limited customers, and limited repeat customers and referrals. There are greater goods in larger numbers than in smaller numbers.

In Adam Smith's epochal book entitled *The Wealth of Nations*, he wrote, inter alia, that "the chance of gain is naturally over-valued," especially if the process is wrongly manipulated to generate profits. Smith added that it may be necessary to "learn from the universal success of lotteries, in which the whole gain compensated the whole loss." There is no doubt that the strength of numbers can generate its own cumulative profits, which in turn can indemnify the future against losses. A shortsighted salesperson may look at the immediate advantage of high profits while overlooking the profits of the future, and miss out on the natural orbit of sustainability and continuous flow of business and profits. Unfettered greed and lack of foresight can often be the hallmark of an unsuccessful salesperson. He only sees the moment and cannot see beyond his nose! He would rather sacrifice tomorrow for today, not realizing that there will always be tomorrow!

To protect tomorrow against bad sales, it is imperative, if not pivotal, to always put customer satisfaction first before profit. While the dealership's policy may put a strong emphasis on profit than on customer satisfaction, it is customer satisfaction that creates sustainability in any business. In order to really have strong and lasting customer satisfaction, it is crucial that a culture of *genuine* customer care is established in the workplace so that customers will feel welcome and become psychologically indebted to the dealership as the only place to do business. When such a genuine culture is enshrined, some customers will always be duty-bound to do business at your dealership, even when your prices may be higher than the competition. The truth is that some customers will pay more for good service even when it is obvious they can get a better deal elsewhere. To have such loyal customers, the excitement has to be genuinely ubiquitous enough to be obvious that it is real. This is not hard to do, as it will shine through if it is genuine!

Building on being genuine can create a successful sales transaction that will carry on, to the future, and create repeat businesses. Being genuine does not translate into bragging about the huge profits made on a particular deal! Being genuine means being sincere and not taking advantage of your customers. While it is good to make profits, it is not always good to make your customers seem like idiots whom you ripped off. If you had a good day and made profits, keep the celebration to yourself by not spreading the word that you had a good profit day. While doing so may temporarily boost your ego and personality, it can also hurt your chances of future sales. You may not understand how this can hurt future sales because you bragged a little. But it can, at least psychologically. Taking advantage of others and bragging about it can have its unforeseen consequences which can rob you off immediate and future opportunities. It is the natural way of things. If you are blessed with a good day, keep it that way!

In sales, a good salesperson will always be focused and aggressive, and unwilling to allow distraction sway him from his objective. The objective of a successful salesperson is to sell and sell until the day is done! A successful salesperson sees the sky as his ultimate limit, and eyes the pinnacle of success as his goal. To achieve this Holy Grail of mindset takes being born with the zeal and hunger to succeed. Just wanting to succeed is not enough. You have to crave and fight for success for success to be yours. Unlike manna from heaven, success has to be earned. There is no faking success. Once earned, it becomes a beacon that shines like a halo over its ultimate conqueror!

One of the reasons most salespeople fail in this not-so-noble but can-be lucrative profession is that they often do not know how to be successful! To be successful in any endeavor, you have to brace yourself for success, and be willing to make the necessary sacrifices that success demands. Success demands that you be determined, dedicated, willing, and aggressive. In the quest for success, there is no room for laziness and fatigue. The motivation that success creates erases fatigues and brings on its own *renewable* energy. Hunger in the process becomes infinitesimal because success assuages physical hunger. The need for nutritional food is often less urgent where success is alive and beckoning! Success quenches physical hunger and replaces it with inner glow of bliss, and solace, which together, create unending psychological satisfaction.

The herald of the inner glow of bliss that success creates builds enthusiasm that becomes part of the successful salesperson's persona. This type of enthusiasm is often imbued with confidence and self assurance. Once enthusiasm is achieved, optimism sets in and takes root. Successful people are always optimistic and enthusiastic about the prospect of achieving more success. In sales, a positive mood and attitude can yield productivity while a negative mood can create the opposite – failure! A positive mood and an enthusiastic mindset can become positively contagious, and impact those who become acquainted with this harbinger of success. Customers appreciate positive people or what experts call the *can-do* people. No one likes negative people because they have a doomsday air about them that runs off potential customers. Negative people are, according to psychologists, associated with unpleasantness and bad luck.

A positive salesperson who believes he/she can make a paycheck when there is only one day left to do so, can achieve his/her goal easily. In the same token, a negative salesperson who believes it is too late to do so will often end up not being able to do so because the faith is not there that it is possible. There is nothing impossible when one is determined, and positive. And in many ways, there is a strong presence of faith in determination and in a positive attitude. And faith as they say moves mountains and such a miraculous feat is not beyond the capability of a positive and successful salesperson.

Another positive characteristic of a successful salesperson is that he does not have time for idle conversations, and when he allows himself to do so, he keeps one eye on the lookout for success. He is ever watchful, even when it seems to untrained eyes that he is slacking. In the psyche, and lexicon of a successful salesperson the word *slacking* does not exist as he works hard to eliminate that word from his world. Positive and enthusiastic salespeople seldom talk about failure as the word does not exist in their world. Their determination and the faith they have prevent the infusion of failure in their life. Failure, to them, is a natural habitat for losers and the lazy. In the domain of success, there is no room for failure or laziness. Every aspect of the life of a true successful salesperson is entirely transformed with optimism and the mindset to succeed and beat the odds. Successful salespeople do not have the time or willingness to dwell on negativity as they are too busy courting success! When faced with the impossible, they often dwell on solutions to the impossible rather than quitting. Quitting is never an option for the determined and positive salesperson. Rather than see an unpleasant and negative situation as obstacles, the successful salesperson sees opportunities. He thrives when faced with challenges.

Like a boxer who wins a fight while under pressure, the successful salesperson knows that pressure is good for him. He thrives under pressure. His worst enemy is complacency and unearned accolades that detractors would pour on him to water down his determination and drive. He sees through the motives of those that would shower him with praises. He knows they are there to create complacency in him, so that he would relax in his aggressiveness. He forbids compliments because he does not believe he has earned enough success to deserve any compliments. Most of all, he abhors detractors that would shower him with praises when he is feeling shortchanged. He refuses to be dragged down by unsavory and unearned accolades. His quest is the reward for his labor, not empty accolades!

Though successful salespeople do not like unearned accolades and empty praises, they do crave humongous results and the sacrificial consequences therein. When it seemed as if things are not going the way they are intended, they do fight hard to correct the course of things. They have no time to blame others as they seek solutions to change the foreseeable doom of failure. They don't want to see the day that failure will be at their doorsteps to deliver the depressing news of defeat. It is the fear of failure that drives the determined salesperson to succeed even when faced with difficulties, and fear of not meeting his personal quota. The one thing the determined salesperson does not do is blame others. He would rather take the blame if things did not go the way he intended. But in his world, things always go his way as he fights to keep it that way. The spirit of aggressiveness that lives and breathes in him does not allow him to fail, and that spirit is like a twin to him, or an alter-ego – a voice that propels him to continue to do well and never to look back. That voice is his salvation and a constant reminder that he is not different from others, that the only thing that sets him apart is his determination and willingness to succeed.

Many salespeople know that hard work pays; and they need the constant reminder that their willingness to work hard, and the dedication they bring to their job, will continue to bolster and boost their success. They are constantly aware that they must do whatever is necessary to succeed, and that reminder always helps them to achieve the impossible. In the horizon of the successful salesperson, it is his actions he believes will determine his output and success. He does not allow things that he cannot control, to bother him. He has his eyes on only one goal, and that is success. He sees himself as being first married to his quest for success before anything else. He is obsessed but not overwhelmingly obsessed to where he becomes depressed when things don't go his way. He does not expect things to go his way at all times as he knows he has to fight for what he wants, with his ironclad determination. He fears something might be amiss if things go his way when it is not earned. He loves the fight for success and enjoys the returns.

Chapter 3

Salespeople's Productivity

Productivity is the lifeblood of any business; and in many ways productivity is organizational sustenance, and without it, organizations would have a short lifespan. In the automobile retail industry, salespeople are the direct producers that bring businesses and opportunities to the industry. An automaker will be doomed without the services of reliable and talented salespeople. And salespeople are the engine that drives productivity in automobile retail industry. And the sad part of the significance of salespeople to retail organizations is that they are often the most marginalized part of the organizational structure. The reason for this is that most automobile retail organizations are structured in a top-down hierarchical culture which often finds salespeople at the bottom of the stratum.

Studies have shown that the reason for salespeople's constant mobility is the indignity they are subjected to, in organizations, including automobile dealerships where they are the pivots of sustainability. At dealerships' top-down organizational structure, salespeople are often relegated to the background as if they don't count in the scheme of things, but in reality the top-down organizational culture will crumble without the services of salespeople who dealerships depend on to sell their vehicles. Dealerships not only have to depend on salespeople to sell their vehicles but to solicit businesses for their survival.

When things are not going well for the dealership and sales and profits are down, salespeople often take the blame for the failure. And when things are rosy, and dealerships are making profits, management and those at the top hierarchy often reap the rewards, leaving salespeople to pick the crumbs, if any. From time immemorial, salespeople have never enjoyed the significance of their pivotal positions in organizations, and this is especially true in automobile retails, where salespeople take blames for everything, from poor customer satisfaction, to poor sales, and customers' complaint. The unending issues and problems that beset salespeople's job satisfaction continue to be that dealerships and their top hierarchies do not respect them, and often downplay their significance. Low morale and insufficient job satisfaction are prevalent in the sales force, according to studies. The reason is that salespeople do not often feel secure on their jobs as they are constantly subjected to the lowliest of tasks at dealerships. While they are not necessarily in the lowest strata of the organization, they are treated poorly, below employees in the lower stratum! Disrespect and indignity continue to plague and haunt salespeople's comfort in organizations such as automobile organizations, according to studies.

The fact that dealerships treat their productive sales-force with scorn and disrespect is almost part of human nature. According to social psychologists, the most important things in our lives often receive the worst treatment, and in many cases are often less maintained, until we lose them, and their usefulness becomes crucial in our lives. Salespeople come a dime a dozen, but talented and skilled salespeople are rare, and dealerships that are lucky to have them often do not realize what they have until they are gone. Good salespeople are like rare gems, and because they are what they are, they often come with high maintenance, meaning they come with their 'heats.' Good things also have their downsides, so it is with talented salespeople. They will bring you the goose, but you have to pay, and sometimes, that price is the hassle that their presence heralds. Just as in life, there can be no gain without pain. With talented salespeople, you will have the gains of productivity if you can take the pains that they bring with it.

While salespeople are the productive organ of dealerships it is really the talented and skilled salespeople that are the real engine of productivity in organizations. Talented salespeople are the ones that sell the most units, and bring the most profits to dealerships. Though they don't often get the respect they deserve, they often make you respect them. They demand their own respects, and by so doing, often run afoul of dealerships' policies, rules and regulations. They set their own rules and do not obey rules set for them. They want to be obeyed! In a way, they are oligarchs in their talented domains. They are the chieftains of their talented realms and anyone that challenges them will always certainly meet with his/her waterloo. Though they are extremely aggressive, they know how to channel their aggressiveness to productivity.

Though talented salespeople are not quitters but they will quit a dealership that does not treat or pay them well. They want to be paid for their skills and talents, and are ready to meet the quotas the dealership is willing to set for them. Sometimes, if not always, they will beat expectations in productivity. But they have zero tolerance for oppressors or wannabe oppressors. They are oppressors themselves and do not like being challenged to a duel, even if they will win. The irony of it is that competitiveness brings out the best in talented and skilled salespeople. The more he is challenged the greater the productivity he brings to the table. And it is often better when there is a monetary incentive at stake for him. His productivity knows no bounds when he has an added incentive to excel and break his own records.

A good organization will know how to feed the engine of productivity that is the talented salesperson. Incentive is the inspiration that propels the inborn productivity in the talented salesperson. When he knows he is being compensated for his talent and skills, he soars and makes the sky his limit. But that engine of productivity will slow down when dealerships attempts to cheat him out of his rightful proceeds. Many greedy dealerships often foolishly try to cheat their talented and skilled salespeople out of their well deserved commissions only to suffer the consequences! It is not wise to limit the engine of your organization's productivity.

Many dealerships believe they can replace talented and skilled salespeople with mediocre, off-the-street people, only to find out the hard way that talents and skills are traits that are limited to a chosen few! You cannot substitute talent with mediocre! A true successful salesperson is indispensable in any organization and to replace him/her can be detrimental to the survival of the organization. Though a lot of dealerships think salespeople are a dime a dozen, good and talented salespeople are hard to find. A lot of salespeople can assume to be great but time always exposes them as mediocre salespeople who cannot hold candle to the real *deal!*

To survive, dealership-franchise organizations have to be able to meet the quotas, set by automakers, and failure to consistently meet a quota can lead to the loss of a dealership-franchise. Many dealerships have been unceremoniously closed and boarded without notice, for lack of productivity. In Houston, Texas, employees came to work one morning to find that their Ford dealership had been boarded up, to the chagrin of the salespeople. The reason Ford took that action was that the dealership had failed to consistently meet the basic sales quota for several months in a row. The owner of the Ford franchise had lost that dealership because he wasn't selling enough vehicles.

Productivity can come in different factors. The first factor of productivity is the ability to move the products that are assigned to the dealership in a timely fashion, while the second aspect of productivity is maintaining sustainability in other areas of the dealership's business such as parts and service, including timely repayments on allocated products.

To keep products selling in a timely fashion requires the astuteness and high ability of salespeople who know how to sell products by exploring the techniques of selling. Yes, techniques, because selling is an art, which embodies the conscious use of skills and creativity. A salesperson will need to be artful in order to be good in his technique, and whenever he is not true to his technique and unable to perform his role, the income of the dealership suffers as productivity would take a fall.

Dealerships need successful salesperson to stay in business, and to a certain degree, salespeople can do without dealerships, meaning they can survive without dealerships, whereas dealerships cannot survive without them. Top management or top hierarchy of dealerships' organizations are not salespeople, or if they can minimally sell, will not survive the hurly burly of the brute force of selling. Those at the dealership's top hierarchy may have at some point tried their hands at selling but had either not done well or were unable to maintain consistency of productivity. In sales, a one-month-magic is not enough to maintain a livelihood, as consistency in productivity will need to be maintained to survive. A talented salesman maintains consistency in productivity and in income, a feat that one-month-magic salespeople are incapable of. And many dealerships who mistake a one-month-magic salesman for a true salesman often find out that they have gambled on the wrong horse!

To ensure the continuity of productivity, successful salespeople have to work very hard. Hard work is often the difference between a good and a bad salesperson. A bad salesperson may perform a one-month-magic in which he sells beyond his capability but is unable to maintain consistency in future months. A good salesperson doesn't have to work hard in maintaining consistency as they often come with his territory of hard work. Most salespeople will have a good month and take the next month off, only to return broke, and disillusioned when they are unable to repeat the same one-month magic. But a good salesperson will not allow a good month to permeate his sense of consistency as he will want to continue to produce at the same high level. A good salesperson knows that consistency in productivity means consistency in income, and will do whatever it takes to maintain continuity.

Good salespeople do not sit around, waiting for businesses to come to them; they often go out and get it. They don't believe that it is impossible to maintain consistent productivity. Superstar salespeople will not fold their arms akimbo, smoking cigarette, and discussing the latest sports' results, and waiting for business to come to them; they know they have to go after the business, and will do so with zeal, enthusiasm, and gusto. Another trait of a superstar salesperson is that he loves to work late to achieve his goal. He often does not like to take a day off for fear of missing out on the action!

Like any superstar in any professions, the superstar salesperson sets his goals and works hard to meet his objective. His productivity knows no bounds as he constantly stays alert for business; as he goes after potential sales. He does not waste his time on fruitless quests for sales. To maintain his high productivity level, he knows he has to be able to discern what can amount to a sale and what cannot. He vets his customers with the keen eyes of a hunter, sizing and making smart decisions about what customers will buy soon or buy in the far future. While he craves both potentials, he often prefers the ones buying soon. He will encourage the future buyer with a tantalizing offer but will not waste too much time on the obvious. He knows snap and uninformed judgment can lead to loss of sales, so he uses diplomacy and tact to discern the good and bad customers.

Superstar salespeople usually work late into the night, sometimes to the annoyance of their supervisors who hate late hours. But the superstar salesman does not care about the feelings of lazy supervisors as his loyalty is to his productivity and objective. He will not compromise in his quest to meet his goals. He knows he may not be the most loved and that he may be hated, but he would rather be a foe than a loser. He knows his success lies in his aggressiveness and hard work, and he will refuse to give up any to satisfy the whims of a lazy supervisor. He knows the same supervisors want him to be highly productive but are unwilling to put in the hours. He sees instantly why they chose to be supervising instead of selling. He knows they could not meet the brute-force demand of selling and had taken the easy way out by becoming supervisors. He knows that he will not allow the lazy antics of a supervisor to derail his productivity.

A superstar salesman will make calls, entice potential customers with good deals, and will often prospect more consistently. He would talk to as many people as would listen to him, and will often strive for greater sales. He is never at rest, even when he is asleep! He is always working and planning. Planning is his means of survival, and he hates vacations as he sees it as a recreation for the lazy. He is overly ambitious and aggressive, and does not care about what his coworkers say about him. He will not give in, even when the prospect of a defeat seems imminent. His success and superstardom lies in not giving in to defeats. He sees defeat as his nemesis and works hard to fend it off on a daily basis. He fights like a determined boxer and does not give in even when he suspects he might lose. He knows if he fights hard and refuses to give in, that he will not lose, and will always win.

Another character trait that promotes productivity among superstar salespeople is the ability to maintain contact and build a relationship with customers. Building a relationship with customers is a character trait that is imbued with creativity, and ingenuity. You have to be a people's person to have this trait. This trait comes natural to some while others may have to fake it. The real success at building a lasting customer relationship is when it is done subconsciously without knowing it is being done! Those who are good at this may not know they have it, and are often surprised at the ease with which they attract customers, and build a lasting relationship with them.

And the naturalness of building a lasting relationship with customers can be infectious in such a beacon-like manner that it permeates customers' awareness. It has its own charm and will sweep anyone in its pathway, in the same smooth and unprepared manner. Effectiveness in building a lasting relationship can result in a commanding productivity for the superstar salesperson. With this character trait, and his effortless ability to explore it, he does not often have to work as hard to achieve his goals in sales. Customers often find him before he finds them! Like a magnet, he attracts customers without having to work as hard as his coworkers.

To achieve effective and consistent productivity, the superstar salesperson makes it imperative to keep in touch with his customers, either by phone or by his professional joviality. Such professional joviality often adds a personal touch to his every transaction that usually makes customers feel at home with him. When customers feel at home with a salesperson and are happy with their transactions, they often send referrals without being prompted to do so. In many cases customers who send their friends as referrals do so because they are satisfied customers, and never because of the referral fee involved. While many customers will cherish the referral fee that comes with referrals, it is always because they were happy with their transactions than because of the accruing monetary rewards. It helps that they get rewarded with a referral fee for their efforts. This is where many wannabe superstar salespeople fail. They always take it for granted that a referral fee is not necessary for satisfied customers who refer friends and family members. Everyone appreciates a reward, no matter how little, studies have shown. Rewarding a satisfied customer who sends a referral increases business and future referrals.

There are many ways that a good salesperson can stay in touch with his customers. The first and mostly overused method is to send a thank you letter or card, while the second is to remember customers' birthdays and anniversaries with a commemorative card. These aforementioned gestures and methods have worked and will continue to do so, but they do not necessarily result in future sales or referrals, according to research. What often results in future sales is the lasting impression that you create at first encounter. Good impression lasts forever and tends to remain enshrined in the minds of grateful customers. If you are going to send thank you cards, birthday and anniversary cards, it may be necessary to add enticing promotions about the specials that the dealership is offering. Many people do not understand the essence of adding enticing deals with such thank you and anniversary cards, but customers do appreciate every opportunity to save money!

And remember that the primary reason for sending birthdays and anniversary cards is to cleverly seek business. And customers know it too that it is all about trying to get their business. They know that deep down that you really don't care about their birthdays and anniversaries, even though they do appreciate the gesture. Adding a little message about the promotions the dealership is having never hurts. Always remember that your customers are not dumb; that they may even know more than you do, and may be more educated in life's trajectories, so taking advantage of them, can be counterproductive!

Some salespeople often go as far as being informal with their customers by organizing breakfast and lunch meetings. In certain transactions this can be ideal but in automobile sales, this does not work and can even be counterproductive. In sales, too much familiarity can result in a no-sale. And depending on the mindset of some customers, this gesture can be misinterpreted. It is often best to be as polite and as friendly as professionally necessary without creating the wrong impression. Certain transactions might result in the need to discuss transactions over coffee or tea, or even lunch; but practical and concrete frontline selling often requires concrete approaches! If your type of sales is intangible, virtual and abstract, talking about it over lunch or breakfast might be ideal.

Productivity can only come about when the right approaches are applied; and known sales techniques are carefully adhered to, without overdoing it. While it is good to have your selling shoes on at all times, it may hurt your sales to oversell a product that does not need overselling. Some products sell themselves, without the added impetuses and inputs of unnecessary explanations or display of product knowledge. In many cases, silence can be more effective than talking! Always remember that silence is golden and that less talk is better than too much talk.

To ensure continuous productivity, superstar salespeople always find ways to attract sales. Superstar salespeople know that consistency in productivity is the only way they can maintain their clouts on the job, and even at home, where monetary imperativeness is highly essential and crucial. Money is important to superstar salespeople, and they cherish the ability to continue to make it on a continuous basis. Their worst fear is an unproductive day, a day they do everything to avoid, even when the prospects of defeat seems inevitable for that day. To maintain consistent productivity, the superstar salesperson knows that luck is not a factor. He does not believe in luck or even a stroke of it. He believes in God almighty, or *Allah*, as the case maybe, but knows that it all comes down to hard work, dedication and loyalty to his craft.

Chapter 4

Salespeople's Dedication and Loyalty

In sales, dedication and loyalty are intertwined. Successful salespeople are dedicated to their profession, and are loyal to their purpose. They have to be in order to maintain consistency of purpose and drive in their continuous quest for continuity in productivity. With superstar salespeople, there is no other loyalty besides the one they work hard to keep, and nurture, and that is to their beliefs, hard work, zeal, and drive. Their loyalty cannot, and should not, be confused and compromised, with loyalty to employers and organizations they work for. They are often not loyal to their organizations for the simple reason that they know that their employers are not loyal to them. For years, they have struggled with marginalization in the workforce, and have succeeded in carving their niches, and the last thing they want is to sacrifice it for nonreciprocal loyalty.

The average salesperson knows that he does not have job security and that the moment his productivity slackens that he will no longer be needed. He knows that his income depends on his output, and to some extent, the dealership's sustainability, *which he commands*! He knows that if he fails himself that he will ultimately fail the dealership, and will be out of work. There is only one loyalty that he knows can yield dividends and that is the loyalty he has to himself and the belief that he will do well. Being loyal to his purpose gives him room to excel and promote his inordinate ambition. His ambition is to sell beyond the scope of imagination, and surpass what is expected of him. He has to always arm himself with the conviction that he will, and must succeed, no matter the circumstances and odds.

As a true craftsman who believes in his skill and ability to excel, he knows that he will have to find a way to survive even when the prospects are slim. In his world, he knows that he is alone in his quest for success. And to keep moving on in the same positive light and direction, he counts on his power of positive thinking, that he will not just survive but will be successful at doing what he believes in, and does best. And he knows that to believe, he will need to be loyal to his cause and be dedicated to the objective of his ambition.

The superstar salesman knows that the hurly burly of his profession can be daunting and confusing, but he has little choices. His other choices were sacrificed long ago in the altar of dedication and loyalty to self, when he made the decision to join the rollercoaster of the sales profession. He knows he could have chosen better, before he made the blind leap into the abyss of the unpredictable profession he now finds himself. And by his choice, he knows the only way out is to be successful, and he has forcefully been bound by that creed. A creed to be successful he has made or, alternatively he would be doomed, he feels and fears. The way out is to be truly dedicated and loyal to his core beliefs and self. He cannot trust the harbinger of his troubles who had forsaken him many years before. And he cannot trust his employers whose only goal is to get the most out of his sweats while leaving him to deal with the carcasses. He has seen many salespeople, who after giving all they could, had withered away to their deaths, with their carcasses left to their relatives to bury!

The superstar salesperson has sworn to leave the stage of his profession when the ovation is still high, and when he is still useful to self. He cannot see that day when he would become old, bent, clumsy and erratic and still plodding and trudging along the lined cubicles and corridors that have become his domain his whole professional life. He knows at some point that he would have to leave before his dusk. He foresees the day he would call it quits from a career that has for long rewarded and belabored him. He has become a slave to his not-so-noble career because he has given his all, and had along the way, gradually withered, as he aged with wear and tear from the profession.

His loyalty and dedication has been both a curse and a blessing. It has been a curse because he has known no other life than the occupation and profession he unwittingly swore allegiance. He has known no other than the career he has been loyal to, all his useful life. At the foreseeable twilight of his career he can only count his blessings and be grateful, yet be beclouded with regrets for robbing himself of other opportunities. He regrets that he didn't allow himself to explore other means before his ultimate decision. Like a marriage where there was no sowing of wild oats, he regrets that he never gave himself a chance to see what else may have been hidden in his stars. He looks back with a forlorn look like one who had found himself in a strange town and had settled without seeing what the other towns had to offer.

But the superstar salesperson has much to be joyful for. He knew it could have been worse, and that things could have turned out ugly and different. Though he cannot help himself with his wondering mind, he has lots to be grateful for. He counts himself lucky for the divine blessings he discovered when he was still in infancy. Though he had wished and craved other more dignifying roles in life, he knows it is not over. There is still hope, even though sunset and twilight are about to cave in, in the foreseeable future. He knows it would not be over until sunset and ultimate heavenly darkness beckons! He is still optimistic that the dream he dreamed at the onset would come true. That dream that has kept his hope alive; that dream of significance, and of the ultimate pinnacle that only life can offer, has yet to make his *landing*. He has conquered his *contingent-reward* profession where he has excelled beyond expectations. He knows the other dream has yet to beckon as has been promised in the dream of yesteryears.

For now, the superstar salesman knows he has to continue with the relentlessness of success, high productivity, and high-income-earning, that has become synonymous with his name. He knows he has become a brand in a way, and that he must keep it flourishing for his mental state. He has seen many who after a while had succumbed to the wear and tear of time. He refuses to be called a *has-been.* He will forever remain the *man* until he quits on his own terms.

One of the most sterling qualities of a successful salesperson is the ability to build and show value, and turn it into sales and profits. A dedicated and loyal salesperson builds and shows value in his craft by setting his mind in a competitive mode, and besting the competition in the only way he knows how – hard work! During the course of his flourishing and successful career, the superstar salesperson has witnessed increased competition in the business he is in, and to make himself useful and relevant, he knows he has to be keenly competitive and better! In a globalized world where cutthroat competition reigns, he knows he may have to find ingenious ways to stay competitive and ahead. Price, he has seen, has become a game of chess, where the customer plays hard to win, and often *wins*. And to not yield and allow the customer to win, he knows, would be detrimental, and may often result in a no-sale, and ultimate poor performance. To stay and remain competitive, the price war must not only be won by allowing the customer to sometimes win, but to find a way to still maintain profitability. Through the course of his illustrious career, he has seen the upsurge of keen competitiveness for the increasingly knowledgeable customers, and has managed to not only stay atop the game but to beat the competition!

As dealerships have become ubiquitous with low competitive prices becoming the new norm, to lure customers, he knows the only way to succeed in the new world order of sales would have to not only be ahead of the competition but to be innovative in using the new norm to his advantage.

Successful salespeople are often aware that price is not the only motivation customers have for buying a particular product; they know that price is just one of the many reasons. Building value, and making the customer believe the product is right for his needs, and will last long enough to assuage and satisfy the essence of it, is an essential part of selling. It can be counterproductive to put the most emphasis on price alone and not the product. The value of the product, if properly showcased and explained, will command a feasible price that would benefit the salesperson and the customer. But to do this, value must be built, and emphasized in the selling process. A superstar salesperson knows that price is not the only reason a customer will be interested in a product, he knows that the product itself, and the inherent value, plays a significant role in the customer's interest.

The cliché that a well presented product will intrigue a customer well enough to induce him to make a reasonable offer may not suffice, if value is not built on the product itself. The way to build value is not to overstress the product features, but to also make the customer understand that your product is better than those offered by the competition. The best way to do this is by concentrating heavily on the relevance of the product to the customer's needs than on the inadequacies of the products offered by the competition. While it is good selling to compare your product with other products out there so that the customer can subliminally see the difference, it is the way the product is presented without overdoing it, that often hits the mark.

A good salesperson knows how to gently take the customer through the sales process without confusing the customer from making an offer. It is easy to bore and confuse a customer out of his decision to buy if the wrong things are constantly said that turns the customer off. Some salespeople believe that small talks about self and customer can be a way to make a customer feel at home and build camaraderie or friendship, but that no longer applies. Some customers can see small talks as patronizing and will be turned off, if not completely angered by it. It is always a good idea to stay and remain relevant. Talk about the things that matter – the product, and not about your son's prowess in the baseball field! You can talk about the weather without making it a topic of conversation. Always remember to stay relevant and to stick to the issue about the product, than about the nonissue!

A superstar salesperson who is dedicated to his craft will not waste time talking about trending politics and sports when he has a product to sell. Sometimes, your views can contradict the customer's views, in which case you can end up putting yourself in the enemy camp by your own carless talks and words. Rather than put yourself in the opposing camps with irrelevant topics, it is imperative to stay focused on what matters most, and that is the immediate need of the customer.

The entire process of selling should be to build value and satisfy the needs of the customers. In doing so, avoid arguing with the customer. It is always a good idea to make the customer think he is right. And sometimes he might just be right! It is not uncommon for the customer to know more about the product than the salesperson. If it comes to where the customer is leading the discussion about the product, immediately take a detour and change the topic as cleverly as possible without raising the customer's suspicion that you are avoiding the subject at hand.

A true loyalty and dedication to one's core beliefs about selling is to first allow the customer to always be right but not to lead you in the sales process! If the customer appears to show superiority in product knowledge, you may have the wrong customer, and chances are that he is not there to buy but to show off his knowledge about the product. A customer that really wants to buy a product will not have the time to try to teach a salesperson about the product! When you encounter a customer showing such pomposity and even questioning your knowledge about the product, you may be wasting your time with that customer. Studies have shown that customers that want to buy a product like a vehicle are in a hurry and hate hanging around the dealership to make a purchase. If a customer appears to not be in a hurry but are asking you questions that they appear to already know, it may not be a good idea to spend too much time with the customer. If you must, try to change the subject to the ongoing promotions that the dealership is offering.

If need be, go into a new subject matter with the customer by asking questions, and talking about credit and financing. You may want to let the customer know that there is zero interest available on the product, if there is, or if not, try to get the customer to come inside, and have a brochure ready to briefly talk about the product. It is never a good idea to open a brochure and start talking at length about a product with a customer who is obviously not there to buy but to shop for a future purchase, which may not be in the foreseeable future.

A true dedication to one's craft will enable you to sensibly, and cleverly discern a flake from a real customer. But be careful! Most assumed flakes have often turned out to be real buyers. You cannot assume a customer is a flake until they start to act flaky. If after test driving a couple of cars, and they start to tell you about an unrelated vehicle that they are thinking of, and will not come inside, to even discuss more, then you have a flaky customer. But wait! Don't assume yet, the customer may be afraid to commit to anything or is just waiting for you to lead him gently into the deal. Many customers may nicely withdraw from committing to make a purchase when a salesperson is a little too hasty and pushy. After you have test-driven a couple of vehicles that the customer may be interested in, then allow the customer a couple of minutes to think before asking him inside. But be careful not to be too eager about getting the customer inside too quickly. The customer may think you are trying to trap and trick him into making a decision. Always remember that the average customer does not trust a salesperson. And when you unwittingly make him suspicious by over talking, and being hasty and pushy, you can inadvertently turn the customer away.

A good salesperson knows how to build value with customers, especially new customers and new prospects. First impression lasts forever, and it is always a good idea for the salesperson to try not to oversell a new prospect as that can recreate old clichés in the customer's mind, about the pushiness of salespeople. You want to be serious and be taken seriously. Don't feed infamous perceptions that salespeople are overzealous and pushy. In a first impression encounter with a customer, you want to first build value in yourself before attempting to build value in the product. The value you build in yourself will enable you to overcome any objection to your presence as a salesperson that the customer may have in his mind.

As a salesperson you are likely to face new and different challenges with each customer. Some customers will have a preconceived notion about you that they will not let go upon encountering you as a salesperson. When that happens, you will immediately know that you have your work cut out for you; that you have a mountain to climb. How you climb this mountain will depend on how you use tact and diplomacy to find a way out. It can be easy and it can be hard, depending on how you have crafted your game. Otto Scharmer in his bestselling book, *Theory U, Leading from the Future as it Emerges*, wrote that "letting go concerns the opening process, the removal of barriers and junk in one's way, and surrendering is moving into the resulting opening." The removal of barriers is helping the customer to shed the preconceived impression about salespeople which may not be favorable to you. You have to immediately use tact to remove this junk perception about you, to allow you to move to the next process of being able to sell the customer, or the sale will be doomed. You have to surrender to the good impression you have set out to create in order to dust the customer's obvious objection to your presence as a salesperson.

When it all comes down to it, you will immediately see that adhering to your self-styled loyalty and dedication, in addition to the imbued sterling personality that you have built as a value to enhance your persona, will create a resounding resulting opening. The process takes mastering the psyche of people and preparing yourself on what to expect. Preparing for the unexpected can eliminate surprises when they do come. But it is all in the technique of selling, if it is to be called thus.

Loyalty, to the characteristic traits of self-made superstar salespeople can be subdivided into different folds. The first is that loyalty has to be all encompassing and embracive without being feigned or subjected to unparalleled conditions that would render its usefulness ineffective. The second is that loyalty has to be inculcated in self so that it can become part of one's beliefs. The third is that loyalty has to be permeable so that it can be felt by those it is meant to impact. And lastly, loyalty must be adhered to in a disciplined manner so that there is no deviation. Achieving these characteristics of self-styled loyalty can have its rewards if one is able to explore and apply its ingrained usefulness towards every transaction and encounter.

On the part of dedication to one's beliefs and conducts, several factors must be adhered to in order to realize the usefulness in transactions and business deals. It is not enough to be dedicated to one's disciplined beliefs; one must also be willing to make the necessary sacrifices that will ensure every action bears positive fruits. Otto Scharmer (2009), posited that many factors can inhibit one's effectiveness by "not recognizing what you see (decoupling perception and talking); not saying what you think (decoupling thinking and talking); not doing what you say (decoupling talking); not seeing what you do (decoupling perception and action)." A superstar salesperson seldom has inhibitive issues as he works towards eliminating barriers that would hamper his effectiveness. This cannot be said of salespeople who often cannot discern between good and bad measures during transactions. Every transaction has its own measure, and in truth, different customer encounters come with different measures. Whereas a less difficult customer may sometimes require a flexible measure than a difficult customer which may require an inflexible measure. But the ability to discern the flexible customer from the inflexible customer can go a long way to c reating an effective sales encounter.

Chapter 5

Salespeople's Obligations and Customer First

Many organizations believe that the needs of the customer should supersede every other need as far as business transaction is concerned. That business philosophy often translates into believing that the customer is always right, whether the customer is wrong or not, it does not matter in the scheme of things. The customer must always be given his/her props if a business is to survive in the ever competitive and evolving business environment. As competition for the ever picky and discerning customers has taken a new turn in favor of customers, businesses understand that a good customer service can make a difference. Many customers will patronize a business because of good customer service, even when prices are higher than its competitors. The reason is not farfetched as customers want to be respected and treated with dignity while making a purchase. Very few customers if any will go to a business environment where they will feel disrespected and treated poorly.

While good customer service can enhance the sustainability of a business, it can also hamper it, especially for organizations that charge for the extra good service they provide. Some organizations go beyond the call of duty to provide additional good customer service and then slickly add it to the tab, without making it obvious to the customers that they are being charged for the added good service! Though many customers will not mind paying extra, price conscious customers may feel that the purported good customer service comes with a price, and is not genuine. If a small segment of customers are willing to pay extra for the good customer service, then those not willing to pay can be a loss to the business.

All business organizations should be able to sell their products and services with good customer service, without making customers pay extra bucks for the service. Many so-called high class restaurants, dealerships, and departmental stores charge extra for the dignifying and respectful business environment they provide for their customers such as respectful employees, free valet parking, 'free' loaners, free refreshments, and other perks that makes the customer feel special.

Impression is crucial when it comes to customers' experience. The greater and better their experience the more positive influence they will create for your business. When a customer has a bad experience in a business organization, that customer will likely tell friends, relatives and neighbors about that experience. And in the age of social media and Yelp, the customer is likely to write a bad review that could damage your business. There will also be customers that will have a good experience and will brag about their good experience to friends on social media. Such happy customers may even go as far as writing a good review on Yelp and other organizations that sponsor reviews on businesses. Good reviews can create more businesses while bad reviews can damage businesses. In a globalized business environment it is imperative that businesses treat their customers well to enable a repeat business and even referrals. The best and most effective advertising is always the word of mouth.

A good salesperson knows how to treat his customers with respect and dignity so as to continue to have more businesses. Successful salespeople know that repeat customers can boost their sales. Repeat customers and referrals can make it easy to get customers than having to stand in front of the dealership waiting for customers in the sun, and sometimes in the rain. If a salesperson treats his customers with respect and dignity he may never have to worry about waiting endlessly outside on the dealership's parking lot for customers. Customers will find him because they know he is good, and will go the extra mile for them, to make their buying experience pleasant.

Salespeople are the representatives of their organizations; and whatever they do will either promote or tarnish the image of their organizations. If salespeople have such powerful dispositions to where they are the mirrors of the organizations they represent, organizations could increase their business by making sure these representatives enjoy job satisfaction so that they can be good ambassadors of their organizations. But *sadly*, many organizations still choose to relegate their most productive human assets to the most marginalized bottom of the strata! What many of these organizations do not understand is that an unhappy salesperson is unlikely to be a good representative of his company. If a salesperson is happy, he is likely to promote his organization in a more positive light, as he would feel he has a stake in the organization's success or failure.

Business organizations should realize that their business reputation or image is only as good as a customer's last experience.

What this means is that just as a good impression lasts forever, a bad impression also lasts forever. People do not forget their bad experience. They are more likely to forget their good experience than they are of their bad experience. Salespeople should be treated with respect so that they can in turn treat their customers with respect. If a salesperson feels he has nothing to lose by being nice or bad since he does not enjoy job satisfaction, he is likely to treat the customer the way he likes which may not benefit his organizations. Not everyone can be a superstar salesperson who is dedicated and loyal to his customer base and who would go to any length to treat his customer with respect and dignity.

Many organizations do not work hard enough to make sure their customers get good service. In a recent study on salespeople's voluntary turnover in automobile dealerships in the U.S., it was found that one of the reasons for salespeople's voluntary turnover and constant mobility from dealerships to dealerships was that they often feel cheated on their commissions or are not getting paid enough for their sales. And if dealership organizations will compensate salespeople well enough, they may end up creating job satisfaction that will in turn create good customer service, and sustainability for dealerships. And dealerships will also enjoy the added impetus of retaining experienced and talented salespeople. On average, talented and experienced salespeople work harder, and produce more than regular salespeople.

Customer first means that organizations are doing whatever it takes to make sure their customers' needs are being met. Meeting customers' needs is not the only way an organization puts customers first. Ensuring that customers are happy with their purchases and that their complaints are taken seriously can be crucial in putting customers first. Putting customers first is not just formulating a policy to do so; it is actually putting it in practice that matters. Some organizations would say they put customers first only to fall short and not really do so. A genuine way of putting customers first is to believe them over your employees in a dispute. But if a serious policy exists, that puts customers first there should never be a dispute that should involve having to choose between employees and customers. If employees are properly trained on the importance of putting customers first, disputes would be decoupled while a genuine environment would be created for customers to truly be treated with deserving respects and dignity. Another way of putting customer first is to create a feedback process that will allow them to review every transaction in a customer satisfaction survey that will depict the state of affairs of your customer first policy.

Customer satisfaction survey will enable your customers to rate their experience on a *Likert* scale, in which customers will be asked to rate their purchase on a scale of 1-10, in which one is *very unsatisfied* and 10 is *very satisfied.* The presence of a well coordinated feedback will allow the organization to constantly monitor, and diagnose where there is a problem in the organization. Remember that your organization depends on its customers to maintain sustainability; and when customers are treated well, they will ensure a continuous flow of business by way of constant referrals of friends, neighbors, and relatives, including repeat businesses. Referrals are the cheapest and most effective form of advertisement for the organization and when it is properly maintained, an organization will never have a downtime. There will always be high-volume productivity.

When using *Likert* scale to measure the level of customer satisfaction, studies show that specificity can best gauge the mood of customers. For example, avoid scales that may confuse customers' answers. It may even be best to make it as simple as possible so that positive and negative answers can be properly discerned appropriately. Another way not to confuse customers' feedback is to make sure the options on the scale are clearly worded to avoid confusion. According to experts, customers can have problems defining their rating if the scale is greater than seven. If the scale is more than seven, customers may pick random answers which may not accurately represent their intended answers, or depict the essence of the survey, and which may render the purpose of the survey meaningless. To properly gauge the level of your customer satisfaction, it may be necessary to keep it short and simple.

Properly designed scales should have fewer ambiguities, if not totally specific. Response options should be well delineated and equally spaced and clear to avoid confusion. It is imperative to make the scale clear, and as specific and as concise as possible so that the customer's time will not be wasted. Scales that takes more than a few minutes of response time should be avoided. Organizations that use scales that take 10 to 15 minutes can only succeed in turning off customers who may want to provide positive answers but do not have too much time to spare. Some customers can be hasty on matters that do not have immediate direct financial benefits to them, and if you must use surveys that exceeds a few minutes, you may want to throw in some incentives for the customer, as a form of inducement. But doing this can be costly and may become an unnecessary but an unavoidable expense. Keeping it simple can be less expensive and less time consuming!

When designing a scale, always make sure every facet is covered, from the least important to the most important, without encumbering the process. If you are gauging how a customer feels about a particular purchase, you may want to ask if the customer was extremely unhappy, happy but not satisfied or extremely satisfied. Generally, scales should be designed on variants that thoroughly explore the customer level of satisfaction or dissatisfaction, without leaving out any option.

Another crucial aspect of understanding customer feedback is to make the responses as logical as possible. It is often imperative to include questions that make sense, and that are less time consuming. The average customer may not have time to answer many questions, and to get the most out of your survey, it might be imperative to stick to the essence of the survey. For example, it may be necessary to stay on the theme of the survey than to deviate into nonissues that may confuse the customer's state of mind. Designing the survey to be as logical, and as concise as necessary, can save the customer time, and the organization unnecessary expenses.

The most effective scale is usually the *Likert* Scale because it is simple and easy and less complex for respondents to understand. The *Likert* scale was designed to measure and understand feedbacks such as moods, attitudes, and perceptions during business transactions, interactions, and services performed by organizations. The scale was designed to measure cognitive and affective components of respondents so that organizational leaders can best understand how to diagnose the problems affecting their organizations. *Likert* scale is popular for several reasons. The first is that it allows businesses to understand customers' state of minds, moods, and attitudes, at the point of service or purchase.

For organizations that want to really put customers first, the *Likert* scale can be a good survey instrument to gauge customers' level of satisfaction and dissatisfaction. Putting customers first also means understanding their needs and how to satisfy those needs. Surveys enable organizations to understand what troubles a customer and how to improve customer satisfaction. If a customer is unhappy with the services provided by an organization, that customer is unlikely to refer friends and relatives, and will not come back to the organization for a repeat business. When this happens, organizations often lose big, though they may not realize it immediately; with time they will, as customers after customers will start to leave because of bad services. Sustainability can thereon become a problem because of the continuous loss of business. Once a bad reputation is created, it is often hard to erase or change it. Bad impressions linger in people's minds far longer than good impressions.

Generally, a good salesperson will find a way to create more businesses by putting customers first in every transaction. While the essence of every transaction is to make profit, if customer service is good, profit will come with every transaction. It might be a good idea to avoid sacrificing customer service for profit, and then losing both in the long run. Though it is true that not all customers can be satisfied and or saved, that no matter what you do some customers will still be unhappy, but it helps to keep to the policy of good customer satisfaction even when it seems some customers are insatiable or cannot be satisfied.

In today's competitive business environment, many customers are aware of the need for businesses to treat them well to ensure future patronage, and as a result they often take advantage of the process by constantly demanding for freebies. When it is obvious that a particular customer is constantly demanding for freebies, it might be a good idea to let the customer know right away that each gift, if any, comes with a purchase. It pays to be honest by telling the customer without mincing words that gifts, where applicable, are only a onetime thing when a purchase is made. The customer might grumble but would be reasonable enough to know that there cannot be free gasoline whenever he is in the vicinity. If the customer knows that gas is free with the first purchase and that subsequent gas or fill-up is not doable, they will stop. Many organizations do offer a free fill-up for a limited number of times, as a form of promotion to entice and lure customers to purchase vehicles, but when that runs out, the customer needs to understand that the process is not continuous.

Customers first also entails being sincere and transparent. The complaints customers often have is that most retail organizations are not sincere, and that there is not enough transparency during sales transactions. While it can be hard to be entirely transparent it can be a good idea to try as much as possible in order to win customers' trust. Many customers do not trust salespeople, and by implication, do not trust retail organizations, especially automobile dealerships. Many customers will not trust a sincere and transparent approach even if it is obvious to them. "The notion that a business is out to make profit and will not care about the customer once a deal is made, is entirely not true," a sales director at a local automobile dealership in Austin, Texas, said. Many organizations still care about the customer when the transaction is over. They want the customer to have a pleasant transaction, during and after the sale.

In today's world of ubiquitous technology, customers have to be treated with care and attention to ensure they do not tarnish the image of organizations with bad reviews on social media and on Yelp, and other review outlets. Many customers will only buy a vehicle or a product from organizations with good reviews. To make sure you are not losing out on the businesses of those that check reviews before making a purchase, you want to make sure your customers are happy. Some customers might leave your place of business with a little unhappiness because things did not go as they intended, but reasonable ones will often realize that nothing is perfect, and will not try to harm your organization with a bad review. There are those customers that are unreasonable, difficult, and always unhappy no matter how much you try, and will give you a bad review regardless of your efforts to please them. It does not matter that some customers cannot be pleased; a good organization will be steadfast in its goal of providing good customer service.

Many business pundits often talk of the need for organizations to have a standard business practice and culture that puts customer first, in order to continue to enjoy repeat businesses. These pundits often emphasize the need for organizations to focus on treating their human assets such as salespeople with dignity and respect so that there will be job satisfaction that will enable salespeople to provide good customer service. It can be hard for an unhappy salesperson to do his job satisfactorily enough to create a good customer service. Though many sales are commission-based, many salespeople do not care about the future of the business as they can go to a different dealership when things go bad. Good salespeople however care about their customers and will go the extra mile to make sure their customers are happy, even when their dealerships are not doing enough to create customer satisfaction.

Many organizations do not realize that the first place to start with providing good customer service is in the workforce. Organizations enjoy high productivity with a happy workforce. That can also translate into a healthy customer first culture that can also be productive. It might also be a good idea for organizations to have a monthly seminar on customer satisfaction so that employees will always be conscious of the need to always provide good customer service. If ingrained into the culture of an organization, the process of providing a good customer service can be effortless as it will be part of the process rather than as an afterthought!

Customer first is not just about satisfying customer needs but making sure customers come first before profit! Some organizations may find this hard to absorb, thinking the essence of running a business is to maximize as much profits as possible. Any organization that sets its policy on profit first before customers will find it hard to maintain sustainability. It can be counterproductive, if not risky to think that putting profit first will not hamper the growth and success of the organization. "There is nothing wrong with making profit and creating a policy that adheres to profit-making; the only problem is balancing the equation," a prominent developer said. Balancing the equation means being able to ensure that profit and customer sustainability perform on equal basis.

In an ever increasing competitive business environment, it is almost impossible to maintain the equilibrium of profit and customer satisfaction. One often outweighs the other, and in most cases it is always profit that overrides customer satisfaction. The reason is that most organizations often place too much emphasis on profit while neglecting customer satisfaction. When this persists for too long, it can erode business longevity and survival. Apple, one of the most valued organizations in the world had for many years placed an enormous priority on profit over customer satisfaction, basing its confidence on the strength of its innovative products. As competition became unexpectedly aggressive, the company found itself in a unique position to readjust to meet the emerging and evolving shift in customer loyalty to its products and competitors' products, to concentrate on customer satisfaction. For years, Apple enjoyed what social psychologists called a cult-following that gave the company a false confidence that it can get away with any behavior even when it was counterproductive, or even disruptive.

Many organizations had been as overconfident as Apple has, and had paid the price with an unexpected waterloo in the marketplace. Blackberry Limited, formerly known as Research in Motion Limited (RM), is the maker of the blackberry wireless handheld devices, which enjoyed a tremendous amount of success for a very long time, until suddenly their once diehard cult-following changed without notice, to a new emerging innovative brand presented by Apple. With the entry of Apple's iphone, in the smart phone market, the end became foreseeable for blackberry as demand fell for its devices. It was not a big surprise to those who had witnessed the tremendous popularity of the blackberry devices, and the obvious overconfidence of Blackberry Limited. The overconfidence that it was invincible made the company vulnerable. Many would say the company created its own waterloo by ignoring the ever changing customer behavior and crave for newer and better innovative products.

Blackberry did not learn from the downfall of Nokia before it, a market it took over with aggressive and innovative blackberry products. By not constantly innovating and investing in research and development, blackberry like Nokia before it, became prone and susceptible to emerging innovative products like Apple's iphone. And as if history hasn't been a good teacher for these once most-valued organizations, history is on the verge of repeating itself with Apple, as its significance has noticeably began to erode in popularity and in innovation.

According to experts, Apple, like Blackberry Limited before it, hoarded cash in offshore accounts while depending on its products to continue to yield new revenues, without plowing the cash into research and development to create new innovations. After years of churning out near identical products and devices, one after the other, it became clear that the company has either lost its innovative quest and spirit or had been visited by complacency. For the first time in many years, the value of Apple stocks have started to plummet, and has become almost unpredictable. Where it was once a firm predictor of value and sustainability, it has become a gamble. The surefooted company has started to experience the first signs of failure, and of decline in its value and significance.

The problem, according to market observers, is that Apple has not lived up to the creed of its founder, Steve Job, who had started out by putting customers first before profit. Many have said that if Job were alive that Apple would continue to innovate rather than slacken in significance and value. Greed, for the most part has been the reasons for Apple's decline, just as it has been the reasons for the decline of blackberry and Nokia. In addition to greed, the company neglected its customer base in its quest to continuously hoard cash.

While customers have been loyal to Apple products, the company has not reciprocated the gesture, experts say. The company executives have gotten richer, while the company itself has gotten richer with hundreds of billions of dollars in its offshore accounts. Many loyalists complained that the hoarded cash should have been poured back into the company to create new innovations while others complained that customers whose loyalty created the company and its wealth have been forgotten in the midst of greed and avarice.

Putting customer first has made many organizations strong, and neglecting that philosophy has also taken many organizations down. A good and sustainable organizational culture should always be conscious of its customer base by continuously nourishing it, to make sure it does not falter. It so happens that many organizational leaders always forget their beginnings and what made their organizations successful. Like a politician who forgets about his constituency once elected, and only returns during elections, Apple, like Blackberry and Nokia before it, may not have been as lucky as many politicians who often get reelected when they return to their constituencies to make the same unfulfilled promises.

Organizations that continue to thrive and enjoy a tremendous amount of success understand the importance of a good customer service and the philosophy of customers first. And several organizations that have failed, met their ultimate waterloo because of poor customer service. Whenever a business is closing its doors, it is always that there is not enough business; and that customers no longer patronize the business. The reason customers will abandon a once prosperous and popular business can always be linked to poor customer service, or poor products. And in the scheme of things, it is all related. Whether customers stopped going to one particular business because of poor customer service or poor product, it is all the same. Whenever the customer needs are abandoned, the consequences will always be failure.

Once upon a time, the social media *Myspace* was so popular that not to have one was akin to missing out on the trendy things in life. And as soon as *Facebook* made its debut, *Myspace* quickly lost the majority of its market share to *Facebook*, and the rest as they say is history. *Facebook* has since grown to dominate the market, and even going as far as gobbling up upstart social media organizations to stay ahead of the competition and to make sure it does not suffer the fate of those that had failed and fallen, before it.

The irony about poor customer service is that many organizations do not take it seriously until it is too late. Successful organizations like *Facebook* for instance have been accused of not paying attention to its customers or subscribers, by not striving to adjust to customer needs and preferences. *Facebook* customers are its subscribers which have recently reached over one billion. As this people oriented business has grown in size, so has its revenue, which is heavily linked to the tremendous popularity of its usage. While there have been an overwhelming number of people on *Facebook*, decisions have often been more centralized than decentralized. If the success enjoyed by the organization is due to the overwhelming number of people that subscribed to its website, it should follow that the subscribers should have a great deal of say on how their image is presented. Lately, there have been complaints that the organization has become more dictatorial, than listening to the needs of its subscribers. This is a bad omen that can spell doom in the long run. This practice can come to bite *facebook* when the monopoly currently enjoyed by the organization is broken. Just like no employee is indispensable, so it is with organizations.

While *Facebook* has continued to buy out emerging competitors, to maintain its hold on the social media market, it cannot continue this crusade for too long. It may come a time that the federal government will step in and say enough is enough. Just like many other organizations where monopoly limits customers' choices, *Facebook* may have to play by the same rule that governs many organizations concerning monopoly. Monopoly, as any capitalist will tell you, is anti-capitalism and limits competition and customer choices. And with traditional organizations, that can translate into an ironclad grip on price manipulation and gouging, and the ability to raise prices that may become a disadvantage to consumers. With *Facebook*, since there is no price gouging in which a seller spikes the prices of goods and services to a level that is exploitative, unreasonable, unfair, and unethical, there may not be a direct monetary disadvantage to its billion-people-strong subscribers. The only disadvantage is that *Facebook* gets to dictate how its subscribers' feeds are posted, and who should see such feeds. And on top of that iron-grip monopoly, the company also gets to dictate the rules governing feeds and friendships on its website.

Experts have often posited that since the website is a people-oriented website, rules should be based on a consensus rather than on a centralized, top-down management. To its many subscribers, *Facebook* seems to be saying you can stay or delete your page if you do not like our decisions. This is not putting customers first. This is organizational despotism at best! No organizations have ever survived with such policies. And if truth be told, no organization succeeds when the choices of its customers are limited and monopolized. The government has not done anything about *Facebook's* monopoly because of the intangibility of its services since there is no actual product involved. But since *Facebook* has become a major player in the economy, it may be just a matter of time before it receives the same scrutiny that organizations that sell actual products are subjected to.

The rules governing customers first is essentially based on sustainability and how organizations plan to remain relevant in an ever increasing globalized business environment. It will be left to the discretion of any organization whether to succeed or fail. For those that want to succeed, the unwritten rule is the same as has been before their existence. If you treat your customers fair and right, the rewards will be multitudinous; but if you don't there will be a short-lived span, or repercussion. The future belongs to the organizations that believe in "leading from the future as it emerges," (Scharmer, 2009). To remain sustainable, organizations have to learn from the past as well as from the future as it emerges. It is not enough to learn from the mistakes of the past but to face and envisage the mistakes that can likely be made from the future and learn from it! This can be hard if an organization does not have a foresight or a vision about what is likely to happen in a future that is unknown and emerging.

But experts suggest that organizations should use the mistakes of those who have failed in the past as a yardstick to expect likely mistakes of the future; and to use past mistakes to learn from, and correct likely mistakes of an emerging future.

Learning from the future as it emerges is akin to thinking of the future and preparing for it and anticipating likely mistakes so that lessons of the past can be used to learn from it. Though it may seemed impossible to learn from a future that has not occurred but when really put in practical terms, and in perspective, it can be more obvious that the future is already with us! And if the future is already here, than we should already be prepared, as it emerges, and be ready to learn from it so that there will be no surprises. *Nokia*, *Blackberry*, *Myspace*, *IBM,* and many organizations failed to lead from the future as it had emerged.

In the automobile retail industry, customers first involves making sure that the customer is happy, satisfied, and willing to refer friends and relatives to the organization. Customers first can also mean that organizations prioritize customers over profits, and not the other way around. According to a recent survey conducted by Kaiser Health poll, "(74 percent) say that pharmaceutical companies are too concerned about making profits and not concerned enough about helping people, while about a quarter (23 percent) say the balance between making profits and helping people at drug companies is about right." Pharmaceutical companies are not alone in this profit-first craze. Many organizations are also guilty of the same unconscionable and counterproductive act that often creates dissatisfaction among customers.

Automobile retail organizations must not emulate the attitude of pharmaceutical companies, and should not be too profit conscious as to forget about the needs and moods of customers. Drug companies know that their products are essential to life, and that patients have very little choices when it comes to prescribed medications. And because of the precarious and vulnerable position of patients, there tend to be a paradigm shift that often favors drug companies over patients. This is not the case with automobile retail organizations where excessive focus on profit over customers can be detrimental to growth, sustainability, and future business.

As far as salespeople are concerned, they need repeat businesses to survive, and cannot depend solely on the dealership's traffic. Most dealerships have limited advertising budget, and as a result depend on salespeople to provide the customers. Many salespeople are often forced to take up this challenge as they have to meet the unwritten quota set for them by dealerships. They know if they don't sell a certain number of cars that their jobs may be jeopardized, and as a result, many do whatever it takes to make a sale, including wooing customers from the neighborhoods they live in, at the supermarkets they shop at, and at the barbershop where they cut their hairs. The salesperson has to constantly advertise his business to have job security, and the dealership depends on salespeople to do what they do best, which is to cajole customers to the dealership to buy vehicles.

In the process of finding means of survival, the salesperson may break one or two ethical code of conduct, which the dealership will overlook, while concentrating on the prospects of potential profits. In this uphill quest, the onerous responsibility of customers first can fall heavily on salespeople who have only one goal in mind, which is survival as they have to make a living. The objective of the dealership is always different from the objective and goals of the salesperson. Whereas for salespeople, the goal is to make a living, while the primary objective of the dealership is to make a profit. The salesperson has to make a profit too as the amount of his commission depends on the size of the profit. The bigger the profit, the higher the commission the salesperson gets from a deal, which can range from 10% to 25%. While this may look big, it can be really small, especially after some dealerships take their fees, and other unimaginable costs out of the profit. A profit of $1000 can dwindle to a profit of $300 or less, after the dealership has deducted its innumerable costs and fees. The net profit, which in this case is $300 or less, is often from which the dealership will pay the salesperson his 10% or 25% commission. And depending on the dealership, a shared referral fee of 50% will also come out of the 10% or 25% commission.

For the salesperson, the only way to survive can be to sell as many vehicles as possible to have a decent paycheck. There are those moments where a customer will walk in and pay whatever price the dealership is asking, thereby netting the salesperson a good commission, but this does not happen often. Most of the deals will generally be low profit commissions for salespeople. And in the midst of these obvious disadvantages, the salesperson will have to make sure he puts customers first or face the debilitating consequences of loss of business.

While the dealership may claim that it puts customers first, it is actually the salespeople that put it into practice. Many dealerships want the business but they do not want the problems that customers bring with every deal. Problems that are often tagged "heats" can be when a customer complains about the mechanical condition of a vehicle, or the absence of an accessory. Many dealerships do not like being bothered with after-sale "heats," and often react negatively when they occur. This is not putting customers first. Putting customers first is when you treat the customer with the same care and attention you gave during the purchase. It is bad business when you argue with your customers and refuse to listen to their complaints, and to satisfy their needs. A good customer care entails assuring the customer that his problem will be taken care of, and even apologizing for the inconvenience that he has to endure during the process. It does not matter whether the deal was profitable or not; as long as a sale is made, the customer should be satisfied, before, during and after the sale.

Automobile dealerships are notorious for their poor handling of customers after a sale is made. This poor handling often comes from the service department where poor customer service is more prevalent. In a recent survey about dealerships' service department, it was found that most customers have low opinion of dealerships' service departments. Most of the complaints about dealerships' service departments include poor workmanship, excessive billing for unfixed problems and in many cases, making the condition of a vehicle worse than when it was first brought in. In one particular survey, a respondent said he brought his car to a Lexus dealership for a brake job, and that few days after picking up the vehicle he found that the problem was still there, unfixed. Meanwhile he had been charged for the job, but the job, according to the respondent was not done, even though the service department claimed it did the job. The respondent said he later took his vehicle to be fixed elsewhere for additional money. And there are many cases like that, where a dealership's service department will argue a customer down about fixing a problem that was not fixed, another respondent said.

Automobile dealerships will need to focus on constantly training and retraining their used car managers on how to handle customers, during and after the sales process. In one of the surveys conducted about customer service at dealerships, 60% of respondents said used car managers are often rude. More than 30% respondents said used car managers are some of the reasons they hate car dealerships. Part of the reasons is that used car managers do not face the same customer service ratings that new car managers face. A new car manager will do whatever it takes to take care of a customer complaint because he knows that the manufacturer will do a customer satisfaction survey to see how the customer was treated, and to gauge the level of satisfaction during the purchase process. The after-sale survey conducted by automakers is intended to see if the customer was happy with the level of professionalism that occurred during the purchase, and if the customer is likely to buy the same brand again or come back to the dealership. In many cases the survey will also gauge the product knowledge displayed by the salesperson during the sale, and if the salesperson was able to explain the features in the vehicle, to the customer's satisfaction.

Customer satisfaction and putting customers first can be multifaceted. It can benefit the organization if done well, and it can doom a dealership if done wrong. A good customer service will promote an organization's business, by helping it to grow and be competitive among its competitors, while a bad customer service weakens competitiveness and repeat business.

Making a customer happy is not just providing everything the customer asks for, it can mean treating the customer with respect, before, during and after the sale. If a customer comes up with a problem that is not fixable, the dealership *can* find a subtle way to make the customer feel that it shares the concerns and problems, and in many cases, *should* go the extra mile to alleviate the customer's problems by just taking care of the problem. While it may cost more than intended to take care of a customer, the reward can come in repeat businesses and referrals.

Organizations have to understand that the business environment is ever changing, and changing with it, and ensuring that customers come first, will not only indemnify an organization against difficult times but also be profitable and sustainable when others won't. Customers, like salespeople, are the lifeblood of any organization and satisfying the needs of customers can pay huge dividends if a policy is created to ensure that a culture of customer satisfaction is defined and enshrined as part of the organization's modus operandi.

No organization can make it with a persistent poor customer service, and the sooner organizations with poor customer service change their ways, the better it will be for the health of their business. A bimonthly seminar on customer service can be a good way to start rebuilding your workforce to focus on good customer service. It is never too late to rebuild a bad customer service. And if it means getting rid of employees with poor customer service attitudes, it might be imperative to do so for the future health of the organization. While employees are dispensable and replaceable, customers are indispensable and irreplaceable.

Chapter 6

Indispensable Salespeople

Employees are replaceable and dispensable but there are certain employees that do not come a dime a dozen because of their high ability and natural knacks for hard work. In sales, salespeople that work hard and sell more products are indispensable to organizations. They are a rare gem, and only a few of them are born, and if truth be told, these calibers of salespeople are in a class of their own. They work very hard, harder than other employees in the organization, and often surprise others with their addictive work habit and ethics. They do not believe in days off, and vacations. They are workaholics, and are dedicated to their ambition to succeed. Their only loyalty is to their goal to succeed, and failure to them, is an enemy that must always be defeated whenever it rears, in their world.

These super salespeople don't go to work to fall asleep on their desks. They are always on the prowl for new deals and businesses. They command the respect of others by the nature of their productivity. They produce in excess of others' expectations. They beat their own records, and work on new milestones. They often aspire for new mileposts as they see the sky as their limit. They only understand one thing, and that is success and the ability to excel even when the odds are stacked against them. On top of their iron-zeal to succeed, they are great optimists who do not entertain any iota of negativity in their world. They wake up in the morning thinking positive, and how to succeed. They do not waver in their desire to beat their own records. Their objective is to create new mileposts to reach, overcome and beat. They create haters and admirers with their work ethics, and devotion to success. And they love haters as they see them as inspiration to succeed; and the zests that spur them on.

On the other side of the coin, are the dispensable salespeople that organizations and car dealerships can get rid of without regrets. These salespeople have no identifiable future ambition and do not care much for hard work and success. They have somehow adopted a defeatist expectation in their lives. They are always the first to get to their desks in the mornings, and the first to leave, unnoticed. Their presence at work is forgettable as their importance is infinitesimal. They are immeasurably and incalculably small in relevance; and their values are arbitrarily close to, but greater than zero! Dealerships will not hesitate to get rid of them for any minute missteps. They come a dime a dozen because of their trademarks, and hallmarks of laziness. Where a superstar salesperson will grieve over the loss of a customer, the non-superstar salesperson will not bat an eyelid or worry an iota. To him those he couldn't sell are flakes and he wouldn't hesitate to walk a potential customer because in his world, everyone is a flake that does not buy from him.

The superstar salesperson sees things differently. He sees every customer as a buyer and tries to make them so, and succeeds 90% of the time. The only reason a superstar salesperson will not sell a customer, which is rare, is usually because the customer couldn't buy or that he does not have the product the customer wants. Oftentimes, he would make the customer buy what he sells as against what the customer wants. He believes the customer's mind can be changed to what he wants them to buy. He does not believe in a customer's objection and discerning picks of his products. In the rare moments that he does not sell a customer, he uses the mistakes made in the process to improve his next opportunity. In essence, the superstar salesperson is a constant learner, who will cast his pride aside to do whatever is necessary to make a sale.

Despite his near uncanny devotion to hard work, the superstar salesperson understands ethics and does his best to adhere to them. And in the midst of his diehard devotion to his ambition to succeed, and hard work to achieve thus, he practices honesty to the best of his ability. He worries and *doesn't* worry! He worries about time and worries that his time will be empty of productivity at the end of the day, if he doesn't work hard. He values his time, and works hard to make sure each day is accounted for in terms of productivity. He can be cruel to himself but not dangerous to his cause. Though he can be cruel to, and critical of himself in his quest to be the best he can be, he knows when to shut it off. He knows not to sacrifice his health for his success. He believes in good health and does everything within his power to make sure he maintains good health. He knows that a good health is paramount to his daily crusade to succeed.

The regular run of the mill salesperson will check the schedule for his day off, making plans for that time, without making plans for a sale! He cares little for a day's productivity. His belief is that manna will fall from heaven to save his day. He often builds castles in a thin air, while daydreaming of being a star someday in an unrelated field. He often brags about things he is not, to create a false admiration. His significance lies in the stories he wants others to believe. He sometimes believes his own stories, and lives a life of falsehood. When it comes to the moments of truth, where his work matters, he wants others to believe that he is capable of what he knows he is not capable of. He tells unfounded stories to buttress his hollowed significance, and to fulfill his emptiness. His lot lies in the falsehood he parades for others to see. Dealerships see him as a liability, a remnant and vestige of real productivity. They will get rid of him at a moment's notice, without qualms. They don't worry about losing anything with him, because to them, he was never anything that meant value.

The reason while some salespeople succeed and others don't is that some come to work, to really work, while others just *show up*. The real significance is in the readiness to work in real time as against going to work to discuss sports and the latest top -picks in the sports community and arena. The superstar salesperson does not care about sports or if he does, cares little. He wouldn't secretly watch sports at work while work is ongoing and while opportunities exist to make a sale. When lazy salespeople are spending two hours at lunch, he is busy prowling and plotting the next sale. The superstar salesperson moves around stealthily, searching for the next sale, mentally calculating, as his eyes watch for the opportunity to make a sale. Where others fret about not making a sale near a day's end, the superstar salesperson is unrelenting, and maintaining his optimism.

There are certain traits that the superstar salesperson adheres to, in his crusade and quest to make a sale. The first is that top salespeople often avoid deception or lies during sales transactions. They know that obvious lies at the point of sale can kill a sale and destroy trust that would hurt potential sale. They try as much as possible to be honest and to avoid outright deception. They know that first impression is important, and work hard to uphold the creed. Top salespeople know that image and personality help in sales. The manner and poise a salesperson brings to the transaction can better his chances of making a sale and of securing a repeat sale and future referrals.

The run of the mill salespeople will tell obvious lies and often be deceptive at the point of sale. They tell lies that the customer can perceive to be lies outright. They are pushy and will tell a customer their product is better than the competitor's products. They often assume the customer is ignorant and that he does not know anything. That is always their first mistakes. They outtalk the customer and often do not listen to the customer's needs. They believe in their mind that selling is talking, that they must keep talking to make a point and a sale. When the customer suddenly tells them he has to go and get his wife, or pick up his son from school, or any excuse to get away, they call the customer a flake. The real flake had unknowingly, unwittingly, outtalked, and killed a potential sale, by *walking* a customer! What some salespeople don't understand is that the average customer is knowledgeable about the product he is interested in, to a certain degree, if not totally. And chances are that the customer may know more about the product than the salesperson. The run of the mill salesperson does not know that it is *never* a good idea to criticize the competition while making a sale. The best way is to often explain the features that differentiate your products from your competitors' products, without seeming to be too elaborative and critical.

Another trait that top salespeople have is that they put their customers first, before anything, in the sales process. A superstar salesperson often approaches a deal with the mindset of *making* the deal without making it too obvious to the prospect. He wants to help the prospect with the right product, without being pushy, and by sometimes *showing* understanding. He knows that customers do not care about the quotas that salespeople have to meet. He knows that customers want a salesperson that will listen to them and help them in the sales process without trying to quickly close the deal and move to the next one. In every sale, the ideal approach is to, often understand what the customer wants and to find a way to skillfully meet those needs. The customer knows that you are out to make a sale. Don't pretend that you are trying to *help* him. In other words, do not insult his intelligence. Many customers hate the use of the word "*help*." They don't need your help in anything. The only help they need from you is to help them with their purchase. Some customers will however truly need your help because of their credit problems. When you have those types of customers, you want to treat them the same way you treat your good credit customers, because your profits might just lie in the hands of the less creditworthy customers!

A top salesperson will quickly apologize for his mistakes without blaming others. Many customers appreciate it when you take responsibility for a mistake, and they especially like it when you apologize. They can act like they are right when they are actually wrong. It is always better to take the blame and to also claim wrong. Give the customer his props as that may only be one of the few moments the customer gets to get his props and be right in the subsets of his life. While doing so, be careful not to be too insignificant in the process. Don't make yourself small and unimportant while owning to a mistake. Try to portray class and sophistication in your poise and diplomacy. It might be a good idea to change the subject as subliminally as possible without sidelining the customer.

Another characteristic trait that helps the top salesperson is that he is not afraid to do what needs to be done to make a sale possible. He often prepares his daily routine with zeal and optimism, without overdoing it. He is careful not to be too eager as that can send the wrong message to the customer. For the top salesperson the goal is to be all that he can be in achieving a sale. Once he masters the act of making a customer comfortable in his presence, he can basically take charge and be able to make the sale possible. Taking charge does not necessarily mean controlling the customer, but retaining the ability to get the customer's attention.

The superstar salesperson is not only an optimist who believes that he can, but one who is good at building trusting relationships with all and sundry. He displays empathy in the sales process, and listens to his customers. He does not prejudge and entertain misguided perceptions about his customers. He builds respect around his image, and often creates a subtle dignity for himself, that customers can perceive and respect.

On the other hand, unsuccessful salespeople have low self esteem and will subconsciously do unpleasant things that can turn off a potential customer. They will smoke in the presence of a prospect, and even use foul and loathsome language that will quickly portray them in a bad light. For customers that believe in the societal debasement of salespeople as untrustworthy and unreliable, and even dishonest, the notion can add to the bad reputation that have become the hallmark of salespeople.

For the topnotch successful salesperson, dignity and hard work are interrelated. He works hard with dignity and drive that often permeates the held psyche of salespeople. With him, there is no substitute for hard work. He knows that his hard work will be defined by the qualitative quantity of his efforts. The quantity of sales efforts can reflect in the high output of the successful salesperson and in the low output of the unsuccessful salesperson. The effort of the unsuccessful salesperson is synonymous with low output, and to a certain degree he has succumbed to his trademark of low productivity and defeat and doesn't care anymore. Though he feels he cannot do better, he really *can*, if he sheds that thickness of self-doubt, and defeatist attitude.

In a way, the unsuccessful salesperson cannot be blamed for his defeatism, or he *can*. Psychologists opined that defeatism is imbued, and imbibed in early childhood where a person perceives himself to constantly lose in every endeavor. But there are those who had shed this low opinion off their image and had moved on to become successful in their chosen endeavors. But for the lazy, easy succumb is his way of saying the fault is in his stars, that he was born to lose.

The knack to succeed and be successful lay in our minds. All fingers are not equal, and in many ways, we are all created differently. Our metabolisms are different in many ways. Each person's metabolism, according to experts, is the sum of the processes in the build-up, of our individuality. The sum of the metabolic activities taking place in our lives can oftentimes define our perceptions, and outlook on things. That sum of our metabolic activities can also translate into hard work and laziness. Hard work to the initiated, with the right metabolic activities, can mean putting enough efforts to create satisfying dividends. To the uninitiated, the wrong metabolic activities can transfigure into low output and negative outlook in life.

Negative outlook in life, according to experts, is what propels defeatism and the notion that one was born to lose in life. That notion of self defeatism is the stuff many unsuccessful salespeople are made of. They believe in failure before it beckons in their direction. In rare moments, the *god* of intervention will take charge of their lives and make things happen in their favor, to ensure the continuity and existence of body and soul. After all, they still have to live, even if it means having to live on the fringes of life, and on good luck.

The successful topnotch salesperson believes in the element of quantity and will work hard to bring quality to the quantity of his output. He believes hard work, intelligence, deep-rooted skill and experience will set him apart from the crop of the sales-force. He believes his hard work will yield him successes, and seldom worries because he knows that his hard work will get him where he wants to be.

Salespeople with integrity have a way of attracting people that is almost surreal and uncanny. The truth is that people are attracted like magnets because of the integrity, honesty, and straightforwardness of the successful salesperson. And because customers come to him, he does not have to work twice as hard as regular salespeople. Or maybe he does, in an intelligent way! The saying that honesty pays, is very true when it comes to the sales profession. Customers will follow a good salesperson wherever he goes because they trust that he will take care of them.

Creating a magnetic, and cult following, takes time and hard work but as words of the salesperson's good deeds travel, so does the good reputation that he has acquired over the years. And because of the high productivity he brings to his job, he makes things easier for his employers. The superstar salesperson often sells more than the total output of an entire sales-force. He does not allow his sales prowess to get in his head as he already knows what he is capable of doing. He does not perceive himself as a one-time performer who will relent after one successful month. He knows his ability to excel lies in his ability to maintain continuity and consistency. He will not have a good month and take the next month off. He believes he must be the best that he can be every month. And by his adherence to his strong beliefs, he is able to outperform his colleagues and peers, on a monthly basis.

Superstar salespeople are not known to be expert in product knowledge. They are often known for their carriage, poise and diplomacy. They speak differently than regular salespeople. Their knack for success lies in hard work rather than in product knowledge. They are generally smarter than the average employee in an organization. Their ability to excel over other employees is not based on luck *but intelligent* hard work. There are two types of hard work. There is the one that takes the exertion of strength with low output, and there is the one that involves the application of intelligent hard work that produces high output. The difference is that the successful salesperson belongs in the latter category. He knows how to manage his time, and to cut to the chase without mistaking a real customer for a flake. He is good at spotting and discerning a flake from a real buyer.

Many successful salespeople know that product knowledge is not an indicator of success in selling and tries to avoid it altogether, if they can. They know that to sell a customer you have to be able to create good impression by being minimally enthused, respectful, and honest during the initial encounter. By being minimally enthused, the salesperson avoids creating wrong impression. He understands the need to be enthused but he wants to be careful not to waste too much time being overly excited when all he must do is to quickly and gently make the customer feel at home and comfortable. When a customer is comfortable, the rest of the sales techniques can be gradual and gentle so as not to create an unhealthy suspicion that could ruin a sale.

Some customers come to the dealership with preconceived notion of distrust of salespeople. And the sooner a salesperson sheds that perception of distrust, the better his chances of making a sale. The words that come out of a salesperson's mouth can either ruin the chances of a sale or quicken the pace of a sale. It is always better to listen to the customers and to allow them to say what they are there for, before grilling them about their reasons for choosing the dealership to make a purchase. It is never a good idea to subject the customer to unnecessary grill. If you must ask questions, ask light and related questions that will not over-pry into the customer's personal life. Too many unrelated questions will make some customers recoil into their shell of nonresponsive when they feel subjected to intense questions about themselves.

Successful salespeople know when to *hold*, and *fold*; and when to gently probe the customers without seeming to pry into unrelated areas of their lives. If a customer is looking for a minivan which seats seven or eight passengers, don't ask the customer how many children he has, as this can be irrelevant. Simply concentrate on the need of the customer which is a seven or eight passenger vehicle. And in the same token, if a customer wants a two-seater car, don't ask if they are married with children as that can be considered an intrusion. Rather than *go there*, simply delve into the needs of the customer which is to find the right two-seater that fits his/her needs. In a nutshell, avoid irritating questions that can send the wrong message. It can be considered inappropriate to ask a female customer if she is married because she is considering a sports car and or a sports sedan. In an era of political correctness, your questions can be misinterpreted and taken wrongly. Concentrate on the obvious needs rather than the *remote essence* of the customer.

Many unsuccessful salespeople are hard to motivate as they already have a low self esteem and innate belief of failure about themselves. They believe bad luck is part of their orbital life, and often find it hard to shake off that unpleasantness of failure that has become their lot. According to social psychologists, such an air of failure can be shaken off, once a person understands that failure or success is not enshrined in anyone's DNA, but in the mind. Once that perception is shaken off, an individual who was counted out, but had the intelligence, experience, and the knack to succeed, will spring out of that defeatist attitude to know success. Many unsuccessful salespeople can become successful if they apply themselves or remember the reasons they chose sales in the first place.

Successful salespeople are *naturals*, and often do things that are in accordance with who they are rather than the products of induced training. They are legitimate tradesmen who know their crafts and often do not know that they do. Their motivation is usually inwardly inspired, in their subconscious state of mind. They operate from an inward sphere, that they are not even aware of most of the time. Perhaps it is that subconscious modus operandi that sets them apart from other salespeople. They are natural born salespeople with hardly any knowledge of their unlimited talent and skill.

Most successful salespeople do what comes natural to them. They talk, behave and act in nature's own direction of things that comes from within. According to Steve Martin's article in the *Harvard Business Review*, successful salespeople do "what comes natural to them," and often possess the type of personality traits that tend to buttress that natural skills and prowess in sales. The first of these traits is modesty, which is said to be coded in nature's directed image of the top salesperson. According to Martin, 91% of top salespeople have "medium to high scores of modesty and humility," in contrast with unsuccessful salespeople who often boasts of their intermittent achievements in sales. Such unsuccessful salespeople, Martin added, are often full of bravado and as a result often alienate more customers than they win.

The second trait, based on Martin's article, is conscientiousness. Eighty-five percent of top salespeople tend to have "high levels of conscientiousness," that describes them as responsible and reliable. They tend to have a stronger sense of duty, responsibility and reliability. In other words, they take their jobs more seriously than their colleagues in the same profession.

The third trait is achievement orientation, which Martin said accounts for 84% scores for top performers. Martin noted that successful salespeople "are fixated on achieving goals and continuously measure their performance in comparison to their goals." Successful salespeople, by their zeal for hard work, and knack for success, are committed to achieving their goals in comparison to unsuccessful salespeople whose level of commitment are often much lower.

The fourth trait, Martin posited, is curiosity, which is categorized as part of a top salesperson's "hunger for knowledge and information." Curiosity accounts for 82% of successful salespeople's levels of crave for knowledge and understanding in their aggressive quest for more sales and productivity, according to research. Since they want to continuously succeed, they are often in search of new knowledge and information, without being conscious of the fact that they are doing so.

The fifth trait is lack of gregariousness. Top salespeople tend to live in their own world and often do things on their own. They have limited friends but are friendly enough to generate high volume of sales. According to Martin, the difference between successful and unsuccessful salespeople is the level of gregariousness or "the preference for being with people and friendliness." Top salespeople scored 30 percent lower gregariousness than unsuccessful salespeople. Top producers are often too committed to their goals to have time to be overly gregarious.

The sixth trait attributed to top salespeople is lack of discouragement. Martin wrote that lower than 10 percent of successful salespeople "were classified as having high levels of discouragement and sadness." On the other hand, 90 percent of unsuccessful salespeople "were categorized as having high levels of sadness." In essence, top salespeople are more optimistic than unsuccessful salespeople. The seventh trait is lack of self-consciousness. According to Martin, self consciousness "is the measurement of how easily someone is embarrassed." Unsuccessful salespeople are easily embarrassed and often prone to excessive sensitivity in the workplace. Since "the byproduct of a high level of self-consciousness is bashfulness and inhibition," unsuccessful salespeople tend to be too self-conscious to be productive because of their high level of bashfulness and inhibition. Martin added that less than five percent of successful salespeople possess high levels of self-consciousness.

Many salespeople often fail because they believe they are not capable of being successful. And oftentimes, when a person believes he cannot, it can become impossible for him to achieve success. The first step to achieving success is to believe that it is possible to do so, and the second, according to social psychologists, is to become determined and obsessed with the idea of making it possible. A dream can remain a dream until it is actualized, experts opined. To actualize a dream, one must be ready to make a personal sacrifice of time and effort. Without that initial sacrifice of time and effort, success can become elusive.

The most successful people in the world today did not give up on success, and they did not grow up with success ingrained in their DNA! Many did not inherit their successes in life. They had to work hard for it. Michael Dell of Dell Computers, worked hard at making his first computer by sacrificing his time and effort to make a success of it. While a premed student at the University of Texas, he put his skill and talent to work by selling upgrade kits for personal computers. Without giving up on success, and believing he could achieve the almost impossible, Dell embarked on actualizing his dream and belief that the "potential cost savings of a manufacturer selling PCs directly had enormous advantages over the conventional indirect retail channel." It was that mindset that spurred him to establish his startup company called *PC's Limited*, which he reportedly started in a condominium. It was a gamble; and the conviction that success was possible with hard work. It worked for Dell, and has worked for many others who became very successful in their various endeavors.

Pessimists often fail in everything they touch because they have a negative attitude about everything in life. They have their own theories about how certain things are done. And in the process of formulating their uninformed theories, they often make up things to embellish their ignorance about things they don't know. They will tell you stories that contrast the real stories and will attempt to make you believe them. In many cases, they will create a tale about things that are not true and present them as truth. They will spend an enormous amount of their time on unproductive things and would blame others when things don't go well for them. Many unsuccessful salespeople fall in this category, and experts believe their problem is due to social handicap that stemmed from their childhood. A lot of people grow up having negative perceptions about life, and often grow into adulthood with that perception; and unless help is sought to change that perception, that person can dangerously be impaired by self-created disadvantages in life, according to experts.

Successful salespeople have no choice but to be optimistic about life, and they often stick to the realities of life, rather than illusions and the unreal. They will pursue goals that are achievable versus mere fallacies. They will not subject themselves to guile and trickery in an attempt to achieve success. In their pursuits of success they will stick to their beliefs and go on a crusade for the advantages that life has to offer. They will not wait for the advantages to fall on their laps. Many successful salespeople believe that the key to success in sales is to be honest first, to themselves, and then with their goals. Self-deception can be detrimental to success in life, and by conventional wisdom, self deception can lead to a downfall and failure. What has become a hallmark of failure of unsuccessful salespeople is that they believe success is *only* achievable through crooked means, and that genuine efforts cannot yield success.

Though there are successes that have been achieved through crooked means, even with those types of successes, hard work is still required. Whether success is achieved through crooked means or through conventional old fashioned and ethical means, it still requires hard work. In most cases, success achieved through crooked means require more work than successes achieved through legitimate means. Successful drug dealers often have to work harder to elude capture in the hands of law enforcement agents. And in addition, they have to constantly be on alert for informants within their turfs to make sure there are no spies within their chain of commands. And that is on top of being creative with new illicit drugs as they have to constantly improve their products to maintain a hold on the market. A drug dealer can easily lose a market share to another drug dealer that comes up with the most appealing and trendy illicit drugs in the market. Drug dealers do not only have to often find ways to improve their drugs but to also make sure they are not being spied on by their own gang members. And all these require hard work!

And the same is true for scammers. Scammers have to constantly stay on top of their game to be ahead of the unsuspecting victim, to succeed in their scams. If they are lousy and incompetent in their game, they will be unsuccessful. The notion that crookedness requires less hard work is incorrect, studies have shown. A crooked operator will usually work twice as hard to deal with the many challenges he has to deal with, compared with the fewer challenges that the legitimate operator will face in every endeavor.

Making and sustaining a deal is different than anticipating a deal and hoping that it can translate into a paycheck. A deal can only translate into a paycheck when the stakeholders in the deal have something to gain from the deal, by actualizing the fundamentals of the deal. Selling a car is different from a virtual or intangible sale. The difference is that you actually get to see what you are buying with a car sale, compared with products that only exist in the senses. With buying a car, you not only see what you are buying but also how it drives, and what color it came in. The visibility of the car at the point of sale makes it a visible unit, while the sale of a club membership or of other intangible units can only be based on trust that the product exists and will satisfy the needs that they are intended.

A successful salesperson in either transaction understands that to make money, he will need to make the buyer believe that a product really exists even if it cannot be seen or touched. The ability to sell is not just to be talkative of the obvious but to impress the customer enough that he is willing to bet his life's savings on the intangible! Buying stocks can represent intangibility because you cannot see nor touch what you are buying. You can only trust the sales representative that what he has sold you is not just a dream but a reality that will yield dividends to satisfy an expectation.

Many unsuccessful salespeople who have problems selling the obvious visible and touchable units, will often have the same failure selling what cannot be seen. To be able to sell, the salesperson cannot have or maintain any feeling of failure. A feeling of failure can be contaminative and reflective in the host, to where everyone can see, and recognize it for what it is. Failure tends to send out its own vibes that the host may not see because it is external and also internal. The external visibility of failure reflects in the demeanor of the host, while the internal perception reflects in the attitude and disposition of the host. Both components of failure speak their own unspoken languages that the onlooker is able to read into, and translate into a meaning.

The successful salesperson does not have the coded feeling of failure to deal with because his optimism prevents the notion of it from the outset. As a striver who never relents in his pursuits, there is only enough room for success! Failure is often denied an abode in his world because his optimism has no tenancy for failure. To host failure, you have to give in, and to yield to it, by submitting to it without a fight. Like temptation to do the unthinkable, the overachiever fights the temptation of failure with hard work. He knows that to yield is to submit to the misery of failure where there is seldom a return to the paths of victory.

The difference between those who want to succeed and those who want to be spectators to the participants of success is that successful people plan, and with fortitude, and utmost determination and zeal, often make success of the end results. The end does not only just justify the means for the believer and host of success; but also pave the way for a life of success that knows no limits.

Steve Job, the founder of Apple, tasted success with the innovative Mackintosh computer that made the computer not only user-friendly but also suitable for all and sundry. When he was forced to leave a company he created, Job would embark on a new innovative venture that catapulted him back to the limelight of success, which surprised his detractors. As his new innovative products began to yield dividends, the beacon of his success was too obvious for his detractors to ignore. Without any hope of continuity, Job's detractors and erstwhile friends would go to any length to bring him back to innovate, enliven and reenergize the floundering Apple. Knowing that there will be no future without Steve Job, Apple's board of directors had no choice but to bring back Job to resuscitate the dying company.

The coming back of Job to Apple also heralded new innovation that would turn Apple around into a new success story. It had to take the return of Job for the company to turn its downward spiral into an upward spiral. Job introduced new innovative products like iphone, ipad, ipod, that would change the way phones have ever been used. The innovative smart phones, tablets and gadgets would immediately take a lion share of the smart phone market share that was then only dominated by blackberry phones. It had taken the innovativeness of Job to reinvent Apple back to a sustainable organization that would create a new cult following.

Steve Job had refused to allow failure to enter his world by instantly rejecting its entrance, and embarking on a new venture. Job opened a new door when the old one had closed on him rather unexpectedly. He did not do what most people who are taken by surprise do by allowing themselves to be derailed and forced into self-induced depression. He fought his way out of the fangs of defeats into the welcoming arms of success. He knew success and had enjoyed the comfort of it, and would not allow it to elude him. He knew that failure could be infectious if allowed to permeate his being, and emotions. He dusted his mind off the intrusion of failure and as he did so, he realized he was greater than the harbingers of failure, and that his orbit would always be populated by success story. It didn't take time for him to realize that he was born to succeed and not to fail.

Those that don't believe in failure can never be cobbled or swooped by its overwhelming folds. Many had been lured into failing but with endurance and fortitude had fought back and succeeded in overcoming the allures of failure. In failure many had found a defeatist solace that had taken them on an inevitable nosedive into nothingness. But with fortitude, hard work and faith, many had overcome failure. Lee Iacocca was fired by Henry Ford II, over a disagreement in 1978, only to find quick successes and fame when he revamped an ailing, and failing Chrysler in 1979. Chrysler was on the verge of going out of business when he took over the company. He had believed that allowing Chrysler to fail would also be his failure. Through a failing Chrysler, he found a new courage and strength to change the course of destiny for a company that was written off as hopeless. Armed with iron determination he knew Chrysler was his chance to redefine and reinvent his image that had been bruised by Ford when he was fired on July 13, 1978, after helping the company to achieve a record profit of $2 billion for that year.

He would bring Chrysler out of looming doldrums and collapse, into a profitable organization, from the precipice of bankruptcy into an organization that was capable of making profit and commanding an enviable productivity that would surprise detractors and critics. He reintroduced the ideas that Henry Ford II had rejected at Ford, to Chrysler and turned them into successes. He didn't revamp Chrysler because he thought the company had a chance to succeed, *he knew* the company had to succeed or he would be swept along with its failure. With Iacocca, failure was not an option. The only way was the way of success. It was with that mindset that he went to Congress to plead for a bailout, in the form of a loan guarantee, telling those that would listen that the failure of Chrysler would also be the failure of capitalism and of free market. He told Congress that if Chrysler was allowed to fail that many employees would be without a job, and that an iconic company would be failed by those that had the power to save it.

Iacocca made a promise to Congress that if a bailout was granted to Chrysler, under a loan guarantee that he would make sure the loans were paid back in a record time, before the scheduled repayment term. And to accomplish his goal, he reinvigorated the workforce by weeding out unproductive workers, and reducing unnecessary overheads. He abandoned the costly turbine engine project, and cut costs in other wasteful areas. He found out soon enough that the company was spending way too much on unnecessary expenditures than on research and development. He figured out that to revamp the ailing company he would have to make necessary sacrifices which included getting rid of employees that were unproductive; and closing factories that were not profitable. The policy to reduce the workforce was not at first popular with the union, but when it became apparent to the union members that the choice was either to get rid of a few unproductive workers and save a large majority of productive workers, or in the alternative allow the company to die and lose the entire workforce, the union was quick to reach a compromise. After all, the essence of the union was to protect the workers, and it chose to save the employments of the majority rather than of the few.

Successful salespeople often employ courage, determination and perseverance in dealing with odds that are often stacked against them. Iacocca had his work cut out for him when he agreed to lead an ailing and troubled Chrysler in 1979. It didn't take long for him to realize that the appointment to lead Chrysler was an opportunity for him to accomplish what others thought was impossible. Henry Ford II had rejected many ideas that Iacocca had had for Ford. Many would say Iacocca accepted the position to reinvent himself after the humiliation at Ford, while others would say he had little choices left for him in the corporate world after the forced exit from Ford. And there are those who would say he was brought to Chrysler to fail, but despite the odds that were overwhelmingly stacked against him, he did not dwell on what couldn't be. Rather, he dwelled on what could be, and he *knew* the only way to do so was to focus on what matters. To him, what matters was getting Congress to agree to a bailout of the company with a loan guarantee. He figured that if he could get on the conscience of congressional members and leaders, and put the burden of allowing Chrysler to fail on their shoulders that they would budge, and they did when it was obvious they had to explain to their constituents and constituencies if they didn't. It was a good strategy and it worked, saving the jobs of many employees, suppliers, vendors, and several stakeholders.

Iacocca's success in revamping an ailing Chrysler was due to hard work, and belief that he could, and most of all, his determination to succeed and to prove his detractors wrong. His style of leadership, which was mostly a bottom-up and decentralized type, allowed him to know and understand the company. It was a shift from the centralized and top-down leadership style that had been prevalent at Ford. With his style of leadership, it became easy for him to achieve success by implementing the ideas that had gotten him fired at Ford. The same ideas that got him fired at Ford would be the ideas that brought Chrysler profits and reinvention. Such productive ideas that Iacocca brought to Chrysler included the introduction of subcompact cars like the Dodge Omni and Plymouth Horizon. Iacocca had seen how the Volkswagen Rabbit had succeeded in Europe and had embarked on the production of the Omni and the Horizon, which became instant successes. As profits poured in, Iacocca would embark on aggressive projects that included the release of the K-car line, such as the Dodge Aries and the Plymouth Reliant in 1981.

As the 1981 recession hit the economy, Iacocca knew that cars that were easy to repair, and most of all, that costs less to repair would appeal to consumers. He introduced the front-wheel drive cars that were inexpensive, small and fuel efficient. The vehicles sold very well, and made the company huge profits that surprised shareholders who were at first skeptical. With renewed confidence, and with successes after successes, Iacocca felt confident enough to release the *Chrysler Imperial*, which was a luxury line with the latest technology of the time. The *Chrysler Imperial* was equipped with electronic fuel injection, along with an-all digital dashboard. The imperial was also an instant success.

Iacocca achieved success when it was thought to be impossible. Like Iacocca, many successful people believe that success is achievable through hard work, optimism, and determination. Iacocca proved that nothing is impossible when one is determined. A successful salesperson knows that success is achievable when he leaves his home for work every day to face skeptical customers with a preconceived notion of distrust. Achieving success often means overcoming that mountain of distrust that is stacked against the not-too-dignified salesman.

Studies have shown that those who persistently work hard and are consistent in doing so, often become successful than those who do not. Working hard does not often guarantee success if intelligence is not applied in the process. Many unsuccessful people work hard but they work hard either in the wrong profession or unintelligently. To work hard to achieve greater results, one must learn to work hard in productive areas than in unproductive areas. Hard work in unproductive ventures does not *often* yield success unless it is continuous and consistent and success-bound. William Shakespeare once wrote in *Macbeth* that "to be thus is nothing but to be safely thus," (3.1.47-71); meaning that it is not enough to do something and be successful but to consistently remain successful and be able to enjoy that success in the long run. While Macbeth's soliloquy pertained to an inordinate ambition to be something that he was not destined to be, it is the belief that success is not earned until it is safely and consistently guaranteed that matters.

In *Macbeth*, the protagonist had worked hard to earn his fame and had been successful at it, but he did not feel fulfilled until he felt the ultimate ambition and success had been achieved. His wife had successfully persuaded him to think of himself beyond what he had achieved, and could be, even if that ambition could not be justified.

But the wife felt it was justified by her reasoning. To her it was not enough to be well respected for being a noble warrior. What would be enough to her, was for him to be the king, even when it would be a wrongful desire that could only be obtained by murdering one who had "built an absolute trust" in Macbeth. She did not care how it was achieved, even if it meant having to kill to achieve it. All she aimed for was that Macbeth should be the king by any means.

Caught between loyalty to the throne and to wife, Macbeth knew that without his wife, the success he had achieved would be nothing; and as a result had quickly learned to recognize where his strongest loyalty lay. Though he would eventually achieve his evil desire to become king, but as he would realized, "to be thus is nothing but to be safely thus," and that would lead to more evil in an attempt to be "safely thus."

In the context of success in sales and in achievement, success can only be truly an achievement when it is safely thus, and guaranteed to be continuous. Achieving a onetime salesman of the month is not success if you cannot continuously do so. Continuous successful performance is what makes a person a true success, and salespeople who continuously perform on a regular basis, are the true superstar of their profession by virtue of their consistent productivity.

The same can also be true of a product. For a product to be a success, it must be consistent in performance. For many years, the innovative iphone has been a consistent performer in the market, outselling its rivals on a constant basis, but the continuity of that performance will be tested by the continuous, or lack of it, innovation of its technology. If Apple rests on its oars and does not invest in research and development to continuously increase the iphone innovation, the product could become vulnerable to being overtaken, where its rivals can take its market shares and become the superstar products, with newer innovations. So it is with a salesperson. If you don't continuously work hard, you are likely to lose your status as a constant performer. With a salesperson, there is no continuous innovation but continuous intelligent hard work. Intelligent hard work is to, often identify areas of weakness and mistakes and be willing to remedy and correct those weaknesses and mistakes so that future performance can be consistent, and enhanced.

The significant difference between those that continuously succeed in sales and those that don't, and those that try but cannot, lies in consistency of intelligent hard work. That consistency of intelligent hard work is imbued with dedication of purpose and loyalty to goals and objectives. That commitment of purpose and zeal also means one's readiness to sacrifice personal convenience, time and effort. Some salespeople that could have been successful will do well in one month and take the next month off. It is hard to maintain consistency on such basis. Success has to be constant "to be safely thus," or it will be a onetime factor.

There are also salespeople that try to work hard, and often do, but because there is no commitment on their part, and because they put other priorities above their goals and objectives, they often falter in their quest to be a true success. To remain a true success, you have to make sure you prioritize your goals and objectives and most of all, you have to be dedicated to the priorities of success which are commitment, dedication, sacrifice and hard work. With strict adherence to the priorities of success, success can be actualized on a regular basis and then be "safely thus," in continuity.

The salespeople that often fail do not show enough commitment in their objectives. Studies have shown that commitment can lead to success but commitment without loyalty to purpose can also be doomed. To maintain an iron commitment to goals and objectives is not the same as sacrificing your family time because of the quest for success. A true superstar salesperson will learn to juggle family and work, and be able to maintain a balance without tipping the scales in favor of the other. Since family and work are important in our lives, the ability to maintain a balance between both is one of the secrets of success. Lazy people will often use family excuse as the primary reason for their failure to achieve success in their professions or intended professions. Experts believe that if the family priority is taken out of the equation that lazy people will still find something to blame for their failure to achieve success.

Successful salespeople will always find time, no matter the pressure of external factors, to achieve success in their lives. One of the reasons superstar salespeople do well is that they are adept at continuously adding value to their customer base. They do this by seeking answers on how to add value to their customer needs. Unsuccessful salespeople often pay more attention to themselves than to their customers by not trying to understand customer needs, and synchronizing the purchase process to customer preferences. To be successful, one must be proactively ready to understand customer needs, and be able to place them above all other priorities at the point of sale. When selling, the only things that should matter should be the customer. One must be ready to not only sell but to deliver value at the point of sale. The two factors are interwoven and must successfully apply in unison during the sales process.

Another important factor in successful selling is that successful salespeople do not have time to complain; when they are trying to work hard. Unlike unsuccessful salespeople that will constantly complain and work less, successful salespeople often devote their time to intelligent hard work, and oiling their commitment and dedication to their goals and objectives.

Sales leads help many salespeople in sales, but many successful salespeople do not depend on leads to achieve success in sales. Oftentimes, successful salespeople create their own leads and are comfortable creating their own sales' niches. Successful salespeople do not like leaning on their managers to provide them with leads in order to make a sale. They would often prefer to go out there and get their own sales. They often prefer to be independent and will do whatever it takes to create a tremendous customer base to achieve success and repeat businesses. They do this by paying attention to their customer needs and continuously working hard to satisfy their customers. With good and successful salespeople, customer satisfaction is important and a priority. Successful salespeople will not wait on their employers to provide a good customer service; they will often do it on their own. They know that their organizations rely on them, to succeed.

Good salespeople know how to build trust so that they can continuously have repeat businesses. They know that trust is built on integrity and will do their best to earn that trust by always focusing on providing what is best for the customers, and for their organizations. Their loyalty is to their commitment, and to their customers, and finally to their organizations. They put customers first in everything, and strive to do their best on a daily basis to meet customer needs.

In addition to building a lasting trust, successful salespeople often create an impression that makes their customers to trust their skills and their abilities to satisfy their purchase needs. In many instances, some customers will not know what they want but will depend on the salesperson to help them with their needs. To reach a position where customers can rely on, and trust a salesperson with their choices and purchases, takes proven trust and reliability.

Chapter 7

Salespeople's Intrinsic and Extrinsic Job Satisfaction

Studies have shown that many salespeople do not have job satisfaction in their profession. In a 2011 doctoral research study published in the ProQuest database, it was found that over 80% of salespeople surveyed do not enjoy job satisfaction in their profession. The reason job satisfaction is almost nonexistent in the sales profession is that selling can be arduous and tough, the survey said. And besides the arduousness of the job, many organizations do not do enough to provide salespeople with job satisfaction or create room for its prevalence.

Intrinsic job satisfaction is a component of the essential nature of human nature that often occurs as a resultant factor of internal derivation and justification. It is a characteristic of a component that comes from within than without; and its existence is attributed to natural occurrence and derivation of satisfaction in every attempt to fulfill an objective. It can also be classified as a crucial metabolic factor that is within a body of things.

Many experts and social psychologists have written that intrinsic job satisfaction is crucial to the wellbeing of employees and the health of organizations. Though intrinsic job satisfaction varies from organizations to organizations, it mainly depends on the individual or the employee. What creates an intrinsic job satisfaction for one employee may be totally different from what creates an intrinsic job satisfaction for another. But one of the essential ingredients of intrinsic job satisfaction, according to social psychologists, is needs and the part they play in aiding an individual's crave for satisfaction in the workplace.

In sales, intrinsic job satisfaction can be due to the level of compensation an employee receives in the workplace, or the level of job satisfaction employees derive from the daily performance of their job. In many cases, happiness and the prevalence of it can also create job satisfaction for many employees. While there is a strong correlation between happiness and money, happiness appears to be a stronger predictor of job satisfaction than money. An unhappy employee who is well compensated is unlikely to have intrinsic job satisfaction. And an employee that receives a small compensation but is happy with the job is likely to have an intrinsic job satisfaction because of the integrity, dignity and respect that comes from the job. To a lot of employees, integrity and dignity account for a higher level of intrinsic job satisfaction than monetary incentives, according to studies.

Making big bucks can have a small proportion of intrinsic job satisfaction if making the big bucks includes frustration, stress, and long hours, to some employees. For a small proportion of employees, making big bucks enable them to derive job satisfaction because the monetary compensation makes up for the hassle they endure in making the big bucks. While this is a justification of a process rather than the natural occurrence of intrinsic satisfaction, it can also be that monetary y compensation creates an internal derivation of happiness that leads to intrinsic job satisfaction.

Attaining a dreamed position in the workplace even if it pays less can also lead to an intrinsic job satisfaction. Many people want to be in charge, and be the boss, but in many of such positions, the rate of compensation is often low, but there is often a greater perception of intrinsic satisfaction. For those who are driven by monetary compensation, getting paid more can create intrinsic job satisfaction. And for this group of people, there is less regard for esteemed positions. These categories of employees do not want positions; all they want is money and the satisfaction it creates for them. In the same token, those employees that seek lofty positions do not often care for monetary advantages.

There is a small segment of employees that want to be compensated for the higher positions they have attained, and for this group of individuals, there is usually a small level of intrinsic job satisfaction. They are very ambitious and in most cases, greedy, and the worst part is that many in this category may not know they are greedy. They are driven by money and the power it brings. And because of their inordinate ambition nothing satisfies them. The only thing that brings any form of satisfaction to them is money; and the more substantial their acquisition of it, the greater the momentary level of satisfaction they enjoy. The reason this group of people do not have intrinsic satisfaction, survey says, is that higher income does not guarantee happiness and as a result not a predictor of intrinsi c job satisfaction.

What one enjoys doing will bring job satisfaction even if it comes with a low level of monetary compensation. A trained medical doctor may not enjoy practicing medicine as a doctor but may enjoy being a medical correspondent for a television network. As a medical doctor he merely fulfils the call but as a medical correspondent and a journalist he may fulfill a long-craved ambition to be a journalist and be on television, traveling to places around the world to find medical reports and news to bring to television viewers and audiences. Being a journalist may pay less than being a medical doctor, but the level of intrinsic satisfaction may be greater as a journalist than as a practicing doctor.

Daniel Gilbert, who is a social psychologist at Harvard University and the author of the bestselling book entitled: *Stumbling on Happiness*, opined that many people do not often know what makes them happy. And because of the flawed and inaccurate idea of what can make them happy, they end up engaging in the wrong endeavors that often brings them unhappiness. An inaccurate idea about happiness can be akin to how we perceive and indulge in things that we feel will make us happy. According to Gilbert, "Few of us can accurately gauge how we will feel tomorrow or next week." And because we cannot accurately gauge or predict our future happiness, it can be almost impossible to guarantee our future level of happiness. What we think will make us happy at the outset may end up making us unhappy in the long run. "That's why when you go to the supermarket on an empty stomach, you'll buy too much, and if you shop after a big meal, you'll buy too little," Gilbert wrote. In essence we make better decisions when we are accurately positioned to do so versus when we have limited choices to make decisions that can sustain our future happiness.

In sales, there are always limited choices at the point of sale, for the salesperson. The choice is to make the sale there and then, or face the consequences of a no-sale. The no-sale consequences can have an extended repercussion of job insecurity which in itself will trigger unhappiness and absence of intrinsic satisfaction. But oftentimes, happiness can occur when a successful salesperson is able to utilize the skill, talent and experience at his disposal to create a sale while delivering value at the same time. But for a salesperson to enjoy job satisfaction in the process he must be able to recognize the vagaries and unpredictability of the profession and be able to find core values in selling. That core value, if properly channeled, can bring intrinsic satisfaction to the salesperson. But the process can be tricky. In the process of trying to satisfy customer needs, and make a sale in an atmosphere that is pregnant with unpredictability, the salesperson may be forced to deal a hand that may lean towards favoring the customer. Though the success of a sale can bring immediate rush of happiness its lasting effect will be short-lived.

The issue that often works against salespeople is how they balance family and work. Many salespeople do not know how to balance spending time with family and having enough time to successfully accomplish a career in sales. And because of this imbalance, many salespeople often end up having to choose between their immediate family and their job. In many cases the job often wins, because of the need to survive. The significance of money is crucial and it is impossible to have a successful relationship without money. Money is needed to pay bills, and buy foods, and the salesperson recognizes that he must fulfill the role of a breadwinner in the family or be damned, and at the same token, he knows he must also spend time with his immediate family or risk losing on that issue. The dilemma most salespeople often encounter is that they cannot balance both equation; and in the interim, unhappiness sets in, and subsequently absence of intrinsic satisfaction.

The best predictor of happiness is said to be the amount of time we spend with loved ones and the relationship therein. According to Gilbert, relationship is more important than money and health. But money is significant in maintaining a good health and a cordial relationship. The absence of money will not only bring disunity in a family relationship but its demise. While studies have shown that relationships can trump money, as a predictor of intrinsic satisfaction and happiness, it is the balance that exists between making money and family time that is perceived to be the predictor of happiness.

Gilbert wrote that people should do "wise shopping for happiness," in discerning the impetus of money and relationship in the quest to achieve intrinsic satisfaction. But happiness as an abstract may seemed secondary to the concreteness of the significance of money in achieving a lasting family cordial relationship and the acquisition of money. A person making $10,000 a year, with a lot of time to spend with family, will be less equipped to provide a better life for his family, and will subsequently create poverty and misery, which in essence will lead to unhappiness and the absence of intrinsic satisfaction. Whereas a person making $50,000 a year is likely to be a better provider, and in a better position to provide a better life for his family even if he spends less time with family.

In an environment where there is affluence at home, and money is not a problem, time and money may become significant predictors of happiness in their various categories. In that sense, money may no longer bring happiness since there is an abundance of it. But the opposite can occur if there is no money and there is more time, than money to spend with family at home. When that occurs, intrinsic satisfaction is likely to be absent as it is likely to be absent when there is more money than time to spend with family. In that respect, Gilbert's assertion that money is not a predictor of happiness can hold.

Many experts have written that money plays a significant factor in creating intrinsic satisfaction in the workplace. Depending on the age of the individual, money can be a factor in happiness, according to experts. But overall, happiness is seen as the overriding factor in intrinsic job satisfaction. Interest and fulfillment are interrelated as predictors of intrinsic satisfaction in the workplace. A person who is motivated by the fulfillment of a job is likely to replace that fulfillment with another job where there is no fulfillment but there is a greater financial reward. A writer who enjoys writing and makes a living from writing will not likely give it up for a different profession that pays more where there is no fulfillment. Fulfillment is an integral part of happiness and of intrinsic satisfaction.

A lot of salespeople are motivated by money because they want to be able to fulfill their basic needs in life. And to a certain degree, being able to fulfill core basic needs can create an intrinsic job satisfaction; even if there is no future guarantee that happiness will be sustained.

Intrinsic satisfaction in the workplace can also come from being happy with the level of treatment one receives from the employer, and the dignity of the job. Many jobs do not have dignity, and respect, and they often bring embarrassment to individuals who are not comfortable with being its practitioners. Studies have shown that the quality of the job one does and the dignity of the position one holds, is a significant predictor of intrinsic satisfaction. A medical doctor for instance that enjoys high favorability among members of the public is likely to be more intrinsically satisfied than a salesperson that is often perceived with suspicion and contempt. The contemptuousness and scorn associated with being a salesman can erode the level of intrinsic satisfaction in a sales job. According to social psychologists, some salespeople find it difficult to identify as salespeople outside their sales environment or during after-work environment because of their level of discomfort with being perceived with contempt and scorn.

Where a medical doctor will proudly introduce himself as one, and where a legal practitioner would also proudly introduce himself as such, a salesperson is not going to exhibit the same pride when he is outside the work environment. The reason, according to experts, is that the sales job does not come with a sense of fulfillment and accomplishment to a lot of salespeople, compared with other respectful professions. In a social gathering, where what one does counts, and where there is no prospect of selling involved, a high proportion of salespeople are going to unlikely introduce themselves as salespeople.

On the other hand, many salespeople see interactions with others, especially outside their workplaces, as an opportunity to solicit for prospects, and canvass for future sales. These categories of salespeople will take business cards with them to social gatherings and would often pass them around to prospective buyers. Experts say that though many salespeople would look for opportunity to make a sale when they are not working, a profound segment of successful salespeople who do not find the sales profession as fulfilling, would avoid introducing themselves as salespeople in such gatherings. They would leave canvassing for business to working hours on the job! In other words, they will not carry their work with them to wherever they go, not because they want to have quality time with their loved ones, but for the simple fact that they are not happy with what they do. If one is not happy with what he does, but is good at it, and is heavily compensated for doing it, there will be the unlikelihood of intrinsic job satisfaction. In this situation, money cannot bring happiness, only fulfillment can.

When most people think of salespeople, the images that often conjure up in their minds, according to social psychologists is one of unpleasantness, sleaziness, tackiness, misleading representations, etcetera. And since many salespeople are associated with behaviors that are dishonest, immoral, coupled with sleazy quality and appearance, the profession is not associated with respect and dignity. There are salespeople who are not comfortable with these characterizations, and who find it repulsive to be called sleazy, tacky, and immoral. Experts believe that negative and unpleasant characterizations can be a strong predictor of job dissatisfaction and absence of intrinsic job satisfaction among salespeople.

Within the profession, and in organizations, salespeople often face the same negative and unpleasant characterization, and to a large extent, marginalization from their managers and supervisors. In 2012, in Houston Texas, a used car salesperson shot and killed his manager for disrespecting him, during a meeting. The salesperson had reportedly been rudely debased and disrespected by the manager during a sales meeting, and the salesperson had left work on that day only to return the next day, with a pistol and shot his boss to death, according to Houston Chronicle. This type of unfortunate incident is commonplace in workplaces where there is a profound absence of job satisfaction, happiness and fulfillment. When interviewed by authorities about his motive for shooting his manager, the 49 year old salesperson lamented that he was disrespected and humiliated by the younger sales manager who had been chosen from the sale-force to manage other salespeople. The older, more experienced salesperson felt disrespected enough to kill to assuage his frustration. And there are often similar cases that are reported in the media where employees kill their supervisors due to anger, disrespect, marginalization, and indignity.

Selling or the art of selling is associated with innumerable stigma that tend to eat into the psyche, moral fabric and fiber of most salespeople that it takes away the modicum of respect or satisfaction they have left. On many occasions, as salespeople, prospects will avoid talking to them even if what they are offering is excellent and will benefit them. The frustration of chasing customers and being scorned and shunned can also lead to job dissatisfaction and unhappiness.

Bargaining over price troubles many customers, and also worries salespeople. It frustrates salespeople when a customer offers a price that is far less than the cost of the product. Many customers will not believe a salesperson when he says he is losing money in a transaction or that a car deal can lose money. And in fact, many customers believe that there is a huge markup that the dealer is always going to make profit, regardless of the negotiated price. That is largely incorrect; many car dealerships have no choice but to move the units in their inventory even if it means having to sell such units far less than they paid for them.

While the bargaining process is part of the norm of doing business, it is the perception and sometimes, the scornful manner of approach that the customer brings to the deal that often puts some salespeople at a disadvantage on the dignity spectrum. They feel they are not worthy of the customer's trust because of the general perception that salespeople cannot be trusted. Though many salespeople will take such humiliating experiences in their strides as part of doing business, some will feel the psychological impact, and will often feel marginalized; and would experience the absence of intrinsic satisfaction from selling. It may pain some sensitive salespeople to think and believe that the public perceive them to be sleazy and immoral enough to be devoid of the truth.

Many unsuccessful and even successful, salespeople are said to be sleazy, and to a large extent, not trustworthy. There have been proven cases where a salesperson will lie, cheat, and even deceive customers to make a sale. According to studies, in automobile sales, thievery among salespeople is very prevalent, and customers are always the victims of such immoral practices. Such sleazy behaviors do not often augur well for other salespeople who do not engage in such sleazy behaviors. No matter how a salesperson strives to stand out as moral and upright, or attempts to, it is often hard to jettison the long-held stigma of sleaziness and immorality.

There is also the general sense of lousiness that comes from the frustration involved in selling. Though many successful salespeople do very well to avoid frustrations, those who have not mastered the art of finding gold in that dust of frustration still find it difficult to cope with the obvious. Successful salespeople will turn frustrations into profitable transactions by simply applying tact and diplomacy in avoiding unpleasantness. As they say, it is all in the game. And successful salespeople tend to create their own job satisfaction and often find intrinsic happiness in the web of frustration that they must wade through in their daily business transactions. The seasoned salesperson knows that survival entails having to apply all his reasonable faculties in the selling process, and as a result will not succumb to any form of frustration that could prevent a potential sale.

Experts believe that selling can be easy and natural if there is enough authenticity at the point of sale. Successful salespeople are known for their authenticities and direct approach that are often devoid of gimmicks, and hassles. The reasons most successful salespeople close 99.9% of their deals is because they are authentic and natural in the way they speak to clients; and they often avoid the traditional gimmicks of trying to oversell. And they attract and retain customers, including repeat businesses and referrals because of the authenticity and honesty they project in the course of doing business with clients.

As most salespeople know, it is all in the game, and that game is often part of conversations that will need to be positive, honest, authentic, and polished to command a sale. A positive and firm but polite conversation will easily create an atmosphere of comfort for the prospect, and to an extent, the salesperson. It is that level of comfort in doing business that can also lead to intrinsic job satisfaction. But to get to that level, one must practice becoming authentic and natural in every business approach. Gimmicks might be good in newspaper advertisements and television advertisings, but when it comes to face to face selling and transaction where body language and eye contact talk in unison, it might be a good idea to be real at that point.

Intrinsic satisfaction can come from knowing you have satisfied a customer when the sale is completed. This level of intrinsic satisfaction might be temporary and fleeting, but it is often there at the point of sale, when a sale is made. Selling has its own sense of accomplishment because the art itself is a task that once accomplished brings its own rush of happiness, even if it is short-lived.

To create and maintain a lasting intrinsic satisfaction on the job, experts believe it is important to cultivate and maintain dignity during the sales process. Dignity, once earned can command respect from customers who will immediately see that you are different from the flock of sleazy, dishonest and immoral salespeople that abound in every sales occupation. By avoiding the indignity of traditional sales techniques, a salesperson can create his happiness without having to rely on his organization to do it for him. Indignity begets disrespect and scorn from the average customer. And to avoid that, one must stand out and apart, and be above the fray of traditional dishonesty in the sales profession.

Relying on trust based selling can also increase intrinsic job satisfaction whereby customers will not only be attracted to you but will bring their friends and family members to do business with you. And the network of family and friends can expand into a pyramid that will increase exponentially beyond the realms of one's imagination and expectation. It pays to be honest and straightforward. The art of selling by itself embodies the use of inborn skill and talent to persuade an unwilling buyer into a buyer; and it is also a series of conversations that usually occur during sales that allows a good salesperson to assess, and structure a sale. This process is often natural as it moves from one natural pattern to the next. It is not hard, experts say, but it can become hard when traditional sales gimmicks are mixed with genuine natural selling, which is the power to command a positive and productive conversation during sales.

The other process is building credibility and this falls into the same category as being authentic and honest. If traditional sales gimmicks and self-created indignities are avoided, credibility can ensue, to where plenty of prospects will be attracted. To do this successfully, trust and integrity, along with dignity must be established.

As a frontline salesperson you want to give a perception of having a profound expertise in the unit that you sell. Doing this does not require having a great deal of knowledge about the product. Matter of fact experts suggest that discussing relevant matters that relate to the business at hand might be better than actually selling. It is easy to sell without selling! What this means is that it can be a bad idea to oversell when presenting a product. You can buttress your chances by simply following the natural order of things, without trying to make the customer believe you are being pushy. Studies have shown that when salespeople act normal and do less selling that they sell more products, and as a result increase their level of intrinsic job satisfaction.

The next most important factor in creating a lasting intrinsic job satisfaction is when a salesperson knows how to coordinate a customer's needs with what he is offering. Collaborating with the customer to identify his needs and fit those needs to match with your product offers can go a long way in making a sale as quickly as possible without wasting the customer's time longer than necessary. Selling is a series of conversations that are structured by successful salespeople to assess, and structure customers' needs, and to build lasting values. The most effective way is to be natural and authentic during the process, and to avoid traditional sales techniques that are associated with gimmicks.

In selling, and during sales, being too eager can often hinder the prospect of a sale than anything else. If during the sale, you act tense, desperate, and unease, the customer is likely to notice it. That sense of unease can shift the onus, and advantage to the customer who may at that point no longer see you as being able to fulfill his needs to make a purchase. The average customer likes confidence in a salesperson. The more assured and confident a salesperson is, the greater the likelihood of making a sale possible. If a customer notices that you are shifty and unease, he is likely to ask you how long you have been in sales, and with that question will come the notion that you do not know what you are doing. Projecting the impression that you are new on the job, when you are not, can be counterproductive. What will give the customer the impression will not be what you say but your demeanor and body language. According to experts, a positive body language and poise can go a long way to creating a strong perception of confidence during the sales process. Displaying and showing a positive demeanor can also create intrinsic job satisfaction when the salesperson is able to fulfill his role of selling, but failure to sell when the possibility is there, can lead to dissatisfaction and the unlikelihood of intrinsic job satisfaction.

While it is a good idea to portray commitment to your craft during sales, it might be a good idea not to be too desperate for a sale. Desperation to make a sale can lead to poor performance; and perception that can make the customer think you are very desperate, that without the sale you are in trouble. It is never a good idea to give out unnecessary signal of distress that you need the sale very bad. A subliminal projection of the philosophy of want versus need can be a strong indicator of desperation, according to studies. It can be easy to gently make it known in a subconscious manner that you want to make the sale but that you really don't need to. Humans have a way of making things difficult for others when they know you really something, according to social psychologists. But the onus of proving that you want to but don't really need to rests on the salesperson to project and exude, so that the customer will quickly understand that subconscious language.

The internal desire of some salespeople to perform better than their colleagues can be stronger in some and weaker in others. Those with stronger desire to perform better are often driven because of the satisfaction they derive from the task; while those with weaker desire are not so driven because the task may not give them enough pleasure or fulfillment. Many salespeople do not work harder than other salespeople because of pleasure or fulfillment; they simply do so because they like to win, and also because they are internally challenged to win.

What motivates some individuals may be different than what motivates others. Some people are motivated because a task may give them a sense of fulfillment; while others may be motivated because of the benefit or rewards that may be in place. A renowned psychologist and theorist, Abraham Maslow, known for creating Maslow's hierarchy of needs that are predicated on fulfilling innate human needs that can result in self-actualization, wrote that certain factors can influence our motivation. According to Maslow, certain needs must be in place before intrinsic motivation can occur. Such basic needs include: physiological needs, safety needs, social needs, esteem needs, and need for self-actualization.

Physiological needs are more urgent in individuals than the other needs. The need to survive by having food, water, air, shelter, clothing and sex, are basic natural needs that are essential to our physical survival. The absence of some of these basic needs can lead to lack of fulfillment, or even demise. To fulfill these needs, we do not need a strong motivation as these needs are essential to our wellbeing. Physiological needs are driven by things our body needs to survive. We often have to work hard to provide food, water, air, shelter and clothing, for self, and families. As for the need for sex, that can be controlled, but the need for food and water cannot be controlled. We can survive without sex but we cannot survive without food, water, and air. Those needs are crucial to our physical survival and wellbeing. Shelter is important but it too can be controlled to a certain extent. Clothing is a must for many of us, but there are societies where clothing is not an essential factor. Many of the physiological needs are essential while others are not so essential.

For many salespeople, the need to satisfy many of their physiological needs may be stronger than those of their colleagues. Those who choose to work harder than their colleagues may have a stronger motivation to fulfill the physiological needs of their families than those who do not have as strong a desire to work hard. But when it comes to the stronger physiological needs such as water, air, and food, the motivation to work hard in order to accomplish those tasks is not optional. Maslow noted that in order to satisfy higher needs, we must first satisfy our basic physiological needs. Satisfying our basic essential needs will allow us to concentrate on satisfying other needs in our lives. In the sales profession, the difference between successful and unsuccessful salespeople is that successful salespeople often satisfy their basic essential needs and then move onward to satisfy their high level needs in life. But unsuccessful salespeople often stay stuck with satisfying the essential basic needs by making those needs the dominant and biggest needs in their lives. Successful salespeople will first satisfy the basic physiological needs in their lives to allow them to concentrate on their higher level needs.

Safety needs, or the need to have safety can have its own motivation that propels us to work hard to satisfy those needs. For many of us, the desire to satisfy such a need may be stronger than others. But the crucial element of satisfying safety needs is more internal with some, while it is not so with others. According to Maslow, we all need safety and security in our lives. Though we all differ in the way and manner we meet those needs, the motivation is driven by factors such as essential components as order, stability, routine, familiarity, control, certainty, health and the environment. Order, or the state of peace, and freedom from confused or unruly behavior, or the state or condition of things, or even appropriate order or functionality, can all derive certain motivation in some people than in others. The need to have order in our lives can serve as a motivation for some while the opposite can occur with others. So it is with stability. Many people seek stability in their lives, while some will not make it an essential factor in their lives.

Having stability, and order can enhance progress in meeting life's challenges. Stability in our lives will enable us to plan for the future, and to meet business and financial obligations. The absence of stability can rob us of the need to face the challenges that life brings our way. We need a stable life in order to progress. A chaotic mind will always create a life of disarray, and be in constant disarray, that will seldom have the time and energy to focus on what matters in life. Instability can reduce safety in our lives. Many successful people work hard to provide safety in their families, but they do so by first ensuring that there is stability, and order, before concentrating on safety.

Familiarity is a component of a safety need which enables us to weave together the factors that provide enhanced safety in our lives. We cannot provide a good safety in our lives without being familiar with the essential components of safety. Such essential components of safety can include having control over our lives, in order to meet the basic needs in our lives. Lack of control can lead to disunity and unstable mental state. The need for control is significant as it helps us to concentrate on important matters that drive our usefulness in life.

Environment, certainty and health are crucial to meeting our safety needs. We can fail in our quest to meet our safety needs if we are unable to cognitively recognize the importance of environment, and the assurance of certainty, and the need for good health in our lives. To move forward in meeting our higher level needs, we must first provide safety needs and the factors that pivot its components.

Social needs are important needs in our lives. Some people are introverts while others are extroverts. Introverts are characterized by introversion or shyness. Whereas extroverts are friendly, sociable, and outgoing people who like to interact. In the context of meeting social needs, or the need for love and belonging, one must be emotionally positive and wired to meet the factors that allow these needs to occur. An introvert may find it difficult to love and belong, while an extrovert will not have issues with belonging. Meeting the essential components of social needs such as love, affection, belonging, and acceptance, can be a challenge for others, while it can be a natural cakewalk for others. For introverts, it can be difficult, while it can be a cakewalk for extroverts because of their love for people. The motivation to meet these needs can vary from person to person, but these needs are crucial in creating happiness in our lives. Happiness, according to social psychologists can lead to intrinsic job satisfaction. The motivation to satisfy social needs can be just as crucial as the motivation to satisfy the needs for food, water, and air, as they all enhance our wellbeing in life. Love, affection, belonging and acceptance are needed to serve as mental stability and to maintain strong positive influence in our lives, and various endeavors.

Esteem needs can be a predictor of job satisfaction among salespeople, according to studies. Esteem needs are important to our mental wellbeing, stability, assurance in life, confidence, dignity and integrity. The respect we get from others can serve as a motivation to have the confidence to concentrate on higher level needs that are crucial in our lives. Most of us want to be respected, and we work hard to be accepted and recognized for our hard work. We repulse being debased or disrespected as that can hamper our ability to command reasonable dignity. The need for self esteem can lead us to channel and harness our strength towards achieving adequacy, competence, independence, and confidence. These essential components of esteem needs can also enable us to nurture the desire for prestige, and to cultivate a likeable reputation. Many successful salespeople perceive esteem needs as a crucial factor in their success. Esteem needs can also be a significant predictor of fame, glory, dominance, importance, and recognition, if properly harnessed to achieve success.

Perhaps the most important factor in the category of needs, according to Maslow, is the need for self actualization. The need for self actualization can lead to success in many areas of our lives. Self actualization can impel humans to achieve greatness because the needs allow us to reach our full potential. This can only occur when we have satisfied the other levels of needs as defined by Maslow. Once the other levels have been achieved, one is able to fully concentrate on the other higher levels of need, and able to function and achieve the best potentials. Though these needs may be met, and we may be able to achieve our full or highest potentials, as humans we are still likely to be dissatisfied, unless we are doing things that fulfill our inner desires.

We cannot be happy until we have reached that level of fulfillment, or we are doing things we love doing. While certain needs can be classified as deficient or inadequate needs because of lack, they can only be met through external sources, via the environment, people or the things around us. Self actualization on the other hand, is a growth need that helps us to reach our highest potential, even though it does not help us with the things we may lack in our lives.

The best part of self actualization is that it gives us room to grow and develop, and it always intrinsically motivates us to do better.

` Extrinsic job satisfaction is distinctively different from intrinsic job satisfaction. Extrinsic satisfactions are derivable from external sources. Some people are motivated because of a promise of an incentive or because there is something to be gained rather than the need to fulfill internal happiness. There are those who will do a job because it satisfies them and makes them happy while there are those who will only do a job because of incentive like money. Whether motivation is due to the need for happiness or fulfillment or due to monetary advantage, each serves a need. And most salespeople will only work if the incentive is strong enough to motivate them. There is small proportion of salespeople that will work because of the love for the job. The reason there is not enough love for the job to justify intrinsic satisfaction is because sales jobs do not command enough dignity and sense of fulfillment to induce a reasonable motivation, according to studies.

Chapter 8

Customer Loyalty and Disloyalty

According to experts, customer loyalty is the gateway, and key to profitability and sustainability. Many customers are loyal to organizations or salespeople that provide prices that tend to benefit them. If the price is right, and the deal is workable, a customer will jump ship and go to an organization that provides the best deal. A customer will not be loyal to anyone, including salespeople and organizations if the price or deal does not favor him. If one organization has a better deal for the same product that you are offering, a customer that was once thought to be loyal will go to that organization, regardless of the perceived loyalty.

Many organizations take customer loyalty for granted, thinking a customer will be back regardless of the price offered; because they think they offer better customer service than their competitors. While a good customer service may command loyalty on many occasions, it is the offering of a better price that actually creates and drives loyalty or disloyalty. And in some cases, a better product or a product that provides greater innovation and design will sometimes be more favored than cheap looking products, even if the price is more reasonable. Many customers are influenced by look, and quality. The better the quality, the more drawn they will be to that product. And if two vendors or merchants are offering the same quality product, price becomes the predictor of loyalty or disloyalty.

Studies have shown that customers will buy a product that meets their needs, and if the price is right, the same customers will buy from a regular vendor versus a new vendor. Customers generally do not care where they buy as long as the price meets their objective or value. And organizations that recognize the importance of price to customers will always do their utmost best to meet such prices so as to keep such customers coming back to them. If a customer buys a particular product from an organization at a higher price than the market price, he is unlikely to go back to that same organization. Many customers will want to justify a reason to go back to an organization where they did not get a fair price in their previous purchase. If there is enough justification, they may go back; if not they will not go back even if the customer service is better.

Fair treatment can also create customer loyalty. If a customer senses that a salesperson did all he could to meet a purchase need, he will come back to the organization because of the salesperson. And in the same token, if other factors influenced a customer to think the organization did not do enough to be fair in pricing and treatment, he/she will not have any reason to be back.

To ensure your customers keep coming back, it is imperative to always work hard to find what will satisfy your customers. If a reasonable or fair price is what it will take, then that should also be the action that the organization should take. The salesperson does not have the authority or power to increase or decrease a price, but the organization does. If a salesperson feels his organization's price is too steep, it might be a good idea to let supervisors know that the same product is going for a much lower price in other organizations. Some salespeople often try to close a customer on their price which may be higher than the price offered by other organizations. This is a wrong way to earn a customer's loyalty. If for any reason there is no way to meet the price the customer is asking, it might be a good idea to explain to the customer the reason why the other organization is able to lower its prices and why you cannot. Justify your reason rather than to try to persuade the customer!

Where justification will not suffice, resort to lowering your price to meet the competitor's price. If the loss is going to be too much in matching the competitor's price, if necessary show the customer your invoice or what you paid for it, and why it would be counterproductive to lower the prices below cost. Some customers will not believe that you will lose money to sell a product because they know most retail organizations usually say that to get the customer to sympathize and buy from them. Many customers think it is a trick some organizations use at every point of sale. The truth is that the dealer might be right. Most organizations such as automobile dealerships want to move their inventories as fast as possible. Any inventory that lasts longer than 80 days is often seen as a must-go-inventory. These old units will often be sold below market price and often at a loss to the organization because of the urgent need to move them.

Customer loyalty and disloyalty can also be due to the product an organization sells. If a customer was previously deemed a loyal customer but because an organization that he/she had previously been loyal to do not sell appealing or trendy products that he likes, such a customer may go elsewhere to meet such a need. Dealers may want to stock a variety of products that are deemed trendy in the consumer community in order to continue to meet the needs of those customers that like being trendy. If the new body style of Impala is the must-have vehicle in a particular neighborhood, a once loyal customer that lives in that neighborhood is unlikely to buy a Ford Fusion from his regular dealer. If the dealer does not have the latest neighborhood-trendy new body style Impala, that customer is going to likely go to the dealer that sells it. In other words, customers will not sacrifice their needs to satisfy a loyalty. They will go where their interests and product desire can be met.

Customer loyalty can oftentimes be unpredictable. A customer that you thought was very pleased with your service can end up in the hands of another person or organization without thinking twice about coming back to you. The reason is that many customers do not think they owe a salesperson or an organization any obligation to be back. Many customers do not feel obligated to one particular salesperson or organization. They want to be free to make their choices without being encumbered to buy from one particular salesperson. And salespeople should not feel slighted when they see their old customers buying from other salespeople. Many customers will not come back if their previous experience was a bad one, or if they feel they were unfairly treated during their previous purchase.

A salesperson should always keep in touch with his customers to make sure the customer remembers to come back to him for a future purchase. Though keeping in touch does not necessarily mean a customer will come back to you, it helps to keep your name in the customer's thoughts when he makes the next purchase. The thing to always remember is that customers will always be customer. Their needs matter more to them than a mere loyalty to a salesperson.

Customer loyalty or disloyalty can be two folds. The first is benefit while the second is advantage. Many customers seek what benefits them if they choose to be loyal, and depending on the accruing benefit, they can be steadfastly loyal or disloyal. If the benefit is persuasive enough, they can remain loyal for as long as the benefit lasts. But if the benefit is weak, they are likely to be unpredictable in their loyalty. The thing to remember is that customers want tangible benefits versus abstract benefits. They want what they can see versus promises that may take time to fulfill or may never be fulfilled.

The second type of benefit that most customers seek in order to fulfill any form of loyalty is advantage. If they know that there is immediate advantage in being loyal, they will be quick to prove their loyalty. If the advantage is not immediately visible, they will likely not have any need to be loyal. In many ways, benefits and advantage are interrelated in that they involve what the customer stands to gain, or not gain, in order to fulfill loyalty.

Loyalty in the workplace is in many ways similar to customer loyalty to organizations. Many employees are loyal to organizations that provide them with job security, job satisfaction, benefits, constant promotions, and stake in the growth of the organization. If an employee believes he has a stake in the organization, and that he is a significant part of its processes and survival, he will do whatever it takes to protect the interest of the organization. On the other hand, if an employee believes his needs are not being met in the organization and that his bosses do not care about his welfare and wellbeing, he will unlikely maintain loyalty to the organization. What many organizations do not realize is that employees will go the extra mile to protect the interests of their organizations if they know they are seen as important players in the organizational process. If they believe they are not important, and that their organizations do not seek their opinions on the things that matter, and that they are just means to an end, they will act in the same manner.

To create employee loyalty, employers need to understand employee needs, and to focus on effectively managing those needs to benefit their employees on a constant basis. Another important factor in maintaining employee loyalty is decision making in the organization. If employees are included in decision making in the organizations, they will feel a sense of belonging, and will protect the organization without being prompted to do so.

With customers, loyalty has the same meaning to them as it is to salespeople, in an organization. A customer will not only bring repeat businesses but will recommend friends and neighbors, including family and friends to the organization, if they believe there is meaning to their loyalty. The keyword here is *meaning*, and how customers perceive such meaning. A customer needs to know that he *means* something significant to the organization in order to maintain adequate loyalty. As to whether the loyalty will be weak or strong depends on how the organization interprets the *meaning* that is silently understood by both parties. While the essence of the *meaning* is not a contract of any kind with obligations to fulfill, it must be significant enough to be perceived as a contract or its essence will be feeble.

In retail organizations, salespeople need to be able to recognize whether their customers have weak or strong loyalty. If the loyalty is perceived weak, the best thing to do may be to find out what can strengthen the loyalty so that it can be beneficial to both sides. If loyalty can be maintained by washing the customer's car whenever he drops by the dealership, it might be a good idea to do so. While it is important to often strive to maintain customer loyalty, maintaining such loyalty must be done with reasonableness or it will put the organization at a disadvantage where it can become counterproductive.

The essence of doing business is to maintain profitability and, sustainability, in order to survive. And to do so, organizations must be careful not to be too eager to give out freebies whenever a customer shows up in an attempt to maintain loyalty. Many customers will take advantage of a situation when they perceive that an organization is too eager to please. If you over please them, they will come to expect such treatment every time, and whenever there is a shortfall in the treatment or freebie, they will immediately take it as a cold reception to their needs or lack of interest on your part, to meet their needs. It is good to be polite and firm at the same time. If one is too polite and too friendly, customer loyalty will be diminished by such over-friendliness. Business must always be business, and focusing on being professional can go a long way in strength ening customer loyalty. To be professional means conforming to unwritten ethical standards of conduct that will not betray, or stray from a formal business conduct. Such a formality must be characterized by upholding a strong personality that will command respect and loyalty at the same time.

Studies have shown that many organizations spend more to acquire new customers than they spend to keep existing ones. To acquire new customers, organizations often spend thousands, if not millions, of dollars in advertising, whereas it costs considerably less to maintain existing customers. If there is no strong customer loyalty, customers will likely leave and may never come back. To make sure customers do not leave and that there is strengthened loyalty, a positive relationship must exist between customers and organizations that can lead to mutual benefits. And to create and maintain such a positive relationship, it is imperative that employees be trained on how to satisfy the needs of customers in order to maintain the continuity of the relationship.

Apart from training employees, organizations must create an atmosphere that gently lures customers without imposing on their senses. This can be done by defining a unique niche that may adhere to customers' sense of comfort and wellbeing. A conducive and cognitively defined atmosphere might be a way to ensure that customers keep coming back.

Customers' disloyalty can occur when they no longer have any need to keep bringing business to an organization that purports to have customer service that does not really exist. A lot of customers believe in action rather than words or promises. Promises tend to feed traditional sales gimmicks and narratives that many perceive to be deceptive. A customer will sense that a promise is not genuine if previous promises were unfulfilled. Salespeople, according to some customers, lie, deceive, and cheat to make a sale. A salesperson will tell a customer an untrue story about a product rather than be upfront with the truth. When there is a perception of falsehood, a customer will not need to be told before going elsewhere where there is honesty.

In a recent survey conducted about salespeople's honesty, it was noted in the random survey that a respondent was so angry that when he had the opportunity to give a feedback about his experience, he gave more than 500 words of handwritten feedback! The respondent mentioned that his personal experience was so horrifying that it took him a long time to recover from the enormity of the deception. The respondent said he was beguiled into believing that a particular product doesn't exist and that they stopped making it, until he visited another dealership and found out that he was fed a lie and deception. He said he had expected more from such a high-end dealership.

A beguiling experience can lead to customer disloyalty, especially if the customer had earlier been loyal to that organization. If it was found later that the organization had been deceptive in taking care of a customer's business needs, the customer will no longer have any need to be loyal to such an organization. Some customers will go as far as writing a bad review on Yelp or other social media to let the world know how they were treated. Reviews can positively and negatively impact organizations. A bad review will drive away prospective customers; while a good review will attract new customers. In today's internet-connected world, many customers depend on reviews to make their decisions. A bad review will quickly inform a prospective customer that such an organization is not a good place to do business.

To avoid creating an atmosphere where a customer will not feel comfortable to do business, it is important that organizations learn to be honest and truthful, in addition to making good on promises. Many customers appreciate organizations that keep their promises. Lies and deceptions tend to turn off customers, especially when such a deception is blatantly obvious. While we cannot all be perfect, it pays to be as close to perfection as possible in business transactions.

Training salespeople to be upright and honest in handling customers' businesses and transactions can create a good image for organizations. Loyalty cannot be earned through sleaziness and untruths. It is a good idea to be truthful, even if the truth is bitter. Honesty pays higher dividends in the long run than untruths. And in today's business, untruths can ruin business reputations, relationships and sustainability.

Social psychologists link untruth with deception and cheating. If a customer believes the notion that an organization is shady, he will tell his friends, relatives, neighbors, to avoid such an organization. Word of mouth travels far and wide, and in many cases more effective than advertising in print and electronic media. In medieval times, advertisings were done through the word of mouth, and even in modern times where media advertising is ubiquitous, word of mouth is still perceived to be more trusted and effective.

Customers are generally unpredictable, and oftentimes the more untrustworthy an organization is, the more some customers can be unpredictable. To constantly predict customers' mood and behavior, organizations must create a culture of honesty and customer predictability. To do this, organizations must be transparent about their modus operandi so that customers can have the option to make decisions that benefit them. Customers do not like to be forced into making decisions that put them at a disadvantage. For example, telling a customer a product doesn't exist when it actually exists can lead the customer to opt for an unintended product that may cost higher. If such a customer discovers the deception later, it may lead to future disloyalty and the demise of repeat businesses and referrals, from the customer, to that organization.

Organizations should always encourage loyalty. Loyalty does not necessarily mean spending money to incentivize customer base. Loyalty can be earned through integrity, honesty, and trustworthiness. Organizations should also inculcate trustworthiness in their workforce so that their sales representatives can be trustworthy enough to conduct honest transactions that do not leave rancor and bad taste in the minds of customers.

Many organizations claim to have policies that encourage trustworthiness and honesty, but few, if any, actually go as far as trying to encourage their employees to be honest and trustworthy. Biweekly seminars and trainings should be used to keep salespeople and other employees on their toes, and in line, so that such policies can be strictly adhered to. It is not enough to say it often, making employees sign a handbook that promotes trustworthiness and honesty can further instill that sense of responsibility in employees. Employees need to know that their organizations are serious about telling the truth to customers. They also need to know that untruths can lead to termination. A constant reminder during meetings can be another way to make sure such policies are strictly adhered to.

In sales, trustworthiness can lead to growth and sustainability. And in addition, trustworthiness can lead to a lasting customer loyalty that can enhance growth. Lack of trustworthiness on the other hand, can lead to poor organizational performance, if not demise. Customers can define the longevity and sustainability of organizations through repeat businesses and loyalty. Studies have also shown that customers are the lifeblood of organizations, and without customers, an organization is unlikely to survive. Many organizations have gone out of business because of customer disloyalty to their products and services. Oftentimes, organizations forget what keeps them in business – customers. And the more aware organizations are about what keeps them in business, the better it will be for their sustainability and longevity.

Recognizing the important role customers play in the organizational process can be a strong indicator of future success.

Knowing and acknowledging that the absence of a strong customer loyalty can be detrimental, is one of the first steps that can help organizations to nurture customer loyalty. Once earned, customer loyalty should be safeguarded and protected. Like a seed planted without adequate care, a customer loyalty that is not safeguarded can die like a seed without care, if not properly taken care of.

There are steps that organizations must take to protect their most valued asset – customers. The first step is to organize, and optimize functions that recognize and reward customers for their loyalty. The second is to promote incentives that can nurture customer loyalty, such as a rebate. The third step is to have a bonus in place that rewards customers who have proven their loyalty for a specified period of time.

Many organizations often use customer loyalty to promote sales and profitability. For instance, automakers occasionally promote customer loyalty programs that reward customers with additional rebate for trading in the brand they previously purchased, for a new brand. Such rebates and incentives only reward customers who are loyal to the brand of products produced by the manufacturer. The idea behind such an incentive is to further reinforce the value of the brand, and to ensure that customers keep coming back to buy the same brand. While this can be a way to create value, and to promote sales, it only works if customers are happy with their ownership of the brand. If a previous Toyota Camry customer is happy with the performance of the car, he is likely to take advantage of the owner loyalty program. But if the customer hasn't been happy with the quality and performance of the Camry, he is likely to try another brand, at a different organization, regardless of the owner loyalty program.

And in many cases, how a customer perceives and enjoys the performance of a product will depend on the efficacy of the service department. For example, a Mercedes Benz S-class owner who has repeatedly experienced problems with the suspension on his vehicle will unlikely buy the same vehicle again, especially if the service department hasn't been very helpful. The experience can even be worse if the dealership's service department does not know how to properly treat their customers with respect and dignity. Many dealerships' service departments are notorious for their poor treatment of customers who bring their cars in for service. Owner loyalty will not work with a customer who dislikes a brand because of poor quality, and appalling service department.

In a research study conducted and published in an International Journal of Management, by Duke Hyun et al, the authors noted that organizations are "failing to gain and maintain a loyal customer base," because of their inability to manage customers' loyal and disloyal behaviors. Using a sample of 159 shoppers, the authors identified three factors that exert significant influence on customers' loyal and disloyal behaviors. Quality and price sensitivity were found to be some of the factors influencing customers' loyal and disloyal behaviors.

Another factor influencing customers' loyalty and disloyalty is how they are able to use the internet to compare various products and prices to make their decisions. If a customer uses the internet to shop for a product and fair price, he is going to be unlikely loyal to any organization. The customer's loyalty will only be to the organization that has the customer's desired product, and offers fair price. If a customer has previously purchased the same product from one organization but the organization has a higher price than its competitors, the customer is going to likely use the internet to shop for the best price; and is going to be unlikely loyal to the organization where he had made a previous purchase. As a result of the internet becoming a convenient shopping avenue for customers to compare products and prices, the "information asymmetries between sellers and buyers are becoming smaller," according to Duke Hyun et al.

Price and product competition can be influencing factors in customers' loyalty and disloyalty. The lower a price is the greater the likelihood of a customer maintaining a product loyalty, and to some extent, loyalty to the organization that sells the product. The quality of the product also matters to the customer's future business with the organization. If the product has met and exceeded the customer's expectation, the customer will likely come back to buy the same product. But only if the price is right! But if the price is not right, the customer is going to likely shift that loyalty elsewhere, where the price is right for the same or a different product.

To ensure that customers always come back, organizations need to create a strategy that can lead to customer retention, and loyalty. Such strategies should include focusing on what matters most to customers and finding ways to satisfy those needs. If customer needs are identified, and met, many of the customers that shop on the internet for prices, will first shop in the organization they feel most comfortable to do business, before resorting to shop on the internet to compare prices. Organizations need to realize that millennial customers are different from customers of pre-internet age where information was limited.

In an internet age where information is only a click away, customer loyalty and how to create quality service should be the new organizational focus. Millennial consumers have access to information customers did not have access to, before the advent of the intent, and as a result, they will only stick with companies that are ready to go the extra mile to create a good customer service. Good customer service can create a loyalty of its own, even where prices matter, studies have shown.

Another significant indicator of customer loyalty and repeat businesses is that customers are inclined to buy from an organization where they feel their needs have been taken care of, and met. The fact that it costs more to acquire new customers than it costs to maintain existing ones, should impel organizations to strategize a plan and a culture to keep existing customers happy so that they won't be advertising for new customers so often. To continuously have a good base for customer loyalty, there is an urgent need for a well structured and defined objective that will promote customer loyalty. A productive and sustainable management objective should focus on customer loyalty and how to sustain it.

Chapter 9

Management by Objective

In automobile retail organizations, management has to be able to define specific objectives and how to achieve such objectives in sequence, so that salespeople can understand their roles. To do this effectively, organizations have to be able to convey their specific objectives clearly, to the sales-force. Management by objective (MBO) or management by results (MBR), in automobile sales, focuses on how organizations define their objectives so that salespeople can understand and agree to them. The idea of the philosophy of MBO is to enable organizations to perform jobs that need to be performed one at a time, to create room for efficient and productive performance.

The philosophy is akin to the philosophy of Adam Smith's division of labor where each employee performs a job he is best suited, to create efficiency. Division of labor has become part of the objective of many organizations, and since its inception, it has allowed organizations to focus on efficiency. With MBO, the goal is to allow organizational leaders to understand how much they can accomplish as each objective is effectively performed. Organization al leaders have to be able to create objectives that are meaningful and relevant to their organization's needs so that set goals can be achieved with productive results. In retail organizations, managers and supervisors have to be able to define their obje ctives well enough so that they can be structured to achieve desired results. And the only way set objectives can be achieved is when management by results or managing to create desired results is working in conjunction with management by objectives. Both have to be working together to achieve desired results, and most of all, employees have to be able to understand what those objectives represent, so that they can be able to agree to them.

The essence of management by objectives or management by results entails organizational productivity and how it can be achieved to create sustainability in organizations. The unfortunate thing is that many organizations create objectives that their employees do not understand, and if they do, do not agree to, and as a result the objectives do not achieve desired results. This usually occurs where standardized objectives are not created to produce results. Management by objectives (MBO) must be properly structured to create desired results or lead to management by results (MBR). One has to define the other. Management by objective has to be able to morph into management by results for the culture of the organization to yield positive results.

If the goal of an organization is to have a positive customer service that is capable of promoting repeat businesses, customer loyalty, and reinforcing trust and honesty in business transactions and practices, all employees must be on the same page or mindset. A salesperson's motivation to sell with positive attitude must agree with the finance manager's goal to sell finance products. If a salesperson does a good job of selling the car and the finance manager does a bad job of selling the finance products, it can lead to bad customer service that can leave the customer with bad impression. Bad impression that occurs due to poor adherence to the goals and objectives of the organization can defeat the purpose of management by objectives and management by results.

In nonretail business environments where organizations are service oriented, objectives have to be set to yield results that can lead to sustainability. It is not enough to have it on paper but to practice how results can be achieved from the objectives of the organizations. Many organizations do not practice what they preach. For example, some organizations preach customer first, but when it comes down to the practical end of it, employees do not often put customers first, and as a result, often end up creating unfavorable impression that leads to loss of repeat businesses and referrals.

Some organizations often have signs posted on the walls of their offices to denote their level of customer care and to urge customers to post good reviews on social media when they have, or have not earned such reviews. Many of the signs often attempt to lure customers with monetary rewards for posting good reviews, but if customer service is bad, no amount of monetary incentive will induce customers to post good reviews. And what most organizations do not realize is that some customers will post good reviews because of the financial reward attached to it, and will tell family and friends the reality of the experience they had during their business with the organization.

Management by objective (MBO) was first propounded by Peter Drucker in his 1954 book entitled, *The Practice of Management*, so that organizations can see why most of their policies do not work, and if they work, why they are not as successful as they should be. Drucker's goal was to bring organizational management to understand the essence of positive management by objective and how the practice of it can yield productive results. In propounding the theory of management by objectives, Drucker also emphasized the importance of its added factor of management by results. The purpose of having goals and objectives is to achieve results, hence management by results (MBR). It is not enough to set goals and objectives, organizations must be able to set feasible course of actions to make sure objectives are adhered to. Each employee must be able to fulfill his/her responsibility in order to ensure objectives are carried out to the benefit of the organization.

For example, a salesperson must be able to understand the objective of his organization along with the course of action to take to fulfill it, in order to have desired results. If it is the duty of the salesperson to sell a product, and perform a proper delivery of the product, he must know and understand the course of action that will produce customer satisfaction in the process. Oftentimes, that will only work if an organization has customer satisfaction as part of its modus operandi. If an organization has set objectives to sell its products and to ensure that the customer is satisfied and willing to return in the future for a repeat business, the organization will make sure salespeople understand what course of action to take to make sure customers are happy with their purchases. Such course of action may include bringing the customer to meet with a supervisor to go through the delivery process once again to ensure the customer's needs have been met. And the process also allows the customer to know who to go to when the salesperson is not around or when there is a grievance with the product in the future.

An effective management by objective must be a process in which employees and supervisors work together to identify the common goals and objectives of the organization, and be able to understand each individual's responsibility so that expected results can be achieved. Organizations have to be able to use the applied measures of MBO to create guidelines for supervisors and employees to ensure there is a meaningful contribution to meet the goals and objectives of the organization. According to Drucker, the core philosophy of management by objective is that employers and supervisors can effectively manage subordinates by creating policies and goals that employees can strive to achieve to accomplish the objectives of the organization. Striving to achieve might not be enough for organizations that want to compete in an environment where cutthroat competition reigns. Employees must not only strive but do their utmost best to ensure that the goals and objectives of their organizations are met. And to do this, each employee must be willing to make the necessary sacrifice so that the future of the organization can be sustained, while achieving desired productivity and profitability.

Successful salespeople tend to make the most sacrifice of working hard to meet their own set objectives in productivity. If organizations can identify the objectives of successful salespeople and align such objectives with their objectives, meaningful productivity can be achieved in the process. There are instances where most successful salespeople have better defined objectives to succeed than the organizations they work for. If management by objective is to produce desired results, organizations have to strive to nurture the productive habit of such successful salespeople to create sustainability.

The essence of MBO is for subordinates or employees to know their roles and responsibilities in order to meet organizational goals and objectives. Part of that roles and responsibilities include making sure employees understand how their roles and activities can ensue in the success of the organization. But to do this, employees must have job satisfaction and be willing partners in working together to achieve the goals and objectives of the organization. In addition, employees have to also know that the sacrifice they are being called to make to achieve organizational objective will also benefit them in the process. The most effective assurance organizations can give to their employees in this process includes fulfilling the personal needs of the employees with rewards and promotions. If employees' needs are fulfilled, they will be willing to work hard enough to ensure the organization is successful in its quest and pursuit to achieve the highest productivity, and to meet its objectives.

Several factors can influence the implementation of MBO and MBR and such factors include motivation and empowerment.

Motivating employees can include a process whereby employees are involved in the decision making process and goal setting of the organization. If employees feel they are important enough to be considered part of the goal setting process, they will be motivated to work hard to achieve the desired results of the organization. Studies have shown that when employees are motivated through empowerment that such process can lead to job satisfaction which can also lead to retention and reduced loss of valued, experienced and skilled employees. Job satisfaction can have a ripple effect of retention and enhanced productivity, and can reduce organizational costs of hiring new employees every time.

Another factor that can lead to the success of MBO and MBR is communication and coordination. Good communication is the key to disseminating information about the objective of the organization to employees so that they can understand what to do, and what actions to take, to make MBO achievable. Coordinating constant and frequent reviews between management and employees with good communication as an apparatus can create a cordial relationship that will enhance opportunities to solve problems that may emanate within organizations.

Communicating the objectives of the organization through effective means will prevent misunderstanding of purpose, including the intentions of those that organizations depend on to implement policies designed to achieve positive and productive results. It is important for organizations to have a flexible channel of communication so that there will be clarity of actions needed to carry out the objectives and goals of the organization. Frequent reviews are crucial to maintaining and fixing loopholes that may exist in organizational objectives. The success of MBO can only be measured by the success of the functions that are created to achieve the desired results. When the functions are in place and coordinated effectively, management by results or that is result oriented will now be the expected outcome. Management by results is subject to the effectiveness of MBO so that intended results can be achieved while working hard to remove problems that may occur in the process.

As a process, MBO can only function when there is clarity of goals so that there will be no misunderstanding as to what actions should be taken to achieve success of the goals. When MBO or MBR first became part of organizational culture of doing business, Hewlett

Packard was one of the initial companies that understood its framework and was able to use it to achieve success and enhance productivity. Hewlett Packard benefited from the applications of the framework of MBO and MBR and knew that success was achievable by adopting the principles of the process, and by ensuring that supervisors and subordinates work and interact in a harmonious workplace to ensure the goals of the organization were successfully achieved.

Hewlett Packard was also one of the initial organizations that embraced the philosophy of MBO to maintain its focus on productivity, sustainability and profitability. The company understood that effective productivity could not be achieved without bringing all the stakeholders within the organization to agree to the objectives that are necessary to maintain and sustain success.

One of the factors that can lead to the success of MBO and MBR is that organizations need to constantly work with those successful and talented employees within their ranks to encourage them to continue to commit to organizational goals and objectives. Successful salespeople and employees are often self motivated, and often do not need to be told what is at stake to continue to achieve and maintain success. Organizations need to recognize the fact that talented and successful employees need to be encouraged to maintain the commitment that comes natural to them by virtue of their dedication to hard work and success. Organizations cannot attempt to dampen the spirit of talented salespeople and employees with policies that are unfavorable to them. While these types of employees cannot be left to do whatever they like, they need to be given the room and flexibility to use their talent to help enhance the growth and productivity of their organizations. It will be counterproductive for organizations to frequently take advantage of the inner drive of talented and self-motivated salespeople and employees by not helping to nurture that inner drive. Providing leads and other motivational apparatus can help add zeal and encouragement to the already motivated and inspired salespeople.

Good employees are hard to find, and organizations like Hewlett Packard, Intel, IBM, etcetera, understood and knew that to make MBO work effectively that employees have to sign on by committing to the process; and were able to use the applications and philosophy of MBO and MBR to achieve success at a time when most organizations were struggling with sustainability in an increased competitive climate. In a corporate climate that is constantly evolving, and changing, organizations have to often change with the times or be left behind. And those that are caught unawares often find out too late that the train of innovation and change had left the station long before they became aware it was there! For example, organizations like Blackberry and Nokia did not understand that they had to change with the times to maintain and improve their innovation. And when new and innovative products came along and took their market shares, they were left with a fringe of the market that was already on the move to embrace the future.

One of the principles of MBO and MBR is the ability of organizations to focus on the objectives that will maintain sustainability on a frequent basis. The process must also be constantly improved so that organizations can understand the importance of having employees to believe and commit to embracing changes that may be necessary to focus on innovation and productivity. And there have to be frequent interactions between supervisors and subordinates so that ideas can be brainstormed to help organizational growth. Frequent brainstorming allows management and subordinates to focus on new techniques that involve the spontaneous contributions of ideas from all employees of the organization. By mulling over ideas together, in a harmonious relationship, solutions can easily be found to problems, as innovation may occur in the process about improving existing products and services that will benefit the organization.

Hewlett Packard did not achieve its success with MBO by not encouraging innovation, and investing in research and development to constantly improve its products and services. The company achieved its initial success by believing in the principles of MBO and MBR and getting its employees to believe in the same philosophy. And when it was obvious to HP that MBO was working to improve its organizational processes, it quickly let the world know that the process works. And it has continued to work for organizations that choose to embrace its principles and objectives.

One of the most significant aspects of MBO or MBR is that it allows subordinates to have a voice in organizational decision making, and it also paves the way for nurturing employees' commitment to the objectives of the organization. Most successful and talented employees like salespeople, often have higher commitment to objectives they set for themselves. And in many cases, these categories of employees set objectives that are often higher than the objectives of their organizations. And organizations must allow these talented employees to prevail in their commitments to work hard to achieve success. It does not often work well to impose commitments upon them as they are not likely to adhere to them, as they already have higher commitments to adhere to. Flexibility is one of the apparatuses of MBO, in the workplace. That flexibility allows talents to flow and flourish so that organizations can benefit. Studies have shown that when employees are given room and flexibility to use their ideas that innovation can occur in the process. And one of the good things about MBO or MBR is that it allows room for employees' empowerment in the workplace.

To enforce the philosophy of MBO or MBR, managers and supervisors have to also believe in the process. They must not only believe that MBO will work but must also ensure that the objectives of the employees in the organization are linked to the objectives of the organization. Managers must have a clear understanding of how the principles of MBO work and how it can benefit their organizations in order to be able to get employees to agree to the process. It will be difficult to convince subordinates to believe in a process that they do not have a clear understanding of.

For organizations to achieve set goals and objectives there must be a unification of purpose and direction among employees and supervisors so that the principles of MBO can be successfully achieved. This process is called maintaining a common goal for the whole organization. The goal must be clear enough for all stakeholders to understand. And the stakeholders involved in this process, in maintaining a common goal include management, subordinates, and anyone or group who will benefit from the organization if it continues to succeed, or who will lose, if it collapses.

Experts believe there are many ways for organizations to manage the principles of management by objectives. One of the many ways includes finding a specific goal to work toward in the organization. If increasing productivity is a goal that must be aimed for, the objective must be clear and concise, with a brevity of expression so that every supervisor, employee, will know that the goal is to increase productivity. And it will be the same if the goal is to maintain profitability. If the goal of the organization is to maintain profitability, there may be a focus to reduce unnecessary overheads and to avoid unprofitable expenditures or ventures that may make it impossible for the organization to reach its goals of profitability. But to do this, everyone must agree to achieve the common goal of helping the organization to maintain profitability.

Organizations like Hewlett Packard, Xerox, DuPont, Intel, and other iconic organizations found the principles of MBO and MBR to be successful. They also realized that to make it work, supervisors and subordinates must believe in the process. The organizations that have successfully applied the principles of MBO have reported considerable increase in sales, and profits. Many organizations have also reported increased productivity. They have achieved their goals by getting their employees to commit to the goals and objectives of MBO. Setting goals and working hard to meet them is not just to increase sales, profits and productivity. Goals can also be set to increase research and development in order to produce innovative products. Tech organizations often focus on frequent research and development by constantly finding new ways to increase the innovation of their products and services. These companies know that the only way they can stay ahead of the competition or to maintain sustainability is to think of the future that is emerging.

Objectives can also be set to improve and achieve positive marketing, services, human resources, finance, information technology, and other meaningful ventures that can enhance growth and sustainability. Many organizations set goals for each department to meet, and work with such department to make sure they have tools and resources to meet those goals. And the same applies for individual employees who may each have goals to meet. If in sales, the goal or objective of the organization may be for each salesperson to meet a certain quota. Some organizations will help their salespeople to achieve their quotas by increasing advertising, and giving them the necessary leads to achieve success. And to do this effectively, organizations cannot select who to give leads to, or practice favoritism, while leaving some salespeople out. If positive and productive goals are to be met, organizations must strive to maintain equilibrium in allocation of leads to salespeople in this respect. Everyone must be motivated and encouraged to meet his/her set goals. Alienating some employees while encouraging others, can be counterproductive and may lead to dissatisfaction among employees.

Many organizations practice favoritism by helping some employees to succeed while leaving others to survive on their own, without help. Good organizations work with all employees to succeed. And one of the principles of MBO or MBR is to motivate *all* employees to commit to work hard to achieve the objectives of the organization. There are different types of objectives. There are objectives that are collective, which involves all employees, and departments, while there are objectives that involve individual employees. For individual employees, goals must be attainable, and every task to actualize such goals must be visualized to see what needs to be done to achieve the goals. And for organizations, goals must also be visualized to see what actions should be taken to achieve set goals. Whether it is individual or collective goals and objectives, there must be commitment to ensure that the fundamental principles of MBO are not lost in the trail.

If the goal is to invest in research and development to find new innovation or to improve existing ones, the department or collective individuals involved must focus on the goal to either create new products or to improve existing ones. And organizations must be willing to invest the funds necessary to achieve this goal. Unnecessary investments in a research that cannot be visualized to meet the needs of the market can be counterproductive. If the goal is to find ways to improve existing products or to create innovation to find new replacements for waning products, efforts should be made to commit to that goal, in order to realize the objective of the organization.

As there has been a paradigm shift in how organizations must adapt to changing consumer needs, it might be necessary to embrace the philosophy of MBO paradigms so that managers and supervisors can effectively be able to determine the objective and strategy to achieve the goals of the organization. If the top hierarchy of an organization sets a goal, based on expert analysis, there should be a timeframe that those goals can be accomplished in order to mitigate losses and meet market demands. In a centralized or top-down organizational hierarchy, top managers often delegate functions to subordinates by appointing those best suited to monitor and control the activities of each department to make sure the goals of the organization are being met. In order to safeguard the principles of MBO and MBR, it might be necessary to appoint a project manager to oversee and monitor the departments of the organization. By doing this, organizations can create efficiency and quality production.

In the absence of a project manager to oversee and monitor each project, goals and objectives, there should be clarity of purpose so that each department, employee and supervisors will be aware of what functions to perform. In MBO and MBR, everyone involved in the process must be able to perform one task at a time, and each task must be as set in the goals and objectives of the organization. While a centralized top-down hierarchy might appoint project managers to oversee and monitor each department, MBO or MBR function best in a decentralized, bottom-up organizational setting, as the process allows for employees' ideas and innovation in the workplace.

Organizational objectives often need to be quantified and monitored in order to ensure adequate accomplishments. To do this, organizations may need to have a reliable communication or information system to manage and monitor relevant objectives that are crucial to efficient productivity. In some cases, employees may need to be incentivized in order to motivate them to work hard to achieve organizational objectives. With MBR, incentives or extrinsic motivation can make it possible for organizations to achieve their objectives. There are employees who are happy with their jobs, and will do whatever it takes to make sure organizational objectives are achieved but these categories of employees do not need extrinsic motivation as they are intrinsically happy with what they do. And because of their intrinsic satisfaction with what they do, they sometimes show more commitment, and work harder, than employees who are extrinsically motivated. Organizations can achieve greater productivity by nurturing the intrinsic happiness of employees who work hard because of the satisfaction they derive from the job. For those types of employees, their satisfaction is mostly from the job, than from monetary gains. These categories of employees often show more dedication and commitment than employees motivated by extrinsic needs.

In retail organizations, MBO or MBR has proven to be successful. Hewlett Packard applied the philosophy to increase its sales of computers and accessories. In sales, for example, a salesperson who loves selling may not necessarily need to be incentivized to meet his quota as the love of selling is already there. But for salespeople who sell for the love of money, and because of the gains they expect and are likely to derive from selling, monetary incentives may be the only way to motivate them. Talented salespeople are often natural in the way and manner they sell. They sell products to customers without overselling because the skill to sell comes natural to them. And they do not need to indulge in traditional gimmicks to sell a product. If they choose to apply traditional sales gimmicks, they may do so for fun, not because they have to, but because they want a reminder that they are still salespeople!

Mnemonic assistance is an integral part of MBO that can also be used by organizational leaders to fulfill set objectives. Mnemonic assistance can enable employees and supervisors to remember what goals are more important to fulfill in order to accomplish the tasks set by their organizations. For example, project managers, and human resources managers, can use mnemonic applications to ensure that set goals are achievable be strictly adhering to the bylaws established to accomplish the objectives of the organizations.

Organizations often set objectives that are based on factors such as: specific goals and objectives, measurable objectives, agreed and achievable objectives, realistic objectives and timeframe. Specific objectives often include what organizations specifically need to accomplish. Such specific objectives can be a quota that needs to be met. For example, automobile franchises such as automobile dealerships have quotas to fulfill in order to satisfy the agreements reached with automakers in the dealer-agreement. If there is a continuous shortfall in meeting the quotas, a dealership may come to the conclusion that a specific objective needs to be reached to meet the quotas. If such specific objective includes incentivizing salespeople with monetary incentives, that will be the specific objective to increase sales. And the specific objective may include focusing on customer satisfaction so that repeat businesses and referrals can be encouraged. And with immediate needs to increase sales, there might be a specific objective to increase advertising to boost, buoy and bolster sales.

Measurable objectives include how organizations that apply the philosophy of MBO or MBR use measurable objectives to increase productivity, sales, profitability and sustainability. In some cases, measurable objective can be applied by project managers to concentrate on time-bound projects so that time and resources will be appropriately used in accomplishing such projects. With measurable objectives, projects are easier to put in perspectives so that goals can be met.

To be smart in achieving set objectives, organizations may need to pay attention to what is attainable and achievable. In addition, organizations must be able to get employees and supervisors to agree on what is achievable and attainable so that objectives can be accomplished without wasting time and money on objectives that are not achievable. For example, in 1979, Lee Iacocca had to abandon the turbine engine that Chrysler had already wasted money and human resources on, after years of seeing no end to the project. Iacocca felt the project was no longer attainable and achievable by quickly abandoning the project for more productive projects. At that moment in 1979, Iacocca needed to direct resources to projects that would rescue Chrysler from collapse, and he felt the turbine engine was a waste of resources at the time.

Objectives may need to be realistic, responsible and adequate to be productive, accomplishable and sustainable. Some projects may look promising on paper but unrealistic when measured against immediate needs of the organization. In a future that is constantly emerging with new products, the objective may be to focus on realistic projects that can enable the organization to be competitive in an evolving global market. If projects are not immediately weighed and measured to meet the needs of an evolving market, organizations might find themselves being sidelined and left behind. To succeed, organizations have to be smart enough to devise objectives that are realistic so that they can be able to maintain sustainability.

Objectives have to be based on timeframes and time-bound projects. Projects have to be measured against the needs of the organization. If a project outlives its usefulness, time and money will be wasted as that project may have to be abandoned. Time-bound objective must be based on a timeframe of organizational needs. For example, when Iacocca suspended and abandoned the turbine engine project, it was because too much time and money had already been wasted on it. If the objective to build the turbine engine had been based on a timeframe, it probably would have yielded positive results. But the project did not have a timeframe and as a result was perceived as a drain on a much needed resources, at the time. Iacocca felt it was a smart move to abandon the project to save resources.

While MBO or MBR has benefitted Hewlett Packard, Intel, and many other iconic organizations, critics opined that if objectives are not adequately understood and communicated that they can lead to misapplication of resources. One of the early prominent critics of MBO was William Edwards Deming, who noted that the process can create poor quality of goods and services if employees are under pressure to meet a production target. The hurry to meet a production target can result in the sacrifice of quality and efficiency as workers will be under pressure to reach their targets by whatever means necessary.

Goods produced in a hurry are likely to lack quality, Deming noted. Another point made by Deming was that employees may not clearly understand the systems, and as a result could misinterpret the objective and end up with poor quality production. According to Deming, a leader with a clear understanding of systems will likely guide employees to appropriate solutions than the pressure to meet an objective. Deming encouraged supervisors and employers to abandon objectives in favor of good leadership. According to Deming, limitations that can negatively impact the efficacy of management by objectives include "setting of goals over the working of a plan as a driver of outcomes," while the second is that the process in contrast under emphasizes the significance of the context in which the objectives are based.

While arguing against management by objectives or management by results, Deming offered 14 principles that can create organizational effectiveness. Outlining the 14 points in his book, entitled: *Out of the Crisis*, Deming pointed out the factors that can create total quality management, which he said is based on quality of production rather than the time-bound objectives that MBO emphasized as a process to accomplish set goals and objectives. The points made by Deming, which in part, reemphasized earlier points made by Peter Drucker on quality production, include: creating a purpose driven emphasis that encourages improvement of goods and services. Emphasis on the production of quality of goods and services, rather than objectives based on a timeframe, will enable organizations to be competitive and to maintain sustainability, so that they will be able to remain in business and able to provide job security for their employees.

Another argument against MBO that Deming outlined in his book includes adopting a new philosophy that will focus on the evolving business climate that will enable organizations to compete effectively with quality production of goods and services. Deming called for a new philosophy that will recognize the changing business environment where the new emphasis is on quality of production rather than the rush to meet set objectives. As new business challenges continue to evolve, Deming said management must awaken to the new reality of the times and learn the responsibilities constantly dictated by evolving global market demands. To do so, organizational leaders must direct their resources toward improving processes to embrace the future that is emerging.

The dependence on inspection to achieve quality creates counterproductive challenges that can reduce quality of goods and services, Deming said. Eliminating the need for massive inspection and emphasizing building quality goods and services will allow multinational organizations to compete and maintain sustainability, especially as quality goods and services are being produced by foreign markets to compete with goods and services produced by Western organizations. Deming called on organizational leaders to focus first on the quality of the goods they produce rather than rushing to meet production targets which may lack quality. This argument reinforces the paradigm shift of quality production of automobiles to the Japanese automakers that started producing quality vehicles and taking more market shares from American automakers that once enjoyed dominance in quality automobile production.

Deming also argued against the practice of building too much emphasis on prices rather than quality. The notion of awarding "business on the basis of price tags," minimizes the emphasis on quality production. Organizations need to cut the cost of production so that prices can be lower, and the products able to compete with products made by competing foreign manufacturers. Reducing overheads to minimize costs, and by reducing the number of suppliers, will create loyalty and trust that will lead to efficiency in the supply chain, Deming noted. Moving towards a single supplier "for any one item," will create effectiveness while minimizing costs will also allow prices to be competitive with foreign products.

To constantly improve quality production of goods and services, Deming called on organizations to constantly improve their processes. Lean production or reducing costs of production will enable organizations to focus on the resources needed for quality production. The process of lean production or reduced cost of production includes eliminating unnecessary overheads, outdated machineries, and unproductive workers.

Job training is another factor that Deming believed would improve processes rather than the focus on objectives without quality. According to Deming, organizations should emphasize training employees on the job, and doing so on a constant basis, so that improvement of goods and services can ensue. If emphasis is placed on constant training of employees on the job, quality production can be the central focus rather than time-bound objectives, Deming outlined. Job training can also lead to innovation as employees will be better equipped with knowledge to deal with the competition that is emerging from the future that is largely unknown.

Good leadership can lead to effective management of both human resources and equipments in the organization. The essence of good leadership is to harness and marshal the human resources, machineries and equipment of an organization, to perform better tasks in order to achieve quality production, and increased productivity. Organizations must overhaul the workforce so that unproductive employees can be eliminated in order to reduce wastes and minimize costs. Eliminating unproductive workers will allow organizations to maintain quality production and to focus on employees who are committed to the objective of producing quality goods and services. Overhauling the workforce will also allow an organization to retire those workers who have aged on the job and are no longer productive.

Fear factor can hinder organizational effectiveness. If organizations are going to succeed, they must drive out fears so that employees can work effectively to reach the goals and objectives of the organization. The difference here is that the focus is to produce quality goods in order to increase sustainability.

Another significant step in quality production is breaking down barriers that exist between the various departments of the organization. The various departments of the organization must be able to work together without any form of barrier in order to achieve the aims of the organization, and to achieve quality production. For example, sales departments, service departments, parts departments, research departments, design departments, and production, must develop esprit de corps to achieve set goals and objectives. Departments must be able to work as a team to prevent production problems that are likely to occur during the production process. Working as a team will enable departments to anticipate and foresee productions mistakes and defects, during the production process and be able to correct them. This process is part of quality control as it prevents issues that are likely to hamper the quality of go ods and services.

In 2001, before the terrorist attack of the world trade center of September 11, 2001, law enforcement agencies in the United States, had information about the terrorists and did not share that information due to the barriers that existe d between the NSO, CIA, FBI, and other agencies involved in collecting information about terrorists in the country. As a result of the barriers, and lack of teamwork, it became impossible for one department to know what the others know. This poor coordinat ion of efforts made it possible for the terrorists to slip into the country unnoticed, to commit the atrocities that took many lives in which planes were used as missiles to destroy the world trade center. The quality of the services provided by the FBI, NSO, CIA and other law enforcement agencies, were eroded, because of lack of teamwork. If teamwork had existed between the various departments, the attacks would have been foreseen, anticipated and measures taken to prevent them. That sharing of knowledge and teamwork would have saved thousands of lives.

In sales, teamwork between the sales departments, service departments, parts departments, and body shop departments, if properly coordinated, can lead to quality services that would increase customer satisfaction and sustainability. Breaking down the barriers that may exist between the sales department, service department, body shop and parts departments, will increase the efficiency of services that can also increase the quality of work a dealership does. One of the problems customers often experience in the car buying process is the shoddy and unprofessional manner of the service and parts departments. If service works in conjunction with the sales departments in the spirit of teamwork, quality of work will ensue, as an efficient service department will increase the quality and productivity of the sales department. Teamwork between the sales and service departments will enable the sales department to know that a customer is ready to trade in his/her vehicle either because of the anticipated cost of maintenance or because the customer feels his/her vehicle is no longer worth spending too much money on, to repair. If there is no teamwork between service and sales, the customer will likely go to a different dealership to trade the vehicle. If information is shared between the sales and service departments about the customer's readiness to trade, the sales department will benefit from making a sale that would, to a certain extent, benefit the organization as a whole.

Teamwork between the various departments of an organization can make it possible to foresee a problem that may be encountered in the production process and be able to prevent them before they occur. Foreseeing and correcting a problem before it occurs increases the quality of goods and services. Unlike the focus on objectives and the timeframe to accomplish such objectives, foreseeing a problem and correcting the problem can prevent inefficiency and incompetence in the delivery, and production of goods and services.

Deming posited that eliminating quotas on the factory floor will increase the quality of work. If the hurry to meet production quota is eliminated, attention will be directed at producing quality of goods and services rather than the rush to meet quotas. Good leadership will enable organizations to concentrate on quality service rather than quota, Deming added. Another obstacle to quality production is management by objectives and management by numbers, which Deming said can create poor workmanship and reduce quality of goods and services because of too much focus on meeting objectives and quotas. To achieve effective production, it is imperative that organizations eliminate slogans, and targets, that demands zero defects, and increased level of productivity, without taking the need for quality production into consideration. Low productivity and low quality can lead to organizational inability to maintain competitiveness and sustainability.

Another significant argument Deming made against MBO or MBR is the barriers that rob hourly workers of job satisfaction, and pride in their workmanship. Focus on quality rather than on numbers will enable workers to enjoy the pride of their workmanship. If the hourly worker can get to see, and have pride in his/her workmanship, organizations will benefit tremendously due to the quality of goods and services that will ensue. Supervisors must change their focus from putting too much emphasis on numbers to putting emphasis on quality.

Deming also called for the elimination of annual merit ratings of management by objectives so that the barriers that prevents employees in management positions and in engineering, from enjoying their right to pride of workmanship can also be eliminated, in order to pave the way for quality of work, and quality of goods and services.

To create effectiveness, and quality production of goods and services, Deming called for the institution of enhanced and vigorous training programs of education and self-improvement in the workplace, in order to bring about innovation, quality of goods and services, competitiveness, and sustainability. Self-improvement will also increase employee confidence to do the job well, and to meet customer needs. Continuous focus on education and self-improvement will also bolster employee satisfaction and increase retention, Deming wrote.

Organizations must get all employees involved in the task of accomplishing the transformation of focus on objectives to focus on quality, Deming noted. The transformation must be all-inclusive so that the job will be done to the satisfaction of the workers, and to the satisfaction of the customers. To do this, massive education and training is required to break with the tradition that has placed too much emphasis on numbers and objectives than on quality.

While quality control, foreseeing and eliminating a problem before it occurs, can increase the quality of goods and services that organizations produce, several factors must be prevented to enable organizations to reach their goals of achieving total quality control. Such factors include lack of constancy of purpose or the inability of organizations to maintain consistency in their pursuit of quality production. Organizations have to be able to maintain and commit to the goal of achieving quality production without deviating from the purpose. It is not enough to have a policy without constantly adhering to it. Policies that are established to enforce the quality of goods and services should be consistent and purpose driven so that employees will believe in it, and be able to do what is required to focus on constantly maintaining quality production of goods and services.

In sales for example, the quality of service to consumers must be consistent with established purpose to achieve organizational goals. Dealerships that sell automobiles for example, must constantly aim to provide quality of service that consumers can appreciate and be loyal to, in order to maintain sustainability. Quality of service in this respect includes ensuring that customer care is based on quality that will promote repeat businesses and referrals. If there is a future deviation from the pursuit of quality customer care, there will be a likely shift of customer loyalty that could result in poor performance and abysmal results.

Emphasis on quick profits or short-term profits is an obstacle to achieving the delivery of quality of goods and services. When there is too much emphasis on short-term, or quick profits, quality might be overlooked in the process, which can lead to poor performance. Organizations must focus on policies that promote sustainability and competitiveness by emphasizing consistency in the delivery of quality of service. The objective of concentrating on short-term profits can be counterproductive and ineffective, in creating efficiency in the delivery of quality of goods and services.

Merit rating and annual review of performance can also be an obstacle to quality production of goods and services, Deming wrote. Focusing on merit rating can shift the emphasis on quality production because employees will be too eager to achieve positive ratings to concentrate on the most important aspect of producing quality products and services. While annual evaluation, based on performance, can incentivize employees to focus on performance, it can also hinder quality delivery of goods and services as employees will be too focused on annual review of performance.

Mobility of management can speed up organizational objectives without necessarily focusing on quality. Emphasis on the mobility of management in order to achieve set objectives can also be counterproductive. Organizations must prioritize quality and avoid excessive mobility of management. The pursuit of quality production of goods and services must be devoid of excessive mobility of management or organizations will risk reducing their sustainability and competitiveness.

Another obstacle to quality production is emphasis on visible figures or numbers. When organizations are too obsessed with numbers, they tend to lose focus of the significance of what matters most to sustainability and competitiveness. Obsession with figures can lead to overemphasis on quotas, and less emphasis on quality production. If organizations are too eager to reach set figures in their production process, they will be too obsessed with that objective that they will lose sight of the need to maintain quality. To maintain constancy of purpose and drive to achieve quality, organizations must reduce their objective to run on visible numbers alone. In sales, too much emphasis is often placed on achieving quotas and numbers while overlooking good customer service, and efficiency. Retail organizations can achieve more in the long run by deemphasizing the obsession to reach quotas at the expense of quality. If quality is prioritized, sales can increase systematically on impulse without the urgency that is often associated with time-bound objectives to meet quotas.

Burgeoning or excessive overheads can hamper quality production as it will lead to scanty resources to focus on the provision of quality of goods and services. Organizations have to learn to reduce overheads in order to focus resources in areas that can create competitive quality products and services. If organizations can reduce unproductive workers, eliminate outdated and slow machineries, and overhaul their processes, the process can lead to the efficacy of, and increase in the quality of goods and services produced.

Deemphasizing long-range planning can be an obstacle to efficient productivity and competitiveness. Organizations must learn to plan ahead so that they can be prepared for the future that is emerging. The future that is emerging often comes with evolving products and services that organizations must either embrace or lose their market shares. Many organizations have oftentimes neglected to plan ahead to meet emerging market demands, only to find out too late that they have lost their market shares because more progressive organizations have stepped in with better products and services.

Many organizations rely on modern technology to solve their problems. While too much reliance on technology to solve problems can be good for the health of an organization, it can also be counterproductive to the delivery of quality goods and services. There is no substitute to human competence. If organizations will focus more on developing their workforce, it can lead to increased quality of goods and services.

Organizations must learn to find long-term solutions to their problems rather than short-term solutions. For example, following precedents rather than developing new innovative solutions can lead to incompetence in the delivery of goods and services. While there are organizations that devote a significant amount of their resources to research and development, to develop new solutions, many organizations often follow existing examples in solving their problems. Organizations need to be ingenious, innovative, and able to deemphasize precedents and existing patterns, to succeed. Organizations cannot maintain sustainability if it cannot foresee a problem and develop solutions before problems occur. The ability to maintain foresight in organizational processes can lead to solving immediate problems which can translate into sustainability and competitiveness.

Embracing problems before they occur can prevent obstacles that can hinder quality production, competence, and efficiency. Organizations cannot continue to defer their problems, thinking market events will provide solutions. It might be imperative to foresee and handle organizational issues as they occur so that there will be no problem in the future that is emerging with evolving products and services. Training employees in a short-term effort to fix long-term issues might not be the way of the future. Experience in foreseeing, and handling issues, can help organizations deal with problems with processes that may prevent the delivery of efficient and competent services. In sales, training new salespeople as substitutes for talented and experienced salespeople, to handle complex issues, can be counterproductive. The saying that management skills cannot be taught in classes is true with training salespeople. Good and experienced salespeople, like good managers and leaders, do the things they do naturally, without classroom knowledge. It is often a mistaken notion that classroom knowledge alone will suffice in inculcating a culture of producing quality goods and services.

Another significant obstacle to organizational ability to produce quality goods and services is that employees that are responsible for 15% of the mistakes in the organization are often blamed, leaving out management that is often responsible for 85% of the mistakes committed, due to inadequate and inefficient system design. If efforts can be made to focus on the 85% mistakes committed due to inadequate system design, unintended consequences can be avoided. Organizations have to learn to focus on the real problems affecting them, rather than often attempting to place blames on employees who are only responsible for just 15% of the problem.

To prevent poor production and inefficient workmanship, organizations must learn to rely less on quality inspection and focus more on improving product quality. While quality inspection is good to a certain degree, the best way to improve the goods and services produced by an organization is to constantly find ways to improve the quality of goods and services. Quality inspectors might sometimes overlook defects that can occur in the production process in order to fulfill a quota. But if efforts are concentrated on improving the quality of goods and services, organizations will eventually benefit more.

Retail organizations, especially dealerships can benefit from quality improvement by constantly finding ways to improve their services. Relying on inspectors for quality can work to a limited degree, if there are no adequate efforts to improve quality. Concerted efforts must be made to constantly improve the quality of goods and services of an organization. The most effective way to do this is through investment in research, development, and in training the workforce so that the talents of dedicated and committed employees can be constantly nurtured. Several ripple effects can occur if employers pay attention to improving the system designs, than putting blames on employees who are only responsible for just 15% of the mistakes that often occur during organizational processes.

If products are designed better to improve services, it will enable organizations to focus on competitiveness in order to meet the challenges presented by the ever evolving consumer market. But if products are not designed better to improve services, organizations will be ill-equipped to compete with other organizations because of inadequate quality of goods and services. Proven quality production techniques that Deming taught the Japanese to improve their products and services immediately after World War II, helped that country to become the second largest economy in the world, in the postwar reconstruction miracles of 1950 to 1960.

The miracles of the postwar economic boom occurred due to improved quality of goods that enabled Japanese companies to take over existing market shares that had become complacent with poor product designs and quality.

Uniformity in product quality is another aspect that organizations can use to improve the quality of their products and services. If there is no higher level of uniform product quality, emphases on quality is likely to shift to objectives which can lead to inadequate preparedness of organizations to meet the challenges of the future.

One of the major reasons Deming was able to help the Japanese to rise from the ashes of World war II, to become the second largest economy in the world in the immediate postwar era between 1950 and 1960, was that efforts were made to improve product testing in the workplace and in research departments. The efforts would pay off as consumers started to see tremendous improvements in Japanese products and services. That improvement led Japanese companies to significantly compete for Western and global market shares. It didn't take long before Japanese companies were commanding a sizable proportion of the global market share. Following the shift in market shares, the paradigm had shifted from rushing to meet production quotas and targets to ensuring that products leaving the factories were produced with the highest quality available.

The renewed emphasis on improved quality of goods and services also allowed Japanese companies to increase the sales of their products and services in the global marketplace. Western companies that had grown complacent with higher emphasis on creating quantity of products rather than improving qualities of their p roducts were taken by surprise by the upsurge of the competition that Japanese companies brought to the global marketplace.

Management by objectives or management by results can enable organizations to reach their production objectives but the philosophy does not emphasis product quality or the improvement of the quality of products and services. While MBO or MBR can help organizations like auto dealerships, or retail organizations to meet their quotas, it can lower organizational competitiveness. And qua lity of goods and services may be sacrificed in the process of rushing to meet goals and objectives.

It is possible to meet objectives and at the same time, improve the quality of goods and services. To do this, organizations must be willing to constantly improve their processes by maintaining uniformity in objective and in quality. In most cases, improved quality of goods and services can increase organizational ability to meet their objectives. But quality cannot be sacrificed for objectives and numbers. It might work better to sacrifice objective for quality in order to produce better products, Deming posited. The opposite can trigger a return to complacency, lack of competitiveness, poor performance and lack of sustainability.

Chapter 10

Total Quality Management

In sales, the quality of a product and the attendant customer care, can build value that can enhance the art of selling. But what drives organizational processes is how organizations manage the essential fundamentals of their resources, to bolster productivity and profitability. The core principle of total quality management (TQM) entails a process in which organizations create a culture to constantly improve their ability to produce, sell and deliver high quality products and services to customers. It is also a process where suppliers' inputs are turned into outputs to meet customers' needs.

Total quality management has enjoyed a tremendous success since its inception in ensuring that organizations focus on top quality production, even though the process has sometimes been overshadowed by the philosophy of lean manufacturing, ISO 9000, and Six Sigma. Regardless of their emergence, they are, according to experts, offshoots of TQM as their basic principles are in many ways similar to the principles of TQM. These similarities will be discussed in details in the chapters ahead.

Total quality management started when organizations in the U.S. and Europe suffered economic setbacks that arose due to the stiff competition from Japanese companies. Overnight, Japan had moved from being a country that was devastated from World War II, to a country that was commanding a viable and strong postwar economy that became the envy of the world. Though a bubble economy, it nonetheless led to panic across industrialized countries that the land of the rising sun had taken over their place in economic hegemony. Having learned the basic fundamentals of producing high quality goods through experts like Deming, Japan soared economically, producing high quality goods at competitive prices. The products were not only in many ways more superior and durable than the products made in the U.S. and Europe the prices were also very competitive, making goods made in Japan more attractive. It didn't take long before Japanese companies led Japan to the forefront of economic hegemony.

Countries that once enjoyed great economic advantages like the United Kingdom became a net importer of finished goods. The majority of those finished goods were coming from Japan; and the U.K. soon became a consumer nation rather than a producing nation. British citizens were favoring foreign goods over domestic goods, especially vehicles and electronics. Domestically produced goods were shunned because of their inferiority, to superior and durable foreign goods, and more importantly because of their lower and competitive prices. Foreign goods were not only better and more durable with superior qualities their prices were also lower than domestic products.

For companies in the West, a new awakening was occurring in production. Since the industrial revolution or the transition to new manufacturing processes that started in the late 18th century that gave the edge in production to Western companies, Western companies had occupied the invincible position of producing quality goods; but complacency had taken over, that created a new lapse in quality production. The goal had gradually shifted from quality production to quotas and numbers. For a while consumers in the West could not differentiate a new product from an old one as the designs were identical, with the same technology. Lack of innovation in productivity, mundane and unattractive brand designs, and poor quality production, had allowed Japanese companies to satisfy the yearnings of consumers in Western countries for better products. These consumers had been forced to take what was available, prior to Japanese companies' emergence in quality production. Japanese products had given them an alternative. Japanese companies not only provided alternatives, but better alternatives at lower prices.

In the U.S. it was becoming clear that unless actions were taken to refocus on quality production that the country would cede its economic hegemony and powerhouse to Japan. It was just a few short years before, that Japan was a struggling nation that was essentially surviving on handouts and aids from Western countries. Now it appeared that had dramatically changed overnight. The techniques that had bolstered quality production in Japan had been taught by American experts who were preaching the principles of quality management and production; as the only way the country could move from the ashes it had found itself after World War II. Japanese companies had taken the principles of quality production to heart, and had acted on them, by producing better products than the West.

The new shift did not augur well for Western companies that were once used to dictating the pace of global production. The transition from hand production methods to machines, including new chemical manufacturing and iron production processes had improved the efficiency of production in the West. The West had dominated industrial production by using innovative water power to increase the use of steam power. The innovative use of machine tools and the rise of effective factory system had led companies in the West to enjoy dominance in industrial production. Industrial revolution had started in the West, between 1760 and 1840, and the benefits had tremendously given advantage to organizations in the West. Rather than capitalize on the advantage by constantly improving their production processes, Western companies had grown complacent, without innovation.

It was when Japanese companies started taking over market shares that were once enjoyed by Western companies that it became urgent to do something to recapture lost market shares. The quest to improve the quality of goods and services in the West gave birth to total quality management (TQM). Though TQM is an offshoot of quality control, it had nonetheless gone further than the principles of quality control. The focus was not only to create quality products but to constantly improve the quality of the products. The obsession was that if the Japanese could do it so could the West. In the United States, the media created a new catchphrase or slogan that read: *if Japan Can - Why Can't We?* Many organizations in the West started to explore ways to improve their processes by refocusing their resources toward meaningful techniques that would herald new innovation. Total Quality Management soon became the new catchphrase in production cycles. Forced to refocus on reexamining the techniques of quality control to see how it had benefited Japanese companies, for organizations in the West, the urgency of the situation had led to confusion as to how to forge ahead. It was in the process of trying to figure out how to best the Japanese-style quality control that total quality management came into existence.

While quality control had helped the Japanese to create better products, it has also created a bubble company that would burst unless adequate safeguards were in place to protect it. On their part, Western companies felt the way to regain lost market shares was to find a way to capitalize on quality control by coming out with total quality management. The idea was to do a soul search to see where things went awry. That soul search was one of the primary reasons for the origin of total quality management. The idea was to come out with a better way to create and manage the quality of goods and services produced by companies in Japan.

The task was an uphill task given the fact that Japanese companies had already made a strong impact in global market. To regain market shares would take more than just a catchphrase and a slogan to create and constantly improve quality. It would take changing the mindset of employees and management who had gotten accustomed to concentrating on objectives of short-term profits, merit rating, and quotas. To have an effective quality management that would create competitiveness, prices would have to be lowered and innovative quality products would have to be produced. Corporate greed had diverted capital resources to compensations rather than to research and development to create innovation. Serious total quality management would mean cutting back on extravagance and on high executive compensations.

Total quality management (TQM) became a Western obsession to regain its erstwhile market shares. In the United Kingdom, it had been inspired by that country's Department of Trade and Industry which was formed in October 19, 1970, during the country's drive to embrace quality control and total quality management. In its 1983 economic slogan a catchphrase had developed, in the U.K., called *national quality campaign* in an attempt to galvanize organizational leaders to move towards instilling quality management in their production processes. In a move that observers called a bold move to increase quality production, the Department of Trade and Industry would later be replaced with a more encompassing Department of Business, Enterprise and Regulatory Reform, and the Department for Innovation.

The essence of the Department of Innovation was to make sure that organizations put more efforts into creating a policy of investing in research and development so that new innovative and quality products can be produced to compete with cheaper and quality oriented foreign goods. The resultant merger of the Board o f Trade with the Ministry of Technology, and the eventual creation of a new cabinet position called Secretary of State for Trade and Industry was to encourage organizations to focus more on quality control, innovation and the technology to enhance quality production of goods and services. While the role of the Secretary of State for Trade and Industry was not to force organizations to change their business practice and culture, it was a role created to let organizational leaders know that the government was serious about embracing total quality management through the innovative production of quality goods and services.

In a British parliamentary move that was highly praised by other Western leaders, the machinery of government led to the creation of the Department for Business. Innovation and skills were prioritized, and it was noted that the Department for Business, Innovation and Skills was established "to build a dynamic and competitive U.K. economy by creating conditions for business success, promoting innovation, enterprise and science, giving everyone the skills and opportunities to succeed." The idea was not only to encourage organizational leaders to focus on total quality management and quality control but to also encourage the citizenry to embrace the various government programs that would train them, and nurture their skills, in order to create innovation.

The British government did not leave the burden of reinventing the British economy to organizations or on the shoulders of organizational leaders, but also formulated a policy to focus on educating the citizenry in science, technology and other related fields. To achieve its goal, the British government had embarked on fostering world-class universities and higher institutions of learning, and promoting what it called an open global economy that would focus solely on new innovation.

Part of the communiqué was the public service agreements (PSAs) that were reached to raise the productivity of the U.K. economy, improve the skills of the citizenry in order to establish a world-class skill base, and to promote world-class science and innovation in the U.K., in order to deliver the conditions for business success in the U.K., and to "improve the economic performance of all English regions and reduce the gap in economic growth rates between regions." To improve organizational processes and to ensure everyone was involved in the goal to strengthen the British or the U.K. economy, the U.K. government added additional set of responsibilities for the new departments which included the following:

The first was to ensure that support was provided for sustaining higher education that individuals and businesses would need to promote innovation through science and research. To do this, the U.K. government created access for individuals to have the skills they need so that they can become equipped with the knowledge and skill needed for the emerging future of growing industries and technology.

To promote and embrace total quality management and to ensure everyone was on board with the principles, the U.K. government also provided for a research funding through the research councils. The idea was to fund the research needed to create innovation and to expect returns for the government's "considerable investment in research excellence." The government saw the investment in research as an income-generating process that would benefit the workforce and the U.K. economy as a whole.

The next process that the U.K. government embarked upon in order to promote total quality management was to create an innovative and entrepreneurial environment where ideas would be put into practice in order to create new quality products, processes, services, and markets, and to in addition transform knowledge into commercial opportunities. The commercial opportunities would pave the way for business opportunities that would lead to growth, productivity, expansion, and creation of job opportunities. The process was to also minimize overheads and to create an environment where bureaucracy and cost of productions are structured towards prioritized areas of production. The goal would be to reduce wastes of resources and to focus more on the areas that are significant, in achieving the goals needed to create new innovation.

The Department of Innovation would also focus on the needs of small and medium sized businesses "and will drive forward the continuing simplification of support to business." The simplification of support will be in the form of flexible access for individuals and businesses to get the support they need to acquire the knowledge and skills they need to reach the goals set by the Department of Innovation.

The focus was not only to promote innovation and total quality management but to also protect the rights of workers and consumers so that they are treated fairly, and able to enjoy the opportunities that are available in what the U.K. government called a "balanced and just economy." The department would also work towards creating conducive environment for business success, developing the economy, and ensuring that domestic products and services are competitive, while strengthening corporate governance to focus on streamlining organizational resources toward meaningful and quality production. The government would also ensure that organizations strive for open markets so that businesses "can trade where they want to and when they want to."

Another focus of the U.K. government to promote total quality management was to support competitive enterprise to encourage positive and strong relationships of the key sectors of the economy. The Department of Innovation would also ensure that government policies were translated into action that drives growth and performance. Part of the process was to continue to improve the quality of goods and services produced by organizations, by focusing on industrial strategy and building on the framework set out in the objectives of the new campaign of *New Industry, New Jobs* that was designed to let organizations understand that improving quality, and creating new innovation will lead to new jobs, which were at the core and forefront of government policies.

The U.K. government would also be accountable for its shareholding in key strategic assets, so that such assets could be harnessed toward strengthening the economy and providing access that will lead to innovation and the creation of new jobs. To ensure that every aspect of the economy was involved in the new economic pursuit to reinvent the economy and to recapture lost market shares, the government would also make it possible for the Department of Innovation to have and share joint responsibilities with the Department for International Development for trade policy and with the Foreign and Commonwealth Office for trade promotion. The idea was to reduce chronic trade deficit and the attendant taste and craze for foreign goods. The job of the Department of Innovation was to create quality domestic products that would have competitive prices that would also be able to compete with foreign products.

To do this, the Department of Innovation would work with Foreign and Commonwealth Office, which is supported by the U.K. trade investment branch of the government. The goal of the U.K. trade and investment office is to provide assistance to U.K. companies that do business with foreign companies abroad. The U.K. trade and investment also provide assistance and support for foreign companies that want to relocate to the U.K. The agenda is to promote the creation of new jobs and innovation.

In the United States, total quality management had first been applied by the Naval Air Systems Commands to promote its quality improvement efforts in 1985. Though the quest for total quality management had been spurred by the then expanding Japanese economic hegemony, it would take much longer before organizations in the U.S. would embrace the drive to promote quality improvement in their products and services.

In the md-1980s, organizations in the U.S. were already losing market shares to Japanese companies and the losses were becoming difficult to ignore, and even with that, progress to embrace total quality management was slow to take off, as many organizations were still embracing the principles of management by objectives (MBO), which many experts like Deming had seen as counterproductive. But when the U.S. Navy embarked on a program to improve the quality of its services, by enlisting civilian researchers to assess statistical process control, it started to send a message to organizational leaders to follow suit.

It all started in the spring of 1984 when a branch of the U.S. Navy asked its researchers to examine the works of renowned quality consultants that had proven successful, and to come up with recommendations on how to improve operational efficiency in the Navy. The works of a renowned consultant like William Edwards Deming became the first recommendations. Deming was chosen because his teachings and principles of quality control had become famous in helping Japanese companies to achieve quality production. It was no secret that Deming had been in Japan teaching organizational leaders and manufacturers the processes involved in achieving quality production of goods and services. Another aspect that the Navy had looked into was the application of statistical process control (SPC).

The process of statistical process control (SPC) would enable organizations to statistically control and monitor their processes. Effective application of SPC methods would enable organizations to operate at full capacities. The use of statistical process control would also help organizations to minimize and eliminate wastes in organizational processes. But SPC only works when there is conformity in the production of goods and services. Conformity entails that products meet specifications so that output can be measured in terms of quality. Tools necessary to achieve product specifications and quality production include control charts or process behavior charts – which is used to determine if manufacturing meets statistical control, continuous improvement, and the focus on new experiments.

In order to fully use SPC to achieve process effectiveness, certain factors must be adhered to. The first is that initial process must be established while the second involves the regular production use of the process. In this second process, those involved in decision making must decide on the aspects of the process to be examined. The 4-M conditions (man, machine, material, and method), and the wear and tear rate of the materials used in production such as machine parts, jigs, and fixture, must be examined for effectiveness in order to achieve efficient production.

The application of statistical process control (SPC) has more advantages over other methods of quality control such as inspection because it focuses on early detection and prevention of problems in the production lines, rather than the correction of problems after they have occurred in production. Statistical process control saves time in the production process and reduces wastes so that efficiency and quality production can be achieved in a timely manner. The attractiveness of SPC is that it reduces wastes, and reduces the time needed to produce a product; and in addition it prevents reworking finished products due to mistakes. In many ways, SPC takes away the headaches of defects that often occur in finished goods such as automobiles.

Though SPC is an effective method of achieving quality production, it has its limitations. One of the limitations often associated with the process includes the elimination of postproduction inspection because of the emphasis on early detection and prevention of problems before they occur. The effectiveness of SPC depends on the skills of those involved in its applications. The process may not be suitable or feasible for some organizations; and it may sometimes be difficult to ascertain when it is suitable or necessary to apply during production. Despite its few limitations, SPC helps manufacturers in identifying, detecting, and prevention of problems during production, and also it increases the rate of production by reducing the time required to produce a product. The application of

SPC entails several processes which include the understanding of the process and the specification limits involved. The other aspect is the elimination of unnecessary assignable sources of variations in order to stabilize the process. But the most crucial aspect of SPC is that it enables manufacturers to monitor the production process by using control charts to detect changes or variation. Control charts are some of the methods involved in the use of SPC by using them to differentiate assignable or special sources of variation in production, from common sources.

The common sources involve those aspects of the process that are expected. Common sources are not nearly as important as assignable sources to the manufacturer. Control charts enable manufacturers to discern between common sources and assignable sources in order to produce efficient, quality goods and services.

Another significant aspect of SPC is the stable process. With this process, whenever the process does not trigger detection rules of the control charts, it means it is stable. When stability has been achieved or when the process does not trigger control chart detection rules, then a process capability analysis may be required to determine the ability of the process to produce conforming products in the future.

The other important aspect of SPC is excessive variation. This is the opposite of the stable process. With this process, when the process triggers the detection rules in the control charts, it means the capacity is low. When this occurs, an analysis may be required to determine and identify the reasons or sources of the excessive variations. To determine the sources, tools such as Ishikawa diagrams or fishbone diagrams often referred to as herringbone diagrams or cause and effect diagrams may be used to determine the causes of the problem. In some cases, it may be necessary to use the design of experiments to explain and describe the variation through hypothesis. Design helps in quantifying the strength of sources of variation through development of standards, staff training, error-proofing, and other fundamental changes to processes or inputs.

The U.S Navy had wanted to improve its processes in order to increase the efficiency of its operations; and total quality management seemed the ideal philosophy to embrace. And with Deming's teachings of quality control proven to be successful in Japan, the U.S. Navy felt it would work for its processes. In 1985, following the recommendation of researchers, the Navy decided to adopt the principles of TQM to improve the efficiency of its operations; and the U.S. Navy rebranded the process as total quality management. As the process became successfully applied by the U.S. Navy, the word had spread that TQM had increased productivity and efficiency in the Navy. Curiosity soon made some organizational leaders to come out and see for themselves how the process works. But the success was more abstract than concrete as the miracles of the results could not visibly be seen. But the success had become noticeable to many federal agencies, as the facts of its success were apparent.

As TQM spread throughout federal agencies, the results led to the creation of the Malcolm Baldrige National Quality Award (MBNQA) in August of 1987. The Malcolm Baldrige National Quality Award was created to recognize business organizations, healthcare and private U.S. enterprises by the President of the United States. The program was under the auspices of the Baldrige Performance Excellence that is managed by the National Institute of Standards and Technology, which is an agency of the U.S. Department of Commerce. The essence of the program is to promote business innovation, and quality production of goods and services. To encourage organizations to strive for excellence in quality manufacturing and production, up to 18 awards are given annually in six eligible categories such as manufacturing, service, small business, education, healthcare, and nonprofit.

In addition, the Federal Quality Institute was created a year later in June 1988. One by one, many federal agencies like the United State Department of Defense, United States Army, and the United States Coast Guard, followed suit and adopted TQM. It didn't take long for the private sector to follow suit by adopting the principles of TQM in order to recapture lost market shares that had been taken by Japanese companies. The goal of the new movement of total quality management was to increase production, and remain competitive in every endeavor, including in endeavors such as bidding for contracts from the federal government. Total quality management entails including all stakeholders in organizational processes and ensuring that there is adherence to efficiency and effectiveness in quality production.

While total quality management was not a policy that was designed to force organizations to strive for excellence in the quality delivery and manufacturing of products and services, it was however a movement that had gradually started, and taken root, in organizational processes. The significance of the urgent move to embrace TQM was that U.S. organizations had been inspired and influenced by the increasing economic hegemony of Japanese economy. Japanese companies sort of sent a clarion call to Western companies to increase the quality of their products or face losing sustainability. For long, many U.S. organizations had taken quality production for granted by not constantly trying to improve the quality of their products. They had sacrificed innovation and efficiency for complacency, greed and quotas, and were paying the price heavily in the form of loss of market shares.

When TQM proves successful in the U.S. Navy, and increasingly became successful among federal agencies and armed forces, many private organizations saw an opportunity to reinvent their processes. And the additional incentive came from the creation of the Malcolm Baldrige National Quality Award, which was geared towards promoting excellence in production and manufacturing. The fact that it is presented to deserving organizations by no less than the president of the United States made it a goal to reach for, by the private sector. There was no greater incentive than the recognition by the United States government for producing quality goods.

The concepts of TQM that the United States Navy adopted, which in many ways became the key concepts that private organizations would later adopt, include focusing on quality and how it is perceived. Meaningful quality production was not only a process but the effectiveness of a process that can only be defined by the end receiver of the goods and services. If a product meets customers' requirements and satisfies them, then the product can be said to have met the standards defined by customers to be quality oriented.

Another key concept for achieving quality production includes making sure that it is an ongoing process to constantly maintain quality. For example, it is the responsibility of top management to direct and maintain quality improvement so that subordinates can follow suit. The responsibility has to start from the top to the bottom in order for the process of quality control and management to be an ongoing process.

A significant aspect of increased quality production stems from systematic analysis of, and improvement, of quality processes so that every facet of quality efficiency and effectiveness can be maintained.

Organizations cannot just have a policy to increase quality production without a systematic analysis that will ensure adequate quality improvement on a constant basis.

Quality improvement has to be on a constant basis to continually benefit output, research shows. If quality measures are not constantly taken, to safeguard and protect the quality of goods and services, total quality management might not be all encompassing and embracive. For effectiveness, quality improvement must be a continuous effort that is conducted throughout the organization.

The Navy had adopted several concepts to apply the principles of TQM. For example, the policy of PDCA or what it called plan-do-check-act or plan-do-check-adjust was a 4-step management process to control and manage continuous improvement of products and services. This process had earlier been called the Deming circle/cycle/wheel; Shewhart cycle, control circle/cycle, or plan-do-study-act (PDSA); or how to essentially improve the quality of goods.

The Ad hoc cross-functional teams which were in many ways similar to quality circles were designed to address process issues that may develop during production. This process involves a group of workers who perform similar functions and who meet regularly to identify, analyze, and solve problems that may stem from their work. The group is often led by a supervisor who would present the solutions reached in these meetings to management. In some cases, the supervisor may allow the workers in these small groups to implement the solutions to the problems as a form of empowerment and motivation, to improve the performance of the organization. This process is an effective way to incentivize the workforce by empowering them to find, and implement the solutions. It creates its own form of motivation and job satisfaction as employees will feel they are part of the decision making process.

In addition to Ad hoc cross-functional teams, standing cross-functional teams are also responsible for the improvement of processes in the long term so that continuous quality production can be achieved. The standing cross-functional teams help organizations to maintain continuous quality improvement by ensuring that there is a constant adherence to quality and the processes setup to achieve total quality management. The task of the standing cross-functional teams is to monitor and control quality improvement so that organizations can be prepared to meet the challenges of the emerging future in organizational productivity and competitiveness.

In addition, active management participation through steering committees will allow management to participate in the processes involved in total quality management. Without active management participation, there will be no serious efforts to continually maintain quality control and effectiveness in order to achieve total quality management. There has to be active management participation in order to ensure that processes are being followed to achieve effectiveness, excellence, and sustainability in the long term.

Another significant apparatus that is often used in maintaining product quality and continuous improvement is the use of, and application of the seven basic tools of quality to analyze issues in the production process. The seven basic tools of quality are effective in troubleshooting issues that may arise in the pursuit of quality production. These tools of quality control are suitable for those employees that may not have in-depth training in statistics, and also because the tools can be used to solve many quality related issues. These basic quality tools include cause and effect diagram, check sheet, control chart, histogram, Pareto chart, scatter diagram, stratification or flow chart.

The seven basic tools of quality were a quasi TQM which originated in Japan after World War II. It was said to have been influenced by the seven famous weapons of Benkei. Musashibo Benkei was a warrior monk and had served Minamoto no Yoshitsune who was himself a general of the Minamoto clan of Japan in the late Helan (794-1185), and early Kamakura period (1185-1333). The seven basic tools of quality were reportedly first introduced by Kaoru Ishikawa who was a management/organizational theorist, and a professor of engineering at the University of Tokyo. Like Deming, Ishikawa had become famous for his quality management innovations. Ishikawa was considered a pioneer in the development of quality initiatives such as the quality circle. Many of Ishikawa's quality initiatives include cause and effect diagram which is also called fishbone diagram that is often used in the analysis of industrial quality processes.

Ishikawa had been tremendously influenced by the works and lectures given to engineers and scientists in 1950 by Edwards Deming. While the fishbone diagram process was helpful in organizational quality management, it was also considered complex by many companies who had started training their workforce in statistical quality control. These organizations had instead focused on simpler methods to avoid the intimidation that many workers felt about the statistical methods.

The seven basic tools of quality made it easier for organizations to statistically control quality and to prevent problems that are likely to occur in the production process. But more complex statistical methods such as survey sampling, acceptance sampling, statistical hypothesis testing, design of experiments, and multivariate analysis, were methods developed to carry out operations research in achieving total quality management.

Total quality management (TQM) had since its inception been seen as a process to continuously maintain quality, innovation and efficiency. It has also been an apparatus that helps organizations to maintain competitiveness and sustainability. Many organizations that had utilized its usefulness have come to see the principles of TQM as the *only* way organizations can face the challenges of an emerging future, in organizational processes.

The United State Department of Defense for instance, saw total quality management as a strategy to continually improve performance in every level and in all its areas of operations. The department applies the fundamental management techniques that are inherent in TQM to improve existing efforts, and specialized technical tools. The department also focuses on improving its existing structures by continually improving all their processes. To create effectiveness, efforts were geared towards improving performance to satisfy objectives such as cost, quality, schedule, operational needs and suitability. With the department, and because of its significance in national security, its central focus was in increasing user satisfaction. The overriding objective of the department was to also build on the pioneering works of management gurus like Edwards Deming and Joseph Moses Juran, and to in addition, benefit from the experiences of organizations in the private and public sectors, in order to continually improve its processes.

In the U.K., total quality management was perceived to be an apparatus to reach quality production, efficiency, competitiveness, innovation, nurturing of skills, science and research and in assisting organizations and individuals to reach their highest potentials. The TQM philosophy was also seen as a strategy that aimed to harness human and material resources in reaching the goals of optimum quality productivity and efficiency.

The International Organization for Standardization fosters TQM as a strategy that galvanizes quality research. The aim of the international organization for standardization is to ensure that organizations focus on a management approach that is centered on quality and the participation of the workforce in achieving a long term success, through customer satisfaction and quality products and services.

On its part, the American Society for Quality pivoted management approach that focuses on quality improvement. Just as with international organization for standardization, the American society for quality, saw TQM as a process in which members of an organization participates in improving processes, products, s ervices, and organizational culture. Many of the philosophies and teachings of management gurus and experts like Philip Crosby, Edwards Deming, Armand Feigenbaum, Kaoru Ishikawa, and Joseph Juran, were adhered to, in achieving quality control and improveme nt.

The Chartered Quality Institute perceives TQM as a philosophy for managing organizations so as to meet the needs of stakeholders. To meet the needs and expectations without compromising ethical values, the chartered quality institute perceives TQM as an imperative apparatus in achieving sustainability and competitiveness.

The Baldrige Excellence Framework which was created by public law 100-107, is a governmental policy that annually recognizes excellence in businesses, educational institutions, heal thcare organizations, and nonprofit organizations that have provided efficient and excellent services in leadership, strategy, customer satisfaction, knowledge management, job creation, employee satisfaction, efficient business operations, and positive res ults in organizational productivity. The criteria for measuring excellence are based on the level of customer satisfaction relative with their satisfaction, with prevailing competition. To effectively measure excellence, organizations will need to constant ly select, collect, align, and integrate data and available information in order to track daily operations.

Managing the workforce to effectively create quality performance and efficiency will be crucial to organizational productivity and sustainability. It is important that organizations understand employees' needs, and be able to align those needs to the needs of the organization in order to ensure continuity, and workforce reduction. Efficient management of the workforce would also minimize the impact of employee reduction when, and if, they become necessary. Several management philosophers believe that rewarding excellence in efficient manufacturing, and service, in every enterprise, is what sustains total quality management. Management theorists like Joseph Juran opined that the Baldrige Award for excellence essentially defines TQM.

Over the years, TQM has been modified with changes that are suitable to the needs of organizations, countries, and governmental agencies that had sought the changes. For example, quality standardization agencies in Belgium, France, Germany, Turkey, United States, Italy, and even in Japan, had standardized or attempted to standardize TQM over the years. In the midst of the various attempts to standardize TQM, ISO 9000 had gradually taken root and superseded the inherent principles of total quality management.

Chapter 11

ISO 9000 and Retail Organizations

In retail organizations, or more specifically, in sales, ISO 9000 can be an integral part of successful sales transactions, if its standards are adopted. ISO 9000 is essentially a series of standards that are developed and published by the international organization for standardization (ISO) that often stipulates, defines, maintains and establishes the effective quality assurance for organizations and service enterprises. It is an aspect of quality management systems standards that are designed to make it possible for organizations to meet the needs of their customers, and stakeholders, while adhering to the quality measures and requirements of their products.

Unlike total quality management, ISO 9000 concerns the basic fundamentals of quality management systems in organizational processes. In addition, ISO 9000 also deals with the eight management principles of the essential standards of quality improvement. The most significant essence of ISO 9000 is that it basically deals with the crucial requirements which organizations that aspire to succeed in providing quality goods and services must fulfill.

ISO 9000 is comprised of, and based on, eight quality management principles which are succinctly defined in ISO 9000:2005. Quality management systems encompass both fundamentals and vocabulary in ISO 9004:2009, and embraced managing for organizational sustainability, and success, which together form a profound quality approach to organizational processes.

The eight principles of quality management include: customer focus, leadership, involvement of people, process approach, system approach to management, continuous improvement, factual approach to decision making and mutually benefitted supplier relationships.

Customer care is crucial to organizational sustainability, performance and existence. Without customers, organizations are likely to fail. Organizations depend on their customers to make it in business, and the success of organizations will depend on the level they are, in understanding customer needs, and how much they strive to meet customer expectations and requirements. To remain competitive, organizations must be able to anticipate and fulfill current and future needs of their customers.

Leadership is a crucial aspect of quality management systems. Good leadership must be able to focus on, and establish organizational unity of purpose, and the direction of the future of productivity and the market. One of the characteristics of a good leader is the ability to create and maintain an environment in which all stakeholders can be involved in accomplishing the objectives of the organization.

One of the most defining qualities of quality management principles is involvement of people in achieving organizational objectives. With ISO, people are the driving catalyst that keeps and maintains organizational sustainability. In many ways people at all levels form the core basis and fundamentals of organizational success. The full involvement of all stakeholders can be a contributing asset to organizational benefits and success. This involvement can be in the form of each stakeholder being able to use his/her abilities to contribute to organizational growth and benefits.

Process approach is another crucial aspect of quality management principle. With process approach, desired result can be achieved more efficiently when organizational functions and resources are both managed as a process. Effective process approach can lead to organizational productivity and growth, if activities and resources are efficiently managed as a process.

Another fundamental approach of quality management principle is the significance of system approach to management. This process involves identifying, understanding and managing interrelated processes in conjunction with quality output. These interrelated processes can contribute to organizational effectiveness, and efficiency in achieving set goals and objectives.

Continual improvement of quality and process is a core principle of quality management principles that focuses on organization's overall quality performance and the imperativeness of making it a permanent objective. Studies have shown that organizations that create continual improvement of quality production and delivery of goods and services often enjoy growth, high performance, financial benefits and increased productivity.

While continual improvement of quality processes are crucial to organizational quality management, factual approach to decision making is also significant in ensuring that organizations base their decision making on correct and accurate analysis of data and information. Factual approach to decision making can increase quality production and reduce mistakes that are likely to occur during the production and delivery of goods and services.

Another core characteristic of quality management principles is the ability of organizations to maintain mutually beneficial supplier relationships. This process is crucial because of the part that suppliers play in organizational productivity and delivery of goods and services. As organizations and their suppliers are interdependent in processes , the ability to maintain and focus on mutually beneficial relationships can boost and enhance the ability of both stakeholders, to create value.

While the essence of ISO 9000 is to create and maintain value, and quality, ISO 9001 enables organizations to build value in the products and services they deliver. For example, ISO 9001:2008 quality management systems sets out a requirement that organizations must abide by in order to create and maintain the delivery of quality goods and services. The requirement contains a 30-page document that is accessible in every country in the world. This process is supplemented by additional two standards which include ISO 9000:2005 quality management systems, both fundamental and vocabulary, and ISO 9004: 2009, which is managing to sustain the success of an organization or quality management approach. Of all the family of quality management systems, only ISO 9001 is audited for third party assessments. The other two quality management systems processes are supplementary and include information on how to maintain, sustain and improve quality production and delivery of goods and services.

Since ISO 9000 deals with the requirements that organizations wishing to fulfill the standard must adhere to, it has become imperative for these organizations to work harder than ever before to meet these standards so that their outputs can increase while maintaining the qualities of the goods and services they produce. The standard also provides guidance and tools for businesses and organizations in order to ensure that their products and services consistently meet their customers' requirements. The principles of the standards ensure that the products and services provided by organizations meet the quality assurance of ISO. Third party certification bodies form an integral part of the process in which independent confirmation is provided that stipulates the requirements of ISO 9001. Organizations must meet the requirements of ISO 9001 in order to fulfill the needs necessary to maintain quality production. As a result of ISO 9001, millions of organizations are independently certified, thereby making the program the most globally used management tools, and accepted certification program that organizations have come to rely on to meet quality production and delivery of goods and services.

Though it is one of the most widely used management tools in the world, ISO 9001, according to critics, can be wasteful and may not be suitable for all organizations. Many critics have opined that some of the requirements that are needed by third party certification bodies to provide independent confirmation which organizations must meet to fulfill the requirements of ISO 9001 may not be relevant to organizational processes and quest for quality production.

While many critics may see ISO 9001 as sometimes wasteful, proponents posited that the process is pivotal to organizational quality production and delivery of goods and services. The adoption of ISO 9001 can be attributable to many factors that are essential to stakeholders, and suppliers. For example, the certification provides confidence and assurance to those who use the services of the organizations. Many product purchasers or consumers for example, would require that their suppliers be certified with ISO 9001 certificate. ISO 9001 certificate gives confidence to consumers that the services provided by suppliers will be honest, diligent, efficient, and quality oriented.

The ISO 9001 certification also gives quality assurance to organizations as it increases customers' satisfaction because of the confidence provided by the certification. Apart from the benefits that stakeholders get from ISO 9001 certification, there is a significant amount of increased productivity and almost guaranteed sustainability due to the certification. Organizations can often be more equipped to deal with emerging competition by being quality certified in ISO 9001. Experts have postulated that organizations tremendously benefit financially for being certified in ISO 9001 due to increased productivity. In addition to high returns, organizations also create workplace and employee satisfaction due to the job security provided by ISO 9001 certification. The reason is because organizations tend to enjoy repeat and flourishing businesses when assurance is provided through certification.

Organizations that are not ISO 9001 certified tend to lose market shares, with attendant low performance and employee dissatisfaction. By implementing ISO 9001 many retail organizations such as automobile retail organizations often enjoy confidence in their products that the certification provides. Customers tend to trust organizations and businesses that are certified or who certify their products. ISO 9001 can also increase financial performance due to increased productivity that often results from repeat businesses and increased traffic to organizations that are certified or whose products are certified. While certification can increase financial performance and increased productivity, the process can be further improved by increasing efficiency in the workforce through effective leadership.

As a member of a family of quality management systems, ISO 9000 came into use when it was published in 1987. At the initial stage when it was published, the fundamentals were based on the BS 5750 standards of British Standards Institution (BSI), which is the national standards body in the United Kingdom. BS5750 is also the equivalent of EN29000, which is the European Standards. The British Standards Institution is responsible for ensuring that organizations adhere to technical standards in products and services. The British Standards Institution also provides certification that meets standards, to businesses.

As businesses continue to work hard to maintain standards through certifications, organizations continue to benefit from increased revenue and sales. In a recent report released by BSI, a remarkable increase of 15% in productivity took revenue to a reported level of £331m. In 2014, revenue was £287.1m, according to BSI reports. In addition, "significant acquisitions boost presence in North America and South Africa," BSI reported. Sales had also increased as new sales orders grew by as much as 21% from the year before. In its 114 year history, BSI continues to positively impact businesses and organizations as growth of 15% maintains the company's consistent and consecutive 16 year record of "annual increases in underlying revenue."

Reported growth and increase in productivity were in part also due to organic revenue which grew at constant exchange by nine percent while 2015 acquisitions added six percent revenue. The BSI report also indicated that "underlying operating profit at constant exchange," also grew by 18%. In general, the total acquisitions added in 2015, increased by four percent profit growth; while net asset was said to have increased by as much as 39% to £78.4m, which was an increase over the year 2014; which saw an increase of £56.5m in net asset value.

As the impact of BSI continues to translate into organizational growth, the company has expanded its reach to embrace more enterprises. According to BSI Chief Executive, Howard Kerr, "Over the past few years BSI has developed into a truly integrated global enterprise, able to serve our clients across the world, while broadening our service into different business streams and sectors." The added principle of organizational resilience was to make it possible for organizations to become strong and maintain healthy processes in their operations so that they can be able to adjust to changes in the emerging future. The principle "is another example of our unique product and service offering, combining our business streams of Knowledge, Assurance and Compliance to work with our clients to ensure their businesses stand the test of time," Kerr added. As an integral part of quality management systems, the principles that established BSI are in many ways the same principles that guide the fundamentals of ISO 9000.

As a quality assurance entity that addresses the various aspects of quality management, ISO 9000 provides standards that include ISO 9001: 2015, which sets out the prerequisites and stipulations for quality management system. The process is to enable organizations to continuously improve the quality of their goods and services, by adhering to standards that are part of the certification process. In addition, ISO 9000: embraces the fundamental concepts involved in providing quality services, and certification. The ISO 9004:2009 entails how organizations can create efficient and effective quality management system that will lead to competitiveness, sustainability and increased performance.

The ISO 19011:2011 also provides guidance on both internal and external monitoring and auditing of quality management systems to ensure that organizations continually comply with the standards. The ISO 9001:2015 sets out the criteria for a quality management system and the only standards that can be certified in the ISO family. While this is not essentially a requirement, it is a quality assurance adherence that benefits organizational processes. Getting certified in this process makes it possible for any organization, small or big, to become certified to ISO 9001. In 2015, over one million businesses and organizations in more than 170 countries have been certified to ISO 9001.

The ISO 9001 is structured on a number of quality management systems that include focusing on customer satisfaction, employee motivation, the motivation of top management, and the continuous improvement of quality production of goods and services. The ISO 9001:2015 also helps to ensure that customers receive consistent and good quality products and services. Organizations that focus on providing consistent quality customer service often benefit and enjoy increased productivity and higher revenue.

It is important for organizations striving for certification to ISO 9001:2015 to make sure that the system works, and to adhere to the fundamental aspects of ISO 9001:2015, for effectiveness. For effectiveness, organizations must perform internal audit to check how its quality management system is working, in order to continually improve quality production and delivery of products and services. In some cases, an organization can invite independent certification body to verify that it is conforming to the standards. This is sometimes done by some organizations that need to continually assess their processes.

Maintaining ISO 9001 can be sector-specific. The reason is that the need for certification depends on the type of products offered by each organization. ISO however has several ranges of standards for quality management systems that are based on ISO 9001 and are adapted to specific needs and sectors of organizational processes. Such organizations include ISO/TS 16949 which deals with automotive products, relevant services and parts organizations. The ISO/TS 29001 deals with petroleum, or petrochemical products and natural gas industries. The ISO 13485 deals with medical devices and accessories. The ISO/IEC 9003 deals with software engineering and relevant fields. The ISO 17582 deals with electoral organizations at all branches and levels of government. The ISO 18091 deals with local government.

Certification can be useful to organizations that want to increase their value, credibility and productivity. It can be a useful tool to add substance and credibility as it makes it possible for organizations to demonstrate that their products and services meet expectations of customers. While not all organizations may feel the need to be certified or to certify their products, some businesses and industries may not have a choice as certification can be a part of a contractual requirement.

ISO 9000 has numerous advantages. One of the advantages is that it enables organizations to improve; but this can only be done through effective quality management. Another advantage is that it can have a good impact on investment, and increase in market shares. It can also increase sales margins, growth, and create competitive advantages. The process can also mitigate litigation that may arise in the course of doing business. In addition ISO 9000 provides guidelines for organizational excellence, and competitiveness, through efficient management of the quality systems. The advantages that can accrue from ISO 9000 can range from improved involvement to better documentation, communication, and cost benefits.

Proven advantages include efficient and effective business operation; and increase in customer satisfaction and retention. The process also reduces audits; enhances marketing, improves employee motivation, awareness and morale. The process also promotes international trade, and increases profits and productivity. In addition it reduces wastes and increases productivity, and provides tools for standardization while allowing organizations to meet the requirements for international uniform quality system. One of the most important advantages is that the process can lead to employee motivation and retention as it enables them to develop pride for achieving excellence on their job.

While proponents argue for, and support the fundamental advantages of ISO 9000 because it can lead to job satisfaction, process improvement, efficiency and reduction of wastes and audits, critics believe too much time, money and paperwork is required for registration. Studies have also shown that quality managers often become overwhelmed by the excessive paperwork and the added time required for registration. In many cases, the registration process creates its own overheads which can be costly.

Another argument against ISO 9000 is that the workplace can become inefficient if too much time, money and excessive paperwork are involved in the registration process. The process that is created to increase efficient and quality production and delivery of goods and services can become a process where quality is not actually improved because of the burden of the requirements. Critics also argue that adopting ISO 9000 can be risky if the resources invested do not generate expected results. The uncertainty of not knowing what resources will be needed, and if the standard will actually improve quality, are some of the criticisms often levelled against the standard. Other disadvantages include the uncertainty of the cost of certification and the added bureaucratic processes that the process entails. And in many cases certification process can fail to galvanize expected quality, and when this occurs, organizations can risk acquiring the attendant poor image and bad reputation.

Studies have indicated that ISO 9001 promotes specification control and procedures rather than the much needed understanding and improvement of quality management systems. Other critics opined that while ISO 9000 can be effective as a guideline, the process of promoting it as a standard can mislead organizations to think that their products are of better quality because of the certification. Though certification can help organizations to provide better quality services, it does not end there; they must still strive to continually improve the quality of their goods and services. Too much reliance on the specifications and guidelines of ISO 9001 may not lead to successful quality production, and delivery of goods and services.

Proponents see the standard as beneficial to organizational processes due to the increased sales margins and growth that can occur, but critics believe that the standard may be prone to failure as some organizations may put certification before quality. Experts have argued that certification is often based on contractual obligation than the need to improve quality. Just having certification without the related substance of quality improvement can be counterproductive and ineffective. For quality to really occur certification must be synonymous with quality – and this is often not the case in organizational processes as the focus is often to pursue certification rather than quality and excellence. Too much focus on certification can undermine efficient performance and quality service, experts noted. Another argument against the process is that certification by independent auditor can create additional overhead due to the added consulting fees that may accrue. Though the standard enables organizations to focus on the delivery of quality services which can lead to positive returns on investments, and increased market shares, including increased productivity, experts opined that organizations can still achieve quality production and services, without ISO 9000 registration.

According to experts, ISO 9001 can still be implemented because of the quality benefits that can be achieved, without necessarily being certified. In other words, an organization can have ISO 9001 for the quality benefits without undergoing the arduousness and hassle of certification.

What ISO systems do is to make sure that organizations adhere to the processes and guidelines needed for quality delivery of goods and services. ISO does not necessarily gauge the effectiveness of the process or how good the processes are; and it does not gauge whether the correct parameters are being adhered to, to ensure quality. Critics further added that ISO does not often validate the effectiveness or robustness of technical solutions which is an integral part of advanced quality planning in tech organizations. In many cases, according to critics, ISO certified manufacturing plants can be ineffective as they may display poor quality performance which may be due to poor technical applications.

Organizations can achieve quality productivity by focusing on the priorities that can lead to increased sales margins and growth without encumbering their processes with unnecessary registrations if it is not actually needed. Certification of products gives a feeling of quality assurance without necessarily delivering quality, research shows. And organizations can simultaneously create quality while providing certification. And if it is going to cost too much time and money to undergo registration, it may be necessary to jettison registration in order to focus on quality. Organizations cannot afford to sacrifice quality for registration and certification. It will not do an organization any good to have a certification paper on the wall without actually delivering quality. Emphasis must be placed on improving the quality of goods and services without devoting resources and expenses toward registration and certification. Quality control managers have often said that excessive paperwork can lead to poor performance and poor quality. Registration should not trump the need for quality as that will lead to an organization's inability to compete. In an internet age and globalized world, the focus should be on the pursuit of quality production and excellence in the delivery of goods and services. Bureaucratic processes that can derail quality should be avoided.

Organizations cannot maintain sustainability and competitiveness if resources are being channelled toward registration and certification, especially when they are not really needed to achieve quality. Organizations can create policies to focus on quality without necessarily becoming a part of the tradition that believes certification is synonymous with better quality.

While certification may sometimes lead to increased sales margins and sales growth, it does not guarantee quality, as the onus to provide quality rests on individual organizations. Many organizations have fallen off the radar of competitiveness by not concentrating on the quality of their products, and by not investing in research and development to ensure that their products are satisfying customers' needs and expectations. Organizations must constantly be current in their researches so that they will not be taken unawares by their competitors, with new innovative products.

Organizations must be willing to go beyond the thresholds of standardization to do things that are beneficial to their processes, and can enhance their products. While conforming to traditional standards can create uniformity and temporary market shares, it is the quality of products and services that can actually take organizations beyond what their competitors are offering. Simply adhering to standards stipulated by a body is not enough; organizations have to be willing to do whatever is necessary for their existential wellbeing that will promote quality production of goods and services.

Chapter 12

Six-Sigma and the Sales-Force

In sales and retail industries, the Six Sigma process can enhance the effectiveness of outputs if organizations are willing to adopt its system approach. Six-Sigma is a disciplined, data-oriented approach that incorporates the methodology of eliminating defects in organizational processes. Six-sigma is also a statistical data-driven approach whereby standard deviations between mean derivative and the closest specification are utilized in production and manufacturing. The process can also benefit business transactions, while enhancing the quality of products and services. It entails a set of techniques and tools needed for process improvement in organizations. As organizations continue to evolve with competition becoming cutthroat, it has become imperative for businesses to focus on doable set of techniques and tools that can enhance their processes.

The purpose of Six Sigma in organizations is to improve the quality of the output of a process by first identifying and eliminating future problems in manufacturing and business processes. Six-Sigma involves using series of quality management methods and tools such as empirical and statistical methods. The process enables organizations to identify talented and skilful employees who are experts in empirical and statistical methods so that proper procedures can be applied in achieving quality productions and services. The process of Six Sigma within an organization is based on a defined sequence of steps that have specific values and targets. One of such defined sequence of targets include defined goals such as eliminating, or lessening the impact of, pollution; minimizing costs, and increasing customer satisfaction while also increasing repeat businesses, referrals and profits.

Six-Sigma was first introduced by Bill Smith and Mikel Harry, while working at Motorola in 1986. Aptly dubbed the father of Six Sigma, Smith studied at the University of Minnesota, School of Management, not long after graduating from the Naval Academy in 1952. He would later join Motorola after 35 years in engineering and quality assurance. His background in engineering and quality assurance paved the way for the concept of Six Sigma which was quickly embraced by Motorola and other iconic organizations like

General Electric. Motorola had applied Six Sigma in all its manufacturing processes and operations by setting a goal to make it a central focus in its business practice. The company had also made it a part of its business culture in its manufacturing and engineering divisions. In 2005, Motorola said Six Sigma made it possible for it to save $17 billion in operational costs.

The term Six Sigma originated from statistical methods that were designed to provide quality in manufacturing processes. Like ISO 9000, it rates manufacturing processes in terms of quality and efficiency. The significance of sigma rating can be measured by the percentage of defect-free products that rated organizations produce. Six-Sigma is said to guarantee that a product will be statistically free of defects. Parts produced under the guidelines of Six Sigma are said to be defect-free. Products that are defect-free tend to create customer satisfaction, in addition to creating credibility and trust in an organization. Six-Sigma helps organizations to produce and deliver quality goods and services.

One of the organizations that had first embraced Six Sigma was Motorola, in its manufacturing processes. The application of Six Sigma helped Motorola to eliminate defects in its parts and products, and to also increase its market shares. Another iconic organization that applied Six Sigma in its operations was General Electric, which started from the time of Jack Welch. Welch had applied it to his operational strategy in 1995. Welch was able to use Six Sigma to successfully improve the quality of GE's output by using the methodology to identify and remove the causes of defects, while minimizing variability in manufacturing and operational processes. Around the same time that Welch had adopted the Six Sigma strategy in 1995, many Fortune 500 organizations also followed suit by adopting the strategy to reduce costs and improve quality.

Another significant advantage of Six Sigma is that it will enable organizations to stay ahead of the competition by improving knowledge and skills necessary for organizational quality assurance. For individuals who seek Six Sigma certification, it has its inherent benefits as employers often use it to gauge the skill and readiness of a potential employee. Many organizations prefer potential employees with talent and skills, and Six Sigma provides these potential employees with the confidence and enhanced skill they need to strive and secure the best positions and top jobs that the level of their skills deserve. While there are several definitions of Six Sigma, the one definition that aptly describes its significance is that it is a measure of quality that enables organizations and individuals to strive for excellence in the production, and delivery of goods and services. Though it is said to be a disciplined and statistics-driven methodology for removing defects, it is also a process that involves six standard deviations that measure essence between the mean and the closest specification limit in organizational processes. These nearest specification limit range from manufacturing to transactional - from product to service.

The data-driven statistical approach of Six Sigma quantitatively explains the performance of a process. In order to accomplish Six Sigma, a process must not produce higher than 3.4 defects per million opportunities. Six Sigma defect is said to be anything outside the purview of customer specifications. Six Sigma opportunities are seen as the total quantity of chances for a defect to occur. Calculating Six Sigma process can be done with a calculator designed for Six Sigma.

The significance of the objective of the Six Sigma methodology involves the implementation of a measurement oriented strategy that is based on process improvement and variation reduction that is usually accomplished through the application of Six Sigma improvement projects. This process can only be accomplished through the use of dual Six Sigma sub-methodologies such as DMAIC and DMADV. The DMAIC process stand for define, measure, analyze, improve, control; and it is an improvement system for processes that fall below specifications that needs improvement. The Six Sigma DMAV process stands for measure, analyze, design and verify, that is also a system which is designed for improvement, and developing of new quality products. This process can be added to existing process if there is a need for incremental improvement.

Another significant aspect of process improvement is lean Six Sigma which is a business philosophy that focuses on improvement by applying lean philosophies in conjunction with Six Sigma methodology. Lean Six Sigma tends to focus on efficiency, effectiveness and the reduction of variability in every aspect of business processes. In manufacturing or service organizations, a lean Six Sigma would be significant and predictable in accomplishing error-free and defect-free production. The implication is that for one out of the innumerable or one million products produced or services rendered at a Six Sigma level, an expected result would be only 3.4 defects with minimum and reduced time. If an order, it would take the same minimum time along with accompanying resour ces, to process.

In organizational processes, performance at a Six Sigma level would result in a significant improvement over other competing organizations. For organizations that operate at a level three sigma the result would be more than 66,000 defects/errors per million opportunities. In such cases, 80% to 90% of the process would not add value to the products and services produced. This occurrence could trigger customer dissatisfaction and organizational inability to compete and accomplish significant market shares. This process can also create a ripple effect that can lead to poor performance and inefficiency. Though Six Sigma continues to improve organizational performance, efficiency and effectiveness, several other organizations had started to experiment with lean manufacturing that would later be referred to as lean Six Sigma.

The lean Six Sigma methodology also focuses on the DMAIC approach which includes defining the problem, measuring process performance, analyzing the cause of the problem, impr oving the process and controlling the improved process by fixing the problem permanently. The lean Six Sigma method and toolset can make it possible for organizations to analyze processes and achieve significant breakthrough improvement if properly abided by. In many ways, lean Six Sigma allows organizations and individuals to find solutions. Such solutions can be how to reduce wastes, defects and improve processes so that high performance can be achieved.

The lean Six Sigma methodology focuses on lean ma nufacturing which is strategized on process flow, and waste issues; while Six Sigma in conjunction, focuses on variation and design, in order to create business and performance excellence. Organizations that have adopted lean Six Sigma include Verizon, Hon eywell, GENPACT, IBM, amongst others, in order to transform efforts toward growth and efficiency. Lean Six Sigma also enables organizations to focus on innovation through research and development in manufacturing, and software development. Lean Six-Sigma places emphasis on efficiency in sales and service performances.

The difference between Six Sigma and lean Six Sigma are few as they are based on similar characteristics. They share similar methodologies and tools as the focus of each philosophy is in process and operational improvement. Though they share similar characteristics, they are different in emphasis and definition. Lean manufacturing or lean Six Sigma focuses on eliminating wastes and in creating efficiency while Six Sigma focuses on eliminating defects, and reducing variability.

One of the numerous advantages of using Six Sigma is that the methodology helps to improve organizational processes by using statistical analysis instead of guesswork to accomplish optimum defects-free and error-free production of goods and services. It creates quality of goods and services, and most of all it reduces wastes by minimizing costs.

The philosophy behind Six Sigma is that it helps organizations to achieve stability and predictable process results. This is usually done by reducing process variation in order to achieve maximum efficiency. One of the things that make Six Sigma different from other quality improvement systems is that a defined process is usually focused on, to achieve measurable and quantifiable results from Six Sigma projects. The other advantage is that Six Sigma increases emphasis on strengthened and passionate leadership and support in organizations. Last but not the least is that it creates commitment to focus decisions on verifiable data and statistical methods instead of guesswork and assumptions.

Apart from helping to achieve sustainable quality improvement, Six Sigma requires commitment from all the stakeholders in the organization, starting from the top to the bottom in the organizational hierarchy. In addition, Six Sigma creates characteristics that can be defined, measured, analyzed, improved and controlled, in achieving defects-free processes.

The Six Sigma methodologies were influenced by Deming's plan-do-check-act cycle or plan-do-check-adjust, which itself is a four step management method that is constantly used in business to control and improve processes and products in organizations. The Six Sigma methodologies are DMAIC and DMADV; and each includes characteristics that are used in accomplishing projects for improving existing business practice, and for creating new products or operational designs.

On the individual phases of DMAIC and DMADV projects, Six Sigma uses, and applies several quality management tools which are mainly used outside the parameters of the Six Sigma process. In the context of interrogative technique, the 5-whys are often used to explore the cause and effect relationships that pinpoint a particular problem. The significance of this technique is to determin e the origin of the cause of a defect by constantly repeating the question why. For effectiveness, every question would create a sequence for the next question.

In addition, the tools necessary to achieve quality management include analysis and variance (ANOVA) or statistical models which are used for analyzing the difference between group means and sequential variations. The next tool is the general linear model which is often identified as Y=XB+U. The Y represents a matrix with multivariate measurements. The X represents a design matrix while the B matrix contains parameters for estimates. The U matrix contains errors which are often assumed to be uncorrelated for measurements even though they generally follow a multivariate normal distribution.

The next significant statistical and fitting tool is ANOVA gauge R&R which means repeatability and reproducibility. This measurement systems analysis technique uses analysis of variance or ANOVA random effects model for assessing measurement systems. This type of evaluation is essentially used for gauging and measuring instruments and test methods.

Another essential tool that is often used as part of a quality management method is regression analysis. Regression analysis is used for estimating the relationships between variables. Regression analysis is part of the techniques for modelling and analyzing variables when examining the relationships between dependent and independent variables. These variables can serve as predictors of outcome when determining the re lationships between the two variables. In organizations, the essence of regression analysis is to clarify how the inherent value of the dependent variable would change when one of the variables vary, while the rest of the independent variables are firm or held fixed.

In addition to regression analysis, correlation is a useful statistical tool for defining relationships between variables. Correlation in statistical terms is a significant broad of statistical relationships between two variables, and their linear relationship with each other. In organizations, correlation can be used to determine a predictive causal relationship between variables.

One of the most widely used tools for measuring and determining the effectiveness of quality management is scatter diagram. Scatter diagram is a form of statistical method that can be used as a quality management tool, using Cartesian coordinates which can specify numerical coordinates to determine the value of variables, for a set of data. This process helps organizations to accurately pinpoint a problem by helping to determine various correlations between variables with confidence intervals.

The inability of many organizations to effectively apply the tools needed to improve and enhance the quality production and delivery of goods and services had resulted in defects and errors which had resulted in millions of products' recalls in the 21st century. Companies that were once thought to be too big to fail in quality control had failed to adhere to the very quality guidelines that had made their brands popular among consumers.

Chapter 13

Salespeople's Fundamentals and the Impact of Recalls

While the introduction of several measures of quality control systems can help organizations to meet their goals, in order to achieve quality, and increase sales and productivity, an effective workforce is what drives productivity and help organizations in meeting their goals. Without a purpose-driven workforce that is disciplined to focus on goals and objectives, organizations will be unable to function effectively. In addition, organizations will be unable to apply the tools and measures necessary to achieve quality, goals, and sustenance.

In retail organizations, salespeople control the source of production as they are the lifeblood of such organizations. They form the core value that creates and enhances growth. If the quality of goods and services are to be maintained and even nurtured, organizations might do well to enhance workplace satisfa ction that salespeople will find conducive to work in, and help their organizations to achieve set goals.

Why do salespeople matter? They matter to organizations that depend on their services, and productivity, to achieve set goals. Such organizational goals can be to improve quality and delivery of goods and services. Organizational goals may be to focus on research, marketing, efficiency and time-bound productivity that are quality oriented. Too often, some organizations would put profit before quality, and would depend on the sales-force to deliver both at the same level. While it is not impossible to deliver profit and quality at the same time, it may be impossible to achieve high profits if certain factors that can lead to quality improvement are over looked. If organizations are to produce error-free, and defects-free products they will need to focus more on prevention so that the job of salespeople will be easier. If salespeople's jobs are made difficult due to constant defects and errors in products that lead to recalls, it can lead to customers' distrust of such products.

Customers understandably hate recalls and they tend to see recalls as evidence of a bad product. In automobiles where there are innumerable recalls, customers may shy away from bu ying such products because of reported recalls. Recalls tend to be bad news for organizations, and that bad news can translate into poor performance and reduced profits. Poor performance and low profits can lead to the inability of organizations to compete for adequate market shares.

In 21st century organizations, the production and delivery of quality goods and services may have been overlooked as more products than ever before have been recalled due to defects. It appears the essence of ISO 9000 and Six Sigma no longer plays significant roles in manufacturing and the delivery of goods and services. ISO 9000 had helped many fortune 500 organizations in the late 20th century to broaden and improve the quality of their goods and services by reducing wastes and minimizing costs in order to create quality of goods and services. ISO 9000 had created a standard that enabled organizations to create quality without sacrificing product effectiveness and efficiency for numbers and quotas. And with Six Sigma and lean Six Sigma, the need to achieve maximum quality had led to the need to statistically improve measures that would prevent defects and errors during the production of goods and services.

The job of salespeople has become harder as the years go by, and as many manufacturers have returned to erstwhile craze to reach quotas without putting quality first. As globalization has led to the integrated global economy that is marked by free trade, free flow of capital, and the increased pool of cheap foreign labor markets, the need to refocus on quality production that will be defects-free have never been more urgent.

As internet has added to the proliferation of information and customer awareness, many Western organizations may be forced to learn from the mistakes of the past that drove market shares offshore to Japanese and other foreign companies. While defects and recalls have also affected foreign companies' products, and has become associated with multinational manufacturers and organizations, including those of foreign countries, the manufacturers that have lesser defects or near zero defects may be poised to control future market shares as the Japanese did in the 1980s.

Toyota and Honda that were once known for the reliability of their vehicles have now become part of the business culture that no longer pay adequate attention to defects-free manufacturing. It wasn't too long ago that the Japanese were renowned for the quality of their products; but the dawn of the 21st century has seen the gradual erosion of the once invincible quality manufacturing of Japanese companies. With the recent recall scandals that put Toyota and Honda on the radar as organizations that have become complacent, that take shortcuts in manufacturing, it will be a matter of time before these companies would start to see a shift in their bottom-lines.

Apart from making the jobs of salespeople harder than ever before, customers' needs no longer appear to be a factor in organizational processes. Where ISO 9000 once focused on meeting the needs of customer and other stakeholders while meeting statutory and regulatory requirements that relate to products, many organizations are foregoing these requirements and sacrificing it for quick profits and quotas. The sector that is left to bear the brunt of the obvious disregard for quality improvement and defects-free production is sales, where salespeople strive on a daily basis to repair the damages caused by the greed of automakers and manufacturers.

Product recalls are the nightmare of salespeople in the retail industry as they must not only work harder to defend their brands but to find reasons to explain the recalls. While there are no justification for recalls, salespeople often try to ease the fears of their customers by reassuring them that recalls do not mean low quality or bad manufacturing. Recalls are nonetheless bad news for organizations and the salespeople that sell the products. The attendant scandals that follow recalls can scare off customers to where the livelihoods of salespeople can be threatened, and suffer the consequences that were dictated by greedy manufacturing executives who made the decisions to forego quality for quotas and quick profits.

The most scandalous and disastrous recalls of all time includes the Toyota recall of 2010 that many observers said was the worst auto recall ever. According to Newsweek, the recall was "the worst handled auto recall in history." The recall had started with faulty gas pedals and floor mats that had led to uncontrolled acceleration. Many Toyota vehicle owners reported that their vehicles were driving out of control, with the gas pedals getting jammed and stuck with floor mats. Many of these Toyota vehicles had ended in ditches, and off-roads, often resulting in deaths. What made the Toyota recall historic was that over 9 million vehicles were recalled by the company, which was unprecedented in the history of automobile industry!

Unlike the Japanese companies of the 1980s that were quality conscious and almost defects-free in their products, Toyota was criticized for not quickly addressing the 2010 gas pedal problems. Many critics blamed the company for appearing to "duck and deny," the existence of the problem. If Toyota had quickly tried to reassure its customers that the problems were being fixed, a damage control would have sufficed. But the company had at first tried to downplay the catastrophic recall by not quickly acknowledging its impact or existence. The impact of the recall had moved Toyota from the number one spot for a couple of years while they struggled to repair the damaged brand that was once known for quality. Some would say that Toyota is still struggling with efforts to repair the damage the scandal did to its brand.

Salespeople selling Toyota vehicles and parts experienced a tremendous decline in their incomes during the same period as Toyota sales plummeted. And the result was the same with pharmaceutical companies selling Tylenol where product recalls drove away customers from the popular medicine to an unprecedented low market shares. Tylenol had two major recalls. The first recall that Tylenol experienced occurred in 1982 that resulted in the deaths of over seven people in Chicago. The cause of the Tylenol related deaths was due to errors in the drugs that were unchecked during the production of the drugs. The errors were that the drug had accidentally been laced with cyanide. Immediately after the Tylenol-cyanide related deaths were announced, the company immediately did the right thing by quickly recalling over 31 million units of the drug.

Apart from the lives that were lost due to the cyanide laced Tylenol drugs that were sold to children and adults, many pharmaceutical salespeople and suppliers were forced to deal with the unpleasant situation that had turned deadly. Many customers felt the company had taken their loyalty for granted and had neglected to properly safeguard and protect their safeties; and millions of customers who had come to rely on the drug to solve their health problems. The media reports that Tylenol was laced with cyanide were so scary that many customers turned away from using the Tylenol products. The result was a significantly and dramatically reduced market share and loss of business for the company. The quality of the product had been sacrificed for quotas and numbers.

For salespeople selling Tylenol, it was a sad time as they felt betrayed by the company. Many of the salespeople felt short of words to explain the cyanide that had been found in the products. Everyone knew that cyanide was a deadly combination wherever it rears its fatal head in products. The notion that Tylenol was careless enough to allow its products to be contaminated with cyanide immediately drew public condemnation.

In 2010 Tylenol would be faced with another debilitating recall that resulted from customers' complaints that Tylenol medicines were causing nausea. It was also reported that the medicines had musty odor. Unlike the 1982 cyanide related recalls, Tylenol handled the 2010 recall poorly by first ignoring the product recall, without trying to quickly take measures to correct the problems. Like Toyota that had tried to downplay the gas pedal issue until it got too big to ignore, Tylenol would do the same. The company would take more than 20 months of the initial complaints, to take action. At the time the company decided to take action, the publicity the defects generated had almost crippled its existence. The attendant recall had been huge, resulting in over 60 million recalls of the medicines. Had Tylenol immediately taken action, the problem would have been averted.

The victims of Tylenol's negligence and lukewarm attitude towards the 2010 defects in its medicines were customers and the salespeople selling the products. Just like the negative impact the 1982 recall brought on the products, the 2010 defects and subsequent recalls were even worse. Whereas the 1982 defects and errors had resulted in the deaths of more than seven people with only 31 million recalls, the not-so-deadly recalls of 2010 that only caused nausea and carried musty odor would result in the recall of 60 million medicines. The difference was in the manner the recalls were handled in both cases. The 1982 cyanide related errors was properly handled with immediate action while the 2010 complaints were ignored until it became widespread, and too big to ignore.

According to critics, poor leadership had been responsible for the poor handling of the 2010 defects that had resulted in over 60 million recalls. Though poor production had been responsible for the defective products, which was due to poor quality management; the mishandling of the 2010 defects and errors was due to poor leadership. If proper guidelines had been in place to safeguard the safety of the medicines, the nausea effect and the musty odor would have been averted. Critics opined that Tylenol failed to adhere to safety standards during the production of the products in both 1982 and 2010. The argument was that it was nearly impossible to avoid errors when producing millions of medicines but critics noted that if proper safeguards had been in place that the products would have been deemed safe for consumption.

For Tylenol, actions were delayed because the company did not act fast enough to address the problem when it first occurred. It would have been much better and cheaper for the company to have had safety and quality measures in place to protect consumers, and to ensure that its products were defects-free.

The Blue Bell ice cream 2010-2015 recall was another major recall that almost crippled the company. For the first time in the company's 108 years history, the existence of the company was at stake as the listeria issue had almost tarnished the image of the company, according to CNN.com. The fatal listeria outbreak had resulted in a nationwide recall, even though the company had reported that there were no confirmed cases of listeria in its products. What had saved the company was that the company took action while denying the claim that listeria was present in its products. The listeria issue was so widespread that it compelled the FDA to investigate listeria monocytogenes in ice cream products from Blue Bell creameries. Following complaints from customers, the government had issued the following:

> The U.S. Food and Drug Administration along with the Centers for Disease Control and Prevention (CDC) and state and local officials are investigating an outbreak of listeriosis potentially linked to certain Blue Bell Creameries single serving ice cream products. Listeriosis is caused by the bacterium listeria monocytogenes.

The announcement prompted the Blue Bell Creameries to quickly expand its recall. The expanded recall was due to the CDC reports of April 20, 2015 that 10 patients had been infected with severe strains of listeria monocytogenes in four states which include Arizona, Kansas, Oklahoma, and Texas. Three deaths were reported in Kansas that resulted from the strains of listeria. Before it came to a head in 2015, the problem had been ongoing since 2010, according to media reports.

Blue Bell made its problems worse by not immediately taking measures to avoid the strains of listeria monocytogenes in its creameries. If the company had established a process to prevent defects and errors, the products would have been safe, and the subsequent bad image and bad publicity would have been averted.

Another recall that resulted in deaths of three people was the e.coli spinach recall of 2006 that resulted in more than 199 people being infected after eating e.coli tainted spinach. According to CDC and media reports, the outbreak was traced to a processing plant in California. The trace of e.coli in spinach had led to multiple brands of spinach being recalled for safety reasons. According to CDC, e.coli can be deadly and is the most dangerous food poison that is known to researchers. Though cyanides in Tylenols are deadly, the e.coli is said to be just as deadly, and one of the most dangerous food poisoning in modern times, according to media reports.

Lack of preparation for the unexpected had made it worse for the company when it failed to prevent its products from getting tainted with e.coli. If adequate safety and quality measures had been taken, the mistakes and errors would have been detected way before the product hit the market. It was even worse when it was reported that over 200 people were infected, with three reported deaths.

Though Six Sigma was introduced to enable organizations eliminate defects and improve the quality of goods and services, not all organizations embraced the concept. Or if they did, they were not practicing or adhering to the methodology. Blue Bell, Toyota, Spinach, and many organizations that had experienced major defects which had resulted in millions of recalls would have avoided the negative publicity and loss of productivity that came with the scandals, if they had applied the philosophy of Six Sigma, according to research studies.

In 2007, Hasbro voluntarily recalled over 1 million easy bake ovens after the company had received over 250 complaints of children getting their hands and fingers caught in the door, with over 80 burn reports. Though Easy Bake Oven is a small oven for kids, it didn't surprise the public that kids were getting their fingers burnt because of the easy access with the product. Critics say kids should not have access to ovens, that it was too early for kids to use ovens because of the potential hazards. But the company voluntarily recalled 1 million of the products that it felt could harm kids, by fixing the issue with the doors.

Rather than the company applying safety measures and improving the quality of its products, it had succumbed to the high demands for the products while sacrificing safety and quality production. Rather than take simple steps to test the products before releasing them, the company had, according to critics, brought the products to markets without adequate measures of testing the products several times to ensure there is adequate safety.

Graco High Chair recalls of 2010 added to the year's already worst records for recalls. While the March 2010 recall brought the total records to three, the issues that led to the recalls occurred systemically and in progressive proportion for sometime before the company took action. A total of 464 complaints of screws lo osening and falling out; with the plastic brackets breaking, added to the additional problems that were causing the high chairs to tip over. Graco recalled 1.2 million units of the product. At the time it got to the media and generated wide publicity, over 1.5 million strollers had been recalled due to fingertip amputation and laceration hazards. What made it worse for Graco was that the company had developed a bad reputation for product recalls. The year 2010 would add to the company's growing bad publicity concerning child safety products recalls.

The company lost a tremendous proportion of its market share as parents started to regard Graco with wariness and distrust. It was said that the company was not doing enough to provide adequate safety for its products. At the outset of its initial production of children's products, the company was known for its quality products and utmost regard for safety. But as its products increasingly became more popular, the company allowed greed and the rush to meet customers' growing demands to overshadow the need for safety and quality. And the company paid dearly with the bad publicity that had occurred in the media as it affected its finances and market shares.

For salespeople selling Graco products, 2010 was a horrib le year as additional bad publicity would affect their sales and livelihood. The company had made it worse when the scandal first broke out by not immediately acknowledging the problem and taking measures to correct them. It was only when over 464 reports of screws loosening and falling out, with plastic brackets breaking and causing the high chairs to tip, that attempt would be made to recall 1.2 million units.

Poor organization and ineffective leadership had made it impossible for the company to seize the opportunity that the first recall presented to rebrand and manufacture quality and safe products instead of the fragile, flimsy and low quality defective products that would result in the 2010 unprecedented recalls. The second and third recalls gave the impression that the company was overlooking safety and quality as it strives to meet market demands for its products. The worsening safety concerns had brought demand to a near halt as demands fell.

Perhaps one of the worst scandals of the early part of the 21st century was the peanut butter scandal when the 2009 recall of the product made customers uneasy and scared to eat peanut butter. The peanut butter cookies that were once everybody's favourite snack became poison as people were afraid to eat the cookies and crackers. The scandal did not just affect peanut butter cookies and crackers but snacks with peanut dust in it. At the time the Peanut Corporation of America felt it necessary to issue a recall following complaints of salmonella contamination and taint, the damage was already too widespread. The recall would affect over 4,000 food products because of the wide usage of peanut butter as an ingredient in numerous packaged foods.

The problem that Peanut Corporation of America had faced was that the company did not apply safety guidelines like Six Sigma techniques and tools for process improvement and prevention. Six-Sigma seeks to improve the quality of the output of a process by identifying and removing the causes of defects while minimizing variability in manufacturing, and delivery of products and services. Salmonella would have been detected and prevented from affecting and contaminating peanut butter food products if the company had taken measures to prevent the defects during production.

The pet food recall of 2007 was another major recall that shook the nation as it enraged pet owners across the nation. For pet owners who spent billions of dollars on pet foods annually, the pet food poison was a disappointment. The Food and Drug Administration (FDA) received more than 14,000 complaints about pet food poisoning, with more than 300 reported deaths of pets across the nation. The 2007 pet food recall was said to be the largest pet food recall in modern history. Many felt pet foods were not getting the same amount of scrutiny and quality attention as human foods. For pet lovers, the news that pet foods were being contaminated with food poison due to negligence or oversight was bad news. Critics say the reason pet foods were affected in such a large scale was because of the reduced scrutiny of pet foods. Since the 2007 pet food recall, efforts have been increased to provide adequate safety and quality to ensure that pet foods receive the same safety scrutiny as any other foods.

While organizations should immediately address complaints about their products, reassuring consumers that their products are safe is not good enough. Organizations should take measures to prevent defects and errors during production by ensuring that quality management systems such as Six Sigma and lean Six Sigma are in place to safeguard and improve the quality of their goods and services. Reassuring consumers that it is safe to continue to consume products that have received numerous complaints is just as bad as complacency; and total disregard for costumers' needs and expectations. Organizational leaders must be willing to take additional measures to ensure that their consumers are happy with their products. Safety and quality should be prioritized by organizational leaders, especially if they want to continue to maintain competitiveness in an ever evolving market.

Perhaps the biggest and most costly recall of the early 21st century was the Firestone Tires recall of 2000. It was at the onset of the millennial when it was reported that the threads in Firestone tires were separating and peeling off, thereby causing accidents. More than 175 deaths and over 700 injuries occurred as a result of the defects in Firestone tires. The problem that had led to the disastrous recall was due to the poor quality of the tires made by Firestone. And it didn't help that the company had at first tried to shift blames for its poor quality production, by first blaming Ford for the problem. If the threads in tires would separate, how was the automaker to blame? Many had asked. But when Firestone could not justify blaming Ford, the company had reluctantly accepted blames for the issues. But not before it ruined the company's image and made the company to sever ties with Ford, a long time partner.

Another company that experienced bad publicity as a result of the recall that shook the company is Thomas & Friends Wooden

Railway Toys, in 2007. The recall was about lead paint and its adverse effect on health. The biggest concern was that the product was potentially harmful to children under the age of six. Since the company quickly made a quick decision to address the problem by correcting the mistakes, there were no reported deaths or any attempt to hide the incident. In addition, no injuries were reported, even though over 1.5 million of Thomas & Friends Wooden Railway Toys were recalled. Though it temporarily affected the image and productivity of the company, the damaging effect also came from the negative press that followed the aftermath of the defects.

Many organizations often neglect to take responsibilities when defects and recalls occur in their products by first denying that there is a safety issue, while quietly taking steps to correct the problem. The lack of pursuit of excellence and the inordinate quest to achieve numbers and quotas often gives the wrong impression that many of these organizations do not care about their customers. An organization cannot survive negative impact of bad publicity. Organization must embrace steps to correct and detect defects, and fix them when they occur. Organizations must continually make serious efforts to improve their products in order to be able to compete. One of the characteristics of Six Sigma is that it allows organizations to detect and fix problems before they occur. No organization can survive when the quality of its products are continually the subject of recalls and complaints.

While product defects and errors can hurt a company's reputation, what can hurt it the most is denial and unwillingness to take responsibility for the problem! When the Firestone scandal broke, the company tried to avoid responsibility by blaming Ford. When investigations revealed that the reasons for the threads in the tires separating were due to poor quality, it was then that the company reluctantly accepted responsibility. Many organizations can shake off bad reputation with time, if the defects that led to the bad reputation are eliminated. But this can be almost impossible for organizations that continue to make the same mistakes of producing defective products, and not making serious efforts to prevent defects and errors in their products.

One of the biggest problems facing many organizations today is how to continually avoid defects and errors in their products. Toyota and Honda that were once known for the quality and reliability of their products have recently faced scrutiny for failure to prevent defects in their automobiles. Since 2010 when Toyota first experienced the worst nightmarish defects and recalls ever, the company still continues to experience defects in its vehicles, years later. Many critics blame the frequent defects in the company's vehicles on top executives who are always trying to cut corners in order to maximum production and fulfil growing demands. There were critics who noted that the Toyota and Hondas vehicles made in Japan do not have the same number of defects like the Toyotas and Honda vehicles made in America.

In 2016 alone, automobile dealerships and automakers have had to deal with the most debilitating recalls ever. The airbag issue that has affected many automakers has led to untimely deaths of many vehicle owners since it was first reported. Many automakers have had to face increased scrutiny due to faulty airbags that often deploy due to extended exposure to consistently high humidity and temperatures. The chemicals in those airbags have sometimes spilled and maimed motorists, sometimes causing deaths and serious injuries. Faulty airbags have added another layer of problems to the already beleaguering recalls that many automobile organizations currently face.

In the 21st century so far, it is as if one problem replaces another, with automakers. And consumers have become weary victims of poor quality manufacturing and lukewarm and lacklustre adherence to efforts to improve quality production. The many standards that are in place to promote quality manufacturing are no longer being adhered to, critics say. For example, the ISO 9000 that allows organizations to ensure that they meet the needs of customers and other stakeholders while meeting statutory and regulatory requirements of manufacturing and production of products, are no longer being implemented. According to experts, organizations need to revisit some of the programs and standards that had bolstered quality production in the past. Such programs as ISO 9000 and Six Sigma can help organizations to continually improve the quality production of goods and services, if properly implemented.

The year 2016 has been especially bad for car recalls. Dangerous recalls like airbags recalls and defective seatbelts have dominated national and international headlines as motorists continue to face danger on the road due to the safety hazards presented by these defects. Defective airbags and defective seatbelts have led to the recall of millions of vehicles across North America, especially in the United States where recalls have affected vehicle owners the most.

Vehicle owners no longer have to only deal with the safety hazards in their vehicles but the inconvenience of waiting endlessly for repairs that would sometimes take months. In some cases car dealerships would be so overwhelmed with defective vehicles that need repairs that they can no longer cope with the millions of vehicles that are recalled, because of the long list of recalled vehicles. Vehicle owners have had to take time off work to deal with problems that are visited upon them by incompetent automakers and parts manufacturers.

The Takata airbag defects have been so huge and prevalent that over 7.8 million vehicles were affected in the United States alone, according to National Highway Traffic Safety Administration. Vehicles affected by defective Takata airbags include Toyota, Honda, Mazda, BMW, Nissan, Mitsubishi, Subaru, Chrysler, Ford, and General Motors. The NHTSA had urged vehicle owners to "act immediately on recall notices to replace defective Takata airbags," to prevent getting hurt by defective airbags that are exposed to high humidity and temperatures. According to NHTSA:

> Responding to these recalls, whether old or new, is essential to personal safety and it will help aid our ongoing investigation into Takata airbags and what appears to be a problem related to extended exposure to consistently high humidity and temperatures. However, we're leaving no stone unturned in our aggressive pursuit to track down the full geographic scope of this issue.

One of the problems that have often affected the ability of many organizations to effectively eliminate defects in their products is the denial that it exists in the first place. When the Takata airbag defects first made news, more than 10 years ago, the company denied that its products were defective even as motorists were being killed by exploding airbags; and automakers were recalling millions of vehicles that were equipped with defective airbags.

In May 2015, when Takata finally admitted that its airbags were defective, and agreed to double the number of vehicles recalled in the

United States to as much as 34 million, which according to the New York Times was "one in seven of the more than 250 million vehicles on American roads, making it the largest automotive recall in American history," it was a little too late. If the company had admitted the problem at the beginning when complaints were flooding government agencies in the United States, more lives could have been saved.

The danger presented by defective airbags can cause deaths. The airbags can explode "violently when they deploy, sending shrapnel flying into a car's passenger compartment," the New York Times reported. As at the time Takata admitted that its airbags were defective, six deaths and over 100 injuries had been linked to the defect.

One of the reasons organizations like Takata was able to get away with such defects for so long was, according to critics, due to the ineffectiveness and lukewarm attitude of the agency responsible for overseeing and protecting vehicle owners. Congress had blamed the NHTSA for being too lax on the industry it oversees by not doing enough to make sure that incompetent and inefficient organizations are made accountable for poor quality products. Poor handling of dangerous industrial products like the Takata airbags defects had been responsible for the hundreds of injuries reported, along with the reported deaths of six motorists. According to New York Times, in 2009, NHTSA investigated allegations concerning the Takata airbags for a few months and would later close the case citing "insufficient evidence," six months later. But current incidents of violent airbags exploding would indicate that NHTSA poorly handled the investigation. If NHTSA had done a good job of properly investigating Takata when the defects were first reported, many lives would have been saved 10 years later. Takata was given the green light to continue its incompetent manufacturing of defective airbags unstopped by the same governmental agency that was created to oversee it.

Organizations entrusted to monitor and oversee manufacturers of consumer products can strive to do a better job of monitoring products that are imported into the country so that consumers can feel protected. While it may not be easy to monitor all imported goods, products that involve safety and the wellbeing of consumers should be retested before they are allowed to make it to the market.

If the government can treat imported goods the same way it treats domestically produced products, many productive lives will be saved. Besides the productive and useful lives that are often lost to low quality products every years, billions of dollars are also lost in medical treatments, drugs, burials and other expenses that bad products create.

Defective products do not only affect adults they affect children who are leaders, innovators, inventors, and merchants of the future. The country loses a tremendous amount of revenue that is lost through the untimely deaths of the young, due to defective products. Congress can enact a law that will compel every manufacturer, importer and organizational leaders to follow standardized guidelines in quality control.

Organizations like ISO 9000, Six Sigma and lean Six Sigma should be reinvigorated to help organizations to improve the quality of the goods and services that they offer to the public. Many manufacturers have resorted to outsourcing, and relocating their manufacturing plants to cheap labor countries in order to minimize the cost of production. Such moves have not only cheapened quality but also made it impossible for monitoring agencies to monitor such products when they eventually make it to the shores of this country. Manufacturers who use foreign manufacturing plants to manufacture their products should be held accountable, liable and responsible for the defects that occur in such products. A punitive measure and or a fine, including prosecution, should be in place to punish and deter erring organizations that import defective products into the country.

Greed has mainly driven many manufacturers to relocate their plants to cheap labor countries where they can pay low wages and not have to pay benefits. With some of these manufacturers, what matters most is the amount they are able to save. Quality is never in the forefront of their decision making. Oftentimes, they would employ a foreign subcontractor to hire local workers who may not be properly trained to do the job. With these foreign subcontractors, the objective is never the same as the objective of the organizations that hired them to do the job.

Low quality products are substandard in nature compared with products that are properly manufactured with quality. Organizations that invest in producing better quality products often enjoy the benefit of producing products that consumers are drawn to. Good products often attract cult-following as words often spread about the quality of the products. Just like words can spread about the bad quality of a product, so can words spread about the good quality of a product. Good news travel fast, but bad news travel fastest, experts say. With bad products, the news often spread the fastest.

In an internet age where information can be disseminated around the world through the social media in milliseconds, and in a matter of minutes, good and bad news tend to spread faster than ever. Organizations that sell defective and low quality products can lose their market shares if another organization springs up with a better product. And in some cases, some organizations can unknowingly divulge their trade secrets by entrusting that secret with a foreign contractor or manufacturer who may not be loyal to the organization.

Organizations like Apple that produces most of its products in China, often risks ending up with low quality products or worse, risks having its intellectual property stolen by the foreign factory that makes its products. Foxconn makes iPhone and iPads for Apple. The same Foxconn makes smart phones for other local manufacturers in China. Samsung is reportedly using Foxconn for its smart phones as well. In addition, Foxconn assembles products for Microsoft, and Hewlett Packard. Recently, Apple was asked to stop selling its iPhone 6 and iPhone 6-plus in China because a Chinese company was also manufacturing and selling similar phones in China. Apple was told that its products were too similar to the smart phones made in China. One wonders who stole whose intellectual property! If Foxconn makes iPhones and iPads for Apple in China, chances are that the same Foxconn also makes smart phones for local dealers in China that may be knockoffs of the real Apple products. Since China is all about protecting the local economy, it sees Apple as the one trying to steal the intellectual property of a local company!

Had Apple protected its products by manufacturing them in the United States, the chances of another company stealing its intellectual property would have been slim, if not impossible. While Apple has been known for its high quality smart phones and tablets, it has also been lagging behind in new innovation. As Samsung continues to come out with improved smart phones, Apple is being gradually swept out of its once invincible pinnacle of tremendous success. Rather than been improving on its innovation, and increasing the quality of its phones, Apple has been hoarding cash in foreign accounts in an attempt to avoid paying taxes on the over $182 billion in its offshore accounts. No wonder the European Union recently fined the company $14.5 billion in unpaid taxes in Ireland. Though the company is reportedly worth over $700 billion, it still borrows to finance its major projects rather than use its own money.

Apple could use some of its cash surplus to invest in research and development so that the company can continue to produce better quality and innovative products. Critics opined that Apple is trying to use its past glory to continue to enrich itself without spending more on new innovation. Experts predict that if Apple continues with the same practice of using existing innovation instead of investing in new ones that the company may end up like its predecessors such as BlackBerry and Nokia, especially if another company is able to trump its current innovation with better products. And the market is already seeing the upsurge in Samsung's smart phone sales, as the company recently became the largest smart phone maker in the world, a position once held by Apple, according to Daily Mail.

While Apple may have become victim of its own greed, and may have inadvertently given out information that involves its intellectual property, the same cannot be said about General Motors whose ignition problems led the company to recall over 1.6 million vehicles. General Motors has had issues in the past that could have totally crippled the company if the government had not intervened and saved the company. But the 2014 ignition scandal took everyone by surprise as it came from nowhere. It came at a time when it was thought GM had moved beyond its chronic faulty mechanical problems that had beset the company during the past decade. The newest of its many problems would be an ignition problem.

The ignition issue came to public attention after the New York Times published a scathing report about the recall of more than 1.6 million GM vehicles with faulty ignitions. The report noted that the faulty ignition problem can lead to a GM vehicle turning off while it is being driven. The most scathing part of the problem was that it said over 260 incidents of ignition failures were reported to General Motors and the National Highway Transportation Safety Administration (NHTSA), and that nothing was done to correct the problems. When the report came out that both GM and NHTSA had neglected to take actions on the complaints that could have saved lives, everyone was enraged and angry, including members of Congress.

The incident led the Senate and House of Representatives to hold bipartisan committee hearings about General Motors and NHTSA. The committee had wanted to find out why NHTSA failed to properly investigate both fatal and nonfatal accidents concerning the ignition switch failures. Following the published report, NHTSA had issued a rejoinder saying that its investigations of the 260 incidents of ignition switch failures failed to find cause for a formal investigation. But it was clear that the agency was merely collecting complaints and storing them in its database without properly addressing the problems. The agency had rebutted congressional inquiry about its inept and lukewarm attitude towards consumer complaints by sending out multiple replies to concerned lawmakers and vehicle owners.

In one particular letter to Congressman Barney Frank dated December 8, 2010, regarding ignition switch failures, NHTSA wrote confirming its responsibility as the federal agency responsible for improving safety on the nation's highways. The letter further added that "we are authorized to order manufacturers to recall and repair vehicles or motor vehicle equipment when our investigations indicate that they contain safety defects in their designs, construction, or performance." The letter added that "however we cannot act on isolated problems or resolve disputes between individual owners, dealers, or manufacturers." But the NHTSA had contradicted itself saying it "cannot act on an isolated problems," when in fact over 260 complaints were received by the agency regarding stalling and ignition switch failures.

According to New York Times, NHTSA's failure to act and to link the frequency of ignition faults, to force a wider investigation, amount to inefficiency and negligence. With heavy scrutiny from congressional committees that oversee consumer affairs, NHTSA would face additional problems, this time, from the justice department. As often the case with the agency, it had managed to shift blames to the automaker saying it was misled by GM to reach the decision that there was no cause to open an investigation about the ignition switch failures. The agency claimed that GM had confirmed that technicians working at GM authorized dealers had claimed they were unable to find the cause of the stalling that had been reported by several vehicle owners. And what had made the situation worse was that GM was said to have followed the recommendations of dealers' technicians, and had refused to provide further assistance to vehicle owners based on dealers' inability to determine the cause of the stalling.

As the Department of Justice focused its case on GM's negligence to act to address the complaints, it became clear that NHTSA would not take blames for the problems and that it would heap the blames on GM. The Department of Justice made it c lear that if it was proven that GM purposefully misled NHTSA with evidence to support the case against the automaker, that the problem could get as bad as the Firestone tires that involves Ford Explorers between 1995 and 2002, if not worse.

Though recalls often occur in automobiles due to the number of vehicles that manufacturers produce yearly, the frequency of the recalls has become a cause for concern to vehicle owners, and lawmakers. The disconcerting part of it is that the problems do not just involve local manufacturers but foreign manufacturers as well. Expert say complacency has taken hold in global manufacturing as competition has increased over the past decade, especially since the dawn of the millennial.

Critics say NHTSA hasn't been acting res ponsibly when it comes to its functions "to order manufacturers to recall and repair vehicles or motor vehicle equipment when our investigations indicate that they contain safety defects in their design, construction, or performance." The reason critics have been so vocal in their criticisms of NHTSA is that the agency has not been doing enough to oversee and monitor organizations as it should, in order to prevent defects. Even when consumers have notified the agency about their safety concerns, all the agency has often done in such cases has always been to contact the manufacturers who in turn would instruct the complainants to take their vehicles to their local dealers for determination of the problem. As if in collusion with the manufacturers, the technicians at local dealerships would often 'diagnose' the problem and send a report that the concerns could not be justified, or nonexistent, to the manufacturer, which in turn would respond to NHTSA that the reported complaints could not be justified. Oftentimes, the NHTSA would close its file on the issue and archive it in "our complaint database."

But the problem would be ongoing and would oftentimes increase in strength and number, sometimes ensuing in the loss of lives and injuries, including new victims. Media reports concerning pre-existing defects that have caused deaths and injuries are usually the reasons that the agency would act, critics say. When it comes to prevention and ensuring that independent thorough investigations are carried out to ensure that defects do not become death traps, the agency has always been ineffective and inefficient, a government official said. Not even congressional complaints would spur the agency to act as was the case with the effort made by Congressman Barney Frank who wrote the agency when he had received a complaint from a constituent about his 2006 Chevy Cobalt that was stalling intermittently.

The same constituent had earlier written to the agency about his ignition problem and when he could not get the help he nee ded, he had written his Congressman. In response to the Congressman's letter concerning the constituent's complaints, the agency had merely replied that the complainant had "filed an online complaint with NHTSA, which we located under complaint No. 1033155 7" and upon which no further action was needed. The agency further added that any complaint submitted through the internet is often automatically "entered into our complaint database." Such database is often reviewed when necessary to determine further act ion. More often than not, the case is archived without action. According to Chan D Lieu, Director of Governmental Affairs, Policy and Strategic Planning, "NHTSA's Office of Defects Investigation reviews and analyzes the data to determine whether an investi gation is warranted." The Director said the complainant in the 2006 Chevy Cobalt intermittent stalling should contact "his local Chevrolet dealership to schedule a meeting with a General Motors district manager regarding the problem," signalling the end of their involvement.

The agency failed to grasp the understanding that the complainant had already explored that area before contacting the agency, prior to contacting his Congressman. In this situation as in many other situations, the agency failed to ade quately respond to a crisis that was brewing that could have saved lives. It was when the crisis was reported in the media that the agency would quickly come out to say it was misled by GM regarding the defects.

Shouldn't the agency have responded to the crisis by conducting an independent investigation of its own without sending the complainant back to the local dealership that had already frustrated him? Shouldn't the agency have directly contacted the local dealership to do something about the intermittent stalling of the 2006 Chevy Cobalt rather than sending the complainant back to the dealership to have a meeting with the district manager, knowing well that such a meeting, if it takes place, would culminate in a futile effort? The issue of accountability and how it relates to a governmental agency totally failed a citizen in distress who had suffered pain and suffering for buying a defective vehicle. The agency failed in its duty to protect consumers and to address defects in products that it was created to oversee. The action of NHTSA also add to the notion that the agency exists only in name and does not do enough to protect customers even when directly contacted by consumers to address their problems. Other critics have said that the agency only react when there is scandal and media reports that reflect the enormity of a crisis. The Firestone tires scandal only became a factor when it became a headline in media organizations. When consumers had complained about the problem, the agency did not take any action but had as usual assigned it a case number!

Assigning a complaint a case number without action does not solve the problem. The agency claimed it uses such data to analyze and determine whether "an investigation is warranted," before even addressing the problem. But there is no known record of the agency *ever* taking action on an archived data that was analyzed and acted on, according to media reports. It has always taken a media report of a crisis to get the agency to act. The Takata airbag crisis and the Firestone/Ford scandals are example where media reports made the agency to take action.

Governmental agencies should be more proactive and responsive to consumer complaints especially when it involves safety, life and death matters. It shouldn't have to become a scandal or a major crisis before an action should be taken. While not all complaints are with merits, every complaint should be treated as if with merit until proven otherwise, to prevent needless deaths and injuries. Automakers have for years gotten away with producing vehicles that are substandard and with poor quality because of lack of adequate monitoring, by the agencies entrusted with the obligations to protect consumers. Congress can enact a law that makes it unlawful for any complaint to be treated with inaction so that consumers can be adequately protected.

Telling a consumer to contact his local dealer to correct a problem when the consumer has already tried that avenue and had been frustrated is not the most feasible way to handle customer needs. In an ideal situation, it should be a representative from the agency who should be contacting the dealer to handle the complaint and to make sure the consumer is treated fairly and his/her complaints handled appropriately. Archiving a legitimate complaint and assigning it a case number does not solve any problem, if anything it worsens the problem as was the case with the Takata airbag. For decades, complaints were swept under the carpet with egregious abandon, only to be taken seriously when numerous deaths had occurred. Consumers should not have to die before a problem can be corrected. It took several deaths before Takata admitted wrongdoing and it was the same with Firestone/Ford defects. This is a miscarriage of justice for consumers whose only voice is supposed to be the agency that was created to safeguard their interests, but *sadly*, it appears those consumer interests have become secondary to the interests of big corporations who determine when to admit wrongdoing and when they should not.

Chapter 14

Why Salespeople Need to Unite and Rebrand

Salespeople are often the most disrespected and scorned professionals in the annals of professionalism, according to research. Like most professions, salespeople did not choose the profession; the profession chose them, by virtue of the way they are genetically coded. Being born to do a particular thing can be akin to being genetically coded into doing something, because it is a natural characteristic of that person to be thus, according to studies. Genetic codes often determine the biochemical basis of a person's heredity which consists of codons in one's DNA and RNA that determine specific amino acid sequence. Codons tend to pinpoint a specific sequence of three consecutive nucleotides that is part of our genetic code. And in many ways, we are predestined to be what we become in life, which means we are chosen to be what we become even before we know it! Science has indicated that our genetic codes direct what we eventually become in life. So, saying that our profession chooses us versus otherwise, tends to be a logical sequence of our genetic code.

The contemptuous situation that salespeople have been predestined to be may have been indirectly created by salespeop le themselves because of the sleaziness many of them have brought to the profession of selling. Studies have shown that when it comes to respectable careers and professions that salespeople rank in the lowest stratum. Their rating was bestowed by societal members who often perceive salespeople as unwelcomed, and sometimes as tolerable nuisance. But not all salespeople fall in this category as some sales professions still command a modicum of dignity and respect. Generally, salespeople are simply just salesp eople; a crop of professional cadre that are barely tolerated to coexist with other notable and worthy professionals.

Automobile sales and door-to-door sales tend to have it worse because of the nature of the terrain they are forced to operate in. Selling cars often entails having to make calls and wait outside the dealerships to greet and show customers around until they find the type of cars they are interested in. In some cases, as an automobile salesperson, your job goes beyond waiting on customers to arrive but to also canvass and solicit for sales in the service department as old customers return to have their cars serviced. Since selling involves going to, and calling, the customer, it may oftentimes be impossible to cultivate respect and dignity since a discreet and mild beggary is often involved, to a certain degree, in selling. One may often have to resort to a certain form of begging, soliciting, and cajoling, to sell a product. But basically, selling is all about trying to lure, in a nice gentle but firm way, a customer to buy a product that he or she may not be quite ready for.

Studies have shown that the average customer is usually 50% ready to make a purchase while the other 50% in him is waiting to be persuaded to make the purchase. It often takes a good salesperson to turn the potential customer into a 100%-ready customer. And to do this sometimes takes a small element of trickery and cajoling. But none of this tactics is ever respectful or dignifying. If it were dignifying it won't be selling, experts say. And if it is too honest, it still won't be selling. Selling has to have some cheats, tricks and deception for it to be selling. It is the same whether one is selling insurance, pharmaceuticals, shoes, clothes, adulterated drugs, bootlegged CD, or even hawking knockoffs. And sometimes if it is too dishonest it defies the logic of selling and becomes an utterly crooked transaction. One part has to be ready to conquer and subdue the other. There has to be middle between two extremes. And in actuality, selling is treading a fine line between two extremes.

Good and talented salespeople know when to do away with extremes. Extremes can lead to a job loss, if not prosecution. To maintain decency and uprightness, one must be willing to make a sacrifice of not toeing any extreme. After a couple of months of near-starvation, a typical salesperson would take the plunge, and starts to act like a true salesman. Though he never did fit in, the problem would be that he wasn't a true salesman and of course wouldn't last. To be successful one must be ready to be dishonest and honest at the same time! Honesty pays in certain situations but it doesn't pay dividends in sales. That is not saying the characteristic of being a good salesperson is dishonesty, it is not! The characteristic trait of good selling is being honest when it calls for honesty and being dishonest when it is needed. But one cannot be everything at the same time!

And in many cases, a lot of customers are just as dishonest in their attempts to get a good deal, as salespeople. The difference is that the one that often ends up with a bad name is the salesperson, not the customer, even when he lies about everything in the purchase process. When a customer says he/she saw the same product elsewhere at a much cheaper price, it may not necessarily be true for if it is true the customer wouldn't be sitting down trying to negotiate. Some customers will tell you after a test drive that they will be back, that they are going to pick up their wives or husbands, in order to get away, having test-driven five to six vehicles for the pleasure of doing so, without even thinking of the salesperson's time. Some customers will say they will be back in order to give the salesperson hope that something is about to, or is going to happen. Customers do this when they feel they have wasted the salesperson's time, knowing they are not ready, or just passing time.

Just like a salesperson will not do well by being too honest, so it is with some customers. If they enter a dealership and say they only want to test drive, that they have no interest in buying anytime soon, many salespeople will avoid the customer. But there are those salespeople that will put on their selling shoes to try to sell a customer who will say he is not buying but just there to test drive. The average salesperson will not waste time with a customer who is not buying, on a test drive. With some salespeople, test drive is a waste of time even though dealerships often encourage it. Some dealerships will even promise customers a reward for coming to test drive. The essence of luring customers to come to the dealership for a test drive is to possibly convince the customer to buy, once he is at the dealership. Studies show less than 10% of these customers will actually buy.

While being deceptive about your readiness to buy, when you are not may not necessarily count as a dishonesty ploy, it is still dishonesty. An honest person will be upfront, rather than hide under the cloak and guise of buying when he knows he is not there to buy or does not even have the wherewithal to buy. When a customer lies, it is not nearly as dishonest as when a salesperson lies. The reason is that the customer gets an easy pass with lying while the salesperson ends up with a bad reputation.

And there are those customers that will knowingly write a bad check for a down-payment knowing there is no money in their accounts. And there are those that will lie, cheat, and bring you fake documents to make a purchase. Some of these subprime customers will sometimes not return the vehicle to the dealer when their information is unverifiable. Whether lying, being dishonest, or wasting your time, the customer does not face the same scrutiny as a salesperson who may often have to deal with the career-threatening debacle of lying.

If the sales profession were like other professions that are protected by membership in the union, perhaps there would be dignity associated with the job of selling. Since there is no prospect of joining the union, as there is no union for salespeople, salespeople can unite by forming an association that will promote unity among them, correct public perception, and rebrand the image of salespeople. Experts believe that not belonging to a union is one of the reasons why disrespect, indignity and job dissatisfaction is prevalent in the profession. If a union exists to protect the interests and needs of salespeople, the public will be compelled to have a different perception and opinion of salespeople.

If salespeople can come together to fight for their rights, and to make the public trust and respect them, there might be a return to job satisfaction and respect. To get to that point, salespeople must be willing to make a sacrifice of time and effort to come together to form a nonconformist association that will command the respect of all and sundry. Lawyers lie all the time to win cases, and oftentimes they cheat to defend their clients, at least 'good' lawyers do, but they don't get tarred and tarnished like salespeople. While lawyers have their own bad reputation for constantly misrepresenting facts, the profession can still be favourably perceived by the public as a noble profession. The same cannot be said of the sales profession that is often perceived to be sleazy, and dishonest, according to studies.

Some organizations often engage in massive fraudulent schemes and practices that make salespeople look like angels in comparison. According to Justin Schultz, a corporate psychologist, "just as character matters in people, it matters in organizations," and since the onset of the millennial, there have been many organizations like Enron, Stanford Financial Group of Companies, Lehman Brothers, that skirted the legal system to make profits through fraudulent financial schemes that shook global stock market to its core. The biggest of them all, Enron, a once colossal natural gas pipeline company, was the seventh largest publicly held corporation in the United States. No one suspected its shoddy business practices that were aided by respectable bankers and advisors, until the company suddenly filed for bankruptcy on December 2, 2001.

According to the Economist, "deceit demands more deceit until eventually the pile collapses under the weight of its own incredibility." In hedge fund and Ponzi scheme swindles, this type of deceit may become an issue that is hard to sustain in the long run, as was the case with Enron and Lehman Brothers Holdings, Inc. Both companies ended in bankruptcies when the center could no longer hold their deceits; but in other professions, constant deceit is a norm. For example, in sales, deceit is part of the modus operandi, while it is also the same in legal practice where lawyers often have to twist the truth, including lying, to win a case. "It is hard to find a successful attorney that is not a sworn, or pathological, liar," a prominent Houston-based lawyer said. "If he isn't a liar then he is definitely not successful," his golf partner quipped. For many organizations, lying is also a norm. In the hedge fund business and or Ponzi scheme where deceit is almost legal, fraud and deceit are part of the modus operandi. Ponzi scheme is an investment swindle in which investors are paid off with money put up by other investors in order to encourage more and bigger risks.

Enron was once a huge organization that had the ears of those in power because of its colossal influence. Once its level of deceit became apparent, the company collapsed, with most of its top executives going to prisons and or 'dying sudden' deaths. In the end, greed, avarice, deceit, and misplaced morals led to the company's demise, while taking with it the lifesavings of those who had gone for the ride. As Warren Buffet puts it, "once a company moves earnings from one period to another, operating shortfalls that occur thereafter require it to engage in further accounting manoeuvres that must be even more heroic. These can turn fudging into fraud." As an iconic organization with power and influence extending to the White House, at the time, the company was thought to be too big to fail. But just when everyone thought the company's future was robust, and infallible, this colossal house of cards that existed in a phantom-like bubble came crashing without notice, taking everyone by surprise, including the hard-earned lifesavings of investors. According to Forbes, "the company's failure in 2001 represents the biggest business bankruptcy ever while also spotlighting corporate America's moral failings."

In the Ponzi scheme debacle of the early part of the millennial that involved Bernie Madoff and many others of his ilk, who took advantage of the loophole in the stock market and investment banking it was a stark reminder that when organizations seem too big to fail, the fundamentals of the structures should be double checked. As a former non-executive chairman of the NASDAQ stock market, Madoff was the quintessential mogul who would not have been suspected of the largest Ponzi scheme that was said to be the biggest financial fraud in U.S. history. As a stockbroker and investment advisor, he represented what it meant to be a successful stockbroker and investor, until his sudden fall from grace. And there were many like him, who became exposed for what they represented. Allen Stanford, like Madoff, operated one of the most fraudulent Ponzi schemes ever. He was until his fall, a prominent financier and sponsor of professional sports. He ran his Ponzi scheme like a criminal enterprise that it was. He built his criminal enterprise beyond the shores of the United States, while maintaining residency in Saint Croix, U.S. Virgin Islands, and holding dual citizenship in Antigua and Barbuda and the United States. Like Madoff, Stanford's fall from grace was imminent and inevitable as his cup of deceits had reached its brims.

Hedge funds may be slightly different from Ponzi scheme but there is a great deal of similarity in how they operate. Hedge fund is a group of investors that take financial risk together to maximize profit or to make a lot of money. Ponzi scheme operators move money around from one investor to other investors in order to encourage bigger risks.

Despite the scandals involving stockbrokers and investment bankers that have, over the years, ruined economies, and individuals, these professionals are still able to command a huge amount of significant respect and dignity in society, compared with salespeople. While salespeople may sometimes tell tales and lure unsuspecting (and suspecting) customers to buy their wares, they do not ruin lives financially as had happened with stockbrokers. The customer may lick his or her wounds but those wounds often heal with time but not so with Ponzi schemes. Ponzi schemes are tantamount to robbing Peter to pay Paul, and in the long run, not paying anyone at all!

The reason stockbrokers and investment advisors have been able to maintain their dignity and respect is that some of them command enormous wealth at their disposal, while salespeople still languish in abject, servile and spiritless condition, and operate in a not-so prosperous business climate that is not associated with huge wealth. Salespeople do not make as much as swindling stockbrokers who often command billions of dollars, at their fingertips. Automobile salespeople are small-time operators who operate in small scales in attempts to eke out a living in a not-too-feasible economic environment. Salespeople are the ones that will grapple with the remnants of a "fake-till-you-make-it" schemes, and downturns in the economy which are too often caused by stockbrokers and investment advisors like Bernie Madoff and Allen Stanford, to name a few.

Salespeople do not ruin economies to where there is a near-global economic collapse, recession and colossal loss of jobs. Though the housing market debacle of the early part of the millennial involved a significant amount of salespeople in its tow the majority of the housing market saga centered around stockbrokers who thrived on speculation of results and aftermaths. Salespeople sold homes that were often inflated by falsehoods perpetuated and perpetrated by mortgage companies and their co-conspirators, including speculators that prospered as predictors of hope and despairs.

As much as salespeople can often be blamed for situations that they are not responsible for, sometimes the weight of making things right falls on the shoulders of salespeople. When business is slow in a retail organization, it is usually the salespeople that would be called upon to work hard in order to increase productivity. When things become robust and good, salespeople are often the least in the hierarchy to get compensated and recognized for the part they play in organizational development and growth. Salespeople do not often get the credit they deserve for organizational productivity and sustenance. When organizational leaders get compensated, salespeople are always left to pick up crumbs or remnants of the crumbs.

While organizations like Enron, Adelphia Communications, Tyco International, WorldCom, were busy pursuing myopic agenda policies that would earn them huge profits, salespeople were busy in nation building in sweltering retail industries such as dealership organizations where they would stand outside in hot weather looking for customers in attempts to make a sale. They did not have the comfort of a plush office where cool air would add to their comfort. They were often subjected to the harshest of weathers, from the dangers of heat strokes to the dangers of pneumonia, and mosquito bites, where Zika virus or disease-carrying insects often share breathing space with them.

For years, salespeople have been the unsung heroes of industrial growth and sustainability. They oftentimes get the last remnants of industrial profitability and the first to face the brunt of organizational misappropriation. They would never get praised or adequately rewarded for their productivity. Their contribution to economic growth overall is immense but they are never told that they are the reason why things are robust. They are never called to share the surplus they have helped to create and generate. They have often watched from the sidelines as top executives pat themselves for a job well done while they look on like servants at the beck and call of their masters.

They might, in quick passing, get a nod of acknowledgement but never one that tells them they have been the harbingers of growth and profitability. While salespeople have often been the engines that drive productivity and sustainability, they have never been given props for their crucial parts. They have had next to naught in job satisfaction and nonexistent job security. When things fall apart, they are always the first to get the boot even though nothing works without them.

When Enron came crashing with sudden bankruptcy, salespeople at the bottom of the rung were the first to be affected. They were the ones seen, with defeat and sadness on their faces, as they carry their belongings, walking out of the offices, which were being forced to close due to the greed and avarice that the executives committed against shareholders, and employees. They had stood watching as Enron pursued short-term gains at the expense of long-term stability. They had not known that while they ignorantly toiled and worked hard to increase the bottom line of the organization that the ledgers were being manipulated to reflect inflated profits that would boost stock prices. Loses were either reduced or were hidden and buried, while revenues were inflated. The soaring stock prices had benefitted the already rich, while the downtrodden poor would later be left to carry the empty coffers that had been emptied and depleted by greedy top executives. They had only known the extent of the deception when the news broke in the media. They had searched for answers and found none. They could only watch as one executive after another were brought to face justice for the heinous crimes of the century that they had committed against taxpayers and investors.

Salespeople that were caught unawares by the fall of organizations like Enron, Adelphia Communications, Tyco International, Lehman Brothers, and WorldCom, had not known that the quarterly reporting syndrome that often pressures organizations to meet earnings expectations would push their organizations to distort the truth about their earnings and growth. They had felt it was the social responsibility of their organizations to promote sustainability through growth and profit to put more people to work and pay their fair shares in taxes in order to promote economic growth and the gross domestic product and gross national product of the country. They had not known that the executives were serving their own interests instead of the interests of the larger society.

When the dust had settled, and many organizations had failed at the dawn of the millennial, a lot of people would suffer loss of jobs, and shareholders and pensioners would lose all they had worked hard for. It had been a disappointing ending to what had once seemed like a promising future, and to most people, a new beginning that would herald a new financial freedom, in which the onset of the internet age would spread wealth and create jobs through a new economic spectrum.

While things came to a grinding halt as once iconic organizations fell belly-up, with empty coffers to show for what was once thought to be a robust ledger, people could only wonder how things had suddenly gone awry. Many of the culprits of these humongous financial misappropriations would later buy justice or try to suppress their roles in the biggest financial scandal ever to hit Wall Street and Main Street at the same time. For the first time ever, people in the Main Street started to see Wall Street for what it really is. They had thought Wall Street was a cash cow that oozes cash whenever speculation favors them. How wrong they were!

Even with that, many stockbrokers were still toasted while those who had fallen off the radar of glory and prosperity headed to prison to serve the punishment that had been meted out to them as a deterrent to would-be wrongdoers. The deterrent lesson of sending corporate wrongdoers to prison would be to re-enact and reinvigorate corporate code of ethics. The corporate code of ethics would be the new foundation in which boards, supervisors, and employees would rely on, when they reach the inevitable fork on the road where illegality meets legality. The code of ethics would recreate new principles that would serve as guidelines when reaching decisions to emphasize short-term profits or long-term stability. It would deemphasize egregious corporate acts.

On their part, if salespeople would unite, their productivity would become the yardstick to measure their worth; instead of it benefitting those at the top of the company's hierarchy. There would be unity of purpose and drive that would herald the dawn of a new beginning for salespeople. Like stockbrokers who do not get tainted with scandalous missteps, salespeople would thrive despite the odds of sleaziness that are stacked against them. They would prosper as their productivity would for once benefit them first before benefitting others in the organizational chart. Salespeople would thereafter enjoy job satisfaction, job security, and the long-craved empowerment that commands respect and dignity.

Empowerment would grant salespeople a voice in decision making, and would put them in positions to help shape the future of their organizations. They would no longer be sidelined and wait for the crumbs that fall off the master's table. They would be the master or part of the authority figures that are the movers and shakers of their organizations. But with lofty positions would come accountabilities and responsibilities. Salespeople would be required to clean their acts, and put their houses in order. They would have to behave in ways that would echo their new positions. They would no longer take money from customers unless such monies are justifiably earned through proper channels. They would no longer collude with customers to deceive banks in order to help procure loans such customers would not qualify for. They would be upright and make good on their promises to be right, just and *legit*.

Being part of the process has its onerous responsibility and salespeople must be willing, and ready to play their parts. "Uneasy lies the head that wears a crown," Shakespeare once wrote; and with the new crown of responsibilities that salespeople would have to wear, a new dawn of responsibilities would mean they have to be more responsible, and be team players rather than playing the role of outsiders who are in it for short returns.

Empowerment encompasses new realities that should be devoid of disrespect and indignity and for salespeople this must be earned. Salespeople must also be unceasingly diligent in their pursuit of workplace dignity, including redeemed perception among members of the public. Rebranding will be necessary to reinvent a new image; and there must be a significant amount of accountability that will erode the old image. That accountability will take into cognizance the requirements embodied in the new responsibility. Uprightness and steadfastness will be the new catchphrases that will herald a new dawn in salespeople's quest for inclusion in the old tradition of elitism and respect.

According to studies, respect is the most fundamental requirement of every salesperson and employee, in organizations. While money might be the primary objective of joining a sales-force, respect is said to be the ingredient that keeps the workplace stable and productive. Lack of respect or the absence of it, often leads to job dissatisfaction in the workforce. So while selling is an attempt to make money, the real factor that drives productivity and increases morale is respect, experts say.

Salespeople that have the power to command respect in the workplace are able to get people to listen to them when they talk. Customers tend to gravitate towards salespeople that are able to command respect as they see it as an ability to cut deals that may suit them. When a customer perceives that a salesperson has no command of respect, he or she may not take the words of the salesperson to mean anything worthwhile. A customer wants to feel he can count on a salesperson to make a deal that will benefit him. Negotiating a deal without having to run back and forth to the manager or to a supervisor for approval tends to frustrate and annoy most customers who may be short on time. Such customers will prefer a salesperson that can reduce the amount of time they have to spend at the dealership, without wasting their day trying to buy a vehicle. With such customers, an empowered salesperson that commands respect makes the buying process pleasant.

Job titles or positions of authority tend to command respect and make the negotiating process speedier, but oftentimes, being authentic and serious when dealing with a customer can command greater respect. The first sign that a customer gets that a salesperson is not being genuine, is when a sense of untrustworthiness and insecurity start to pervade the atmosphere that otherwise would have been pleasant and conducive. Some customers can detect when a salesperson is being insincere and fake. These perceptions can ruin a potential prospect. When a salesperson is real and upfront, customers often get drawn to such a salesperson as they feel they will get the best deal possible.

Even if the salesperson does not have the final say about the final price, the idea that sincerity is evident is enough to create trustworthiness. And oftentimes, being authentic can create the foundation for earning respect. Experts believe that to earn respect one has to be willing to give it. Seeking respect without being ready to earn it may not augur well for the seeker. A customer that walks into a dealership or a place of business by being disrespectful will ultimately leave the dealership or place of business with disrespect in-tow. In the same token, a disrespectful customer can sometimes be tamed to understand and believe that not everyone wants to be disrespected in a transaction process. The best antidote to disrespectful customers is to try as much as possible to maintain civility, and to observe being cool, calm and collected. Sometimes, when a customer sees that you are not yielding to the direction of disrespect that he or she is creating and promoting, there might be a detour in the behaviour that could become respectful to you and the business at hand.

One of the major characteristics of selling is maintaining optimism when in the presence of a customer, and even when you are not in the presence of a customer. Customers like optimism in a salesperson. Studies have shown that customers gravitate toward salespeople with positive attitudes than salespeople with negative attitudes. And positive attitudes can easily be observed or gleaned by customers at first glance. And first impression at the initial stage can immediately herald a sense of trustworthiness that will turn a prospect into a buyer.

But the ability of the salesperson to effectively sell and maintain dignity at the same time will be better enhanced if there is a cohesive unity among salespeople where rules, ethical guidelines are enshrined in an informal constitution or memorandum of association. Such a unity of purpose and trade mission might be better enforced in a bylaw that will set out the rules, and regulation that govern salespeople in this proposed association.

While any meaningful association will be informal at infancy, it will at least portray civility in otherwise unruly salespeople. Some salespeople are perceived by many customers to be rude, uncivil, gruff and brusque but there are salespeople that are kind, willing and ready to portray themselves as true and real. But oftentimes they don't get the opportunity to do so because some members of the public are often already prejudiced by long-held impression that salespeople are not trustworthy. And if truth be told, many customers who come to dealerships or to business organizations do not often come with a sincere purpose. They come to either take advantage of a sale, get the best price possible, or if need be, use untruths to get the best price. If a customer is buying a product where negotiation is allowed, a typical customer may say he has seen the same product at a cheaper price elsewhere and will want you to take his word for it. But in some cases the customer may not be telling the truth and is just trying to get you to lower the price. Why this may not entirely be a dishonest move and may be part of the bargaining process, it is still based on untruthfulness.

While a customer is always right, regardless of the situation, it is the sincerity and optimism that the salesperson brings to the process that ultimately defines the transaction, not the untruthfulness or the disrespectfulness of the customer. And if a salesperson portrays an insincere behaviour in the process, the prospect of a deal becoming a reality can become slimmer, if not impossible. The process of buying a vehicle and selling it can be fundamentally different from buying or selling clothes and shoes. In selling shoes, the negotiating process is absent as the transaction is often limited to paying the price on the tag without the unpleasantness of back-and-forth negotiations. Some customers would prefer that the price tags on shoes and clothes be negotiable at departmental stores and malls, but no such luck, as the essence of such merchandise is to make the buying process haggle-free.

Selling and or buying a vehicle require bargaining because of the cutthroat competition in the business. The fact that auto dealerships are ubiquitous makes the vehicle buying process a frustrating one, mainly because the customer wants the best deal and knows there are dealerships that will provide it if you don't; while the dealer wants to be able to make a profit. In the bargain process, the customer always wins while the dealer always loses, though customers do not actually believe that dealerships can lose money selling a vehicle. Ninety percent of the time, new car dealerships often lose money in the negotiating process, especially when haggling with a customer who is determined to get his desired price or go somewhere else to get the price. No dealership wants to lose a deal but they will if the loses are insurmountable. If a customer insists on getting the price he wants, and the dealership is unyielding, the customer will of course go where such a price is possible. In these negotiating processes, a customer may become unruly and would call the dealer names for wasting his time but in reality it is the customer who may have wasted everyone's time by his unreasonable offer and demands. But in abiding by business ethics, the dealer will take the blame and move on, hoping that the next customer will be a little bit more understanding.

The buying process can be a unique process. If a customer comes to the dealership to look at a $25,000 vehicle with a bad credit and expects a payment of $300 or less, with no money down, chances are that the customer will leave disappointed. The reason is simply that the math does not add up. Even at zero percent, it is impossible to get a payment of $300 or less on a $25,000 vehicle. Financing a vehicle for 60 months or 72 months will be higher than $300 per month, unless the customer is willing to invest a substantial amount of money down to reduce the amount financed. And if the credit is bad, the situation is even worse as the interest rate will be much higher. A customer with unreasonable expectation is going to be likely disappointed if he cannot get the payment he is looking for.

Oftentimes a customer with a fairly good education will come to the dealership requesting unreasonable payment for a significantly higher vehicle, with a questionable credit, and would be disappointed and angry when it is not doable. In such situations the dealer will need to maintain a positive professional poise to ensure the situation does not degenerate into an unwelcome scene that will distract other buyers from doing business. It is impossible to sell every prospect but a dealer will aspire to try to sell everyone that walks through the door. Not every customer is worth selling. There are some impossible customers that may have to be left alone for the sake of business continuity. Just like life itself where we cannot have everything, so it is with customers. We cannot have all customers, because some customers might be unreasonable to where communication is impossible.

In a conducive unity of purpose that is regulated by an informal bylaw and or memorandum of association, it might be necessary to have clauses that instruct salespeople on the dos and don'ts of selling and what customers to avoid and to embrace. Bracing oneself for the selling profession will take tact and diplomacy and a sense of authenticity, including a positive disposition. It is not just enough to be ready to sell one must be ready for the unpleasantness of selling, in a selling situation that is devoid of respect and dignity.

Uniting and coming together to fight for a common cause will increase awareness about salespeople's new quest for respect and dignity. If the awareness is made known to the public that a new image is in the making, then the public will buy into it when it becomes obvious that the sleaziness that was once attributed to salespeople has been jettisoned for civility and uprightness. A new image may not be enough for this uphill task of image building as a new attitude will be needed so that the public can begin to see salespeople in a different light. The notion of portraying the profession as a productive profession instead of a crooked and sleazy profession will need all stakeholders to be brought on board. All salespeople will need to conform to the new standard of conduct that will be dictated by the newly enacted bylaws.

Promoting a purposefully driven ethical conducts will enhance salespeople's sense of self esteem. This process will give salespeople a sense of value and make them more attuned to what customers want. And it will also compel them to act kindly towards customers. In addition, it will ultimately increase their sales and productivity. Enhanced self-esteem will enable salespeople to properly listen and engage in conducts that are respectful and productive. This process will reduce frictions with customers; and in situations where friction is imminent, civility and politeness will prevail.

In the absence of purposefully driven ethical conducts, the old tradition of sleaziness will be ubiquitous to the detriment of productivity and profitability, and the downward spiral of craved dignity and respect, in the sales profession. And this aberration often occurs when salespeople lack the ability to uphold self esteem and egos. Salespeople usually behave poorly when they have low egos and diminished self esteem. The absence of a sense of value and self esteem can lead to poor teamwork and the inability to work effectively with other employees in the workforce.

Social psychologists say that when salespeople have increased self esteem that they are able to work well with other employees, and able to increase customer satisfaction. A low self esteem salesperson will lack self-confidence, and will be difficult to work with. Confident salespeople are often easier to work with, and are more efficient and able to give straight answers to customers.

Salespeople with low egos often interpret questions as criticisms because of their low sense of value. Studies have shown that salespeople with low self esteem and low egos are often nervous and edgy. And during sales transactions they often misinterpret honest questions the wrong way and oftentimes create unhealthy situations when they feel cornered. These types of salespeople are usually diffident, and do not perform very well in sales. With proper interaction and adequate intermingle with other experienced and more confident salespeople, low self esteem salespeople can be reoriented to become productive. But this process can only come about if there is room for reorientation and enhanced self esteem for willing low performing salespeople. Another debilitating situation that most low performing salespeople often face is that they are likely to jump to conclusions without properly listening to facts. High self esteem salespeople will usually listen and make reasonable decisions based on facts.

While good foundational training can often remove low confidence and diffidence from some salespeople, many usually remain unchanged because of their naturally diligent disposition. This is usually not the case with salespeople with positive attitude and with high self esteem who knows how to maintain proper poise and calm, and to relax and approach a prospect without assuming the worst. A good salesperson will not easily jump to conclusions; and that is because his positive attitude makes him better equipped to handle volatile situations and how to find gold in the dust of uncertainty.

Another characteristic trait about low self esteem salespeople is that they do not often give straight answers. Generally, good salespeople will steer their new prospects into making a purchase without trying to take unproductive shortcuts that could turnoff a prospect. But the reverse is the case with low self esteem salespeople who will usually take the easy road that is often less travelled by those willing to make a sale. Low self esteem salespeople will often cultivate the habit of exploring shortcuts to turn a prospect into a buyer. This usually results in a disaster that can easily turn a prospect into a window-shopper.

Low self esteem salespeople frustrate prospects who often find it difficult to get straight answers to their concerns and questions. This dilemma usually adds to the issue of credibility that the low self esteem salesperson may already have, which may ultimately lead to a no-sale as it will ruin every opportunity to make a sale. High self esteem salespeople usually do well in this area as they see an opportunity for a sale when a customer asks questions, and has concerns.

Low self esteem salespeople can cultivate a positive go-getting habit of turning prospects into buyers by becoming more confident in the way they approach and talk to customers. Facial expression and body language can enhance confidence if positively positioned to do so. Strong business culture that promotes training and confidence-building seminars can help reorient salespeople that are naturally diffident and unable to turn prospects into buyers.

Dealerships and organizations that are engaged in direct sales like automobile sales can work with their salespeople to help them build confidence and value in their personalities. This can be done by ensuring that low performing salespeople get enough rest, and are ready to perform when they come to work. Helping salespeople to overcome their nervousness can increase their credibility and trust that will in turn increase sale. In other words, salespeople have to learn to earn the trusts of their customers.

Forming a union that will buttress understanding and increase the confidence level of salespeople will make it possible for a new image to emerge among salespeople. That new image will be one that will entirely rebrand how salespeople think, and operate in business environments. Organizations that are sales oriented will benefit a great deal as there will be a noticeable increase in the sales margins, profits and general productivity. A rebranded sales-force will give a new understanding and perception about salespeople that will inspire a new trust, respect and dignity from members of the public. Instead of the sales profession being associated with sleaziness and deception, it will be a new vineyard of collective uprightness and decency.

Though unionization will redefine the essence of salesmanship, and salespeople's image, it will also benefit members of the public who will no longer be frustrated by the old cadre of salespeople who thrive in deception, fraud and crookedness. Rather than being protective or on their guards in the presence of salespeople, potential customers or prospects will be free to enjoy the benefit of shopping for the best value and bargain before making an informed decision about buying. Customers will no longer anticipate the worst when in the presence of salespeople as the new crop of rebranded salespeople will make shopping a pleasant experience. Serious efforts will be made to change the old and long-held perception about salespeople by members of the public who will now have to deal with a different brand of salespeople. Rebranding will give the profession a new outlook that will attract positive and ambitious young men who will not be worried about entering a profession that is tainted with indignity, sleaziness, pushiness, and unruly salespeople.

As the new avant-garde salespeople will emerge from the rubble of the old guard who thrived in deceptive practices, new intelligent ways of selling will also accompany the new emergence that will benefit the profession and customers. Refocusing on a new outlook will be twofold. The first will be to recreate an atmosphere of civility in the sales environment that will be patient, tolerant, and respectful of customer's time and investments. As the new intelligentsia of rebranded salespeople emerges, respect and dignity will gradually take hold, and emerge as well to erase the old perceptions of thievery, crookedness and sleaziness.

Chapter 15

Rebranding Salespeople's Mindset and Leadership Styles

The sales profession, according to studies, has for time immemorial been subjected to both psychological and subconscious abuse and contempt that has made the profession unattractive to the members of the intelligentsia and the educated. Though it can sometimes be profitable and lucrative, sales has been decidedly avoided by the young and educated who are not comfortable with the level of taint and indignity in the profession. Unless push ed by circumstances that make it difficult to survive in other worthy professions, educated people do not often see the sales profession as a worthwhile profession to engage in. Studies have shown that the level of disrespect associated with the sales prof ession often makes it difficult for educated members of the public to make a career out of sales.

Experts believe that rebranding the mindsets of salespeople will also change the perception of members of the public about salesmanship. That perception will shift from negativity to positivity if the apparatus for change are effectively adopted, experts say. But changes in the mindsets of people in general do not occur overnight as a damage that took years to take root will also take an equal amount of time, if not longer, to change. Change in general takes time, and oftentimes, changing from negativity to positivity takes longer. It is quicker to destroy than to rebuild. A structure can quickly be destroyed whereas it takes time and efforts to build a structure. Getting it destroyed can be done within a day but it takes months, and sometimes years, to build a structure, whether concrete or abstract.

Rebranding can occur among salespeople with the help of organizations that will stand to benefit more from such psychological rebranding. If training can herald such rebranding and change the attitude and persona of salespeople, then organizations that depend on salespeople to achieve their productivity should do so. Training can entail a perennial process that con stantly refocuses the mindset of salespeople on the objective of the organization while perennial seminars can serve as a reminder to salespeople not to lose focus of the objective of the organization. To achieve this perennial training that could herald new rebranding, organizations must be willing to invest adequate time and resources to ensure that the rebranding objective is achieved. Having the policy on paper will be meaningless if concerted efforts are not made to push the objective and make it a part of the organizational culture or policy.

The rebranding process should not just be limited to new salespeople that are entering the profession, it should mostly concentrate on existing salespeople who have been on the job long enough to have become part of the tradition of salespeople who thrive in deception. While incoming salespeople can be easier to instruct on the new focus and policies of an organization, old employees may not be so easy to change as they have gotten used to getting away with their old habits. But organizations can change this by gradually using training to weed off old unproductive habits, and weaning them of poor personality, into the new brand of adopted personalities.

Another area of opportunity that organizations can learn to focus on in creating an environment of productive and customer-friendly, and good-image sales-force, is to use the essence of empowerment to psychologically establish responsibility that will compel all stakeholders, including salespeople, to change into habits and behaviours that will not tarnish their organizations. If a salesperson believes or thinks he has as much to lose as the organization he works for by not doing things that will benefit the organization, he will do whatever it takes to ensure that the organization's interests are protected. And another thing is that the salesperson will no longer see the organization he works for as employment but as an investment that he must protect for his interests as well as for the interests of the organization.

Using the power of empowerment to compel salespeople to be more responsible has its advantages as well as its disadvantages. The most obvious is that it recreates a new understanding and responsibilities that often make salespeople do things the organizational way, rather than their way. If a salesperson has an image to protect, he is going to very likely do everything possible to protect it. And in a situation where a salesperson is seen as a representative of the organization he works for, whatever that salesperson does reflects the modus operandi of the organization he works for. If he does something good by treating the customer right, it will reflect as a positive mark for the organization, not the salesperson. But if the salesperson does something bad, the resultant bad image will also reflect as a negative mark that the customer will either spread among friends or use as a reason not to ever do business with the organization in the future.

In many ways, as a representative of the organization he works for, by virtue of his selling, the salesperson becomes in broader terms, an ambassador of the organization. What the salesperson does or does not do, will either enhance or hamper the reputation of the organization. By the foregoing analysis, it can pay dividends for organizations to sometimes invest more in their human capital so that productivity and sustainability will be enhanced for the future that is emerging.

Job satisfaction can also herald a new set of characteristics that will create new traits among salespeople. If a salesperson is satisfied with his organization, he will want to do things that will enable him to keep that job, if anything, at least for the sake of the satisfaction he derives from the job. The situation will be different for salespeople that do not derive any form of job satisfaction from their employment. For such salespeople, the chances of trying to be good representatives of their organizations are slimmer and gloomier than that of happy employees. But organizations can change this mindset by creating a workplace that promotes job satisfaction, and focuses on job security and retention. Studies have shown that salespeople with job security tend to be happier than salespeople who do not believe they have job security. And there is also the key issue of loyalty.

Salespeople will be loyal to the organization they feel has their best interests. If they feel that the organization will be there for them when things go awry with their personal lives, they will in turn be there for the organization as far as protecting the interests of the organization. The old saying that 'to whom much is given much is expected' can be significant in weighing what factor serves as a predictor of a salesperson's readiness to look out for the interests of the organization he represents.

What most organizations do not know, or neglect to acknowledge, is that an unhappy employee often makes an unhappy representative of his organization. If that employee is a salesperson, the situation can be further worse for the organization as an unhappy salesperson can do an irreparable damage to the organization. A salesperson that is unhappy with his job will not be a good ambassador or representative of his organization. And in the same token, an unhappy salesperson is likely to move from one organization to another, in search of a greener pasture, compared with a satisfied salesperson that will stay to contribute his quota to his organization's growth. In a recent study about salespeople's constant mobility from one dealership to another, it was found that a significant proportion of unhappy salespeople will leave their organizations for another, for better pay, intrinsic satisfaction, and respect. If unhappiness is an important factor in a salesperson's decision to leave one organization for another, then organizations should do more than just a lip service to ensure that salespeople are at least happy with their jobs.

It might be a good idea for organizations to have an explicit policy that promotes salespeople's job satisfaction rather than having an implicit policy that would often attempt to promote job satisfaction. There are certain factors that may induce a salesperson to want to work in an organization until he is ready to retire. One of such factors is a pleasant work environment that promotes feasible programs that enhances workplace recreation, joviality, jollity, but firm and serious workforce. Most organizations like Google, Facebook and several Silicon Valley companies, including some new modern organizations, have established facilities that promote employees' comfort on the job. Such an environment also buttresses innovation, and brainstorming that is devoid of pressure and micromanagement. What these Silicon Valley high-tech employers are promoting is an environment where their employees can feel at home and work, without actually feeling the pressure of working. Several organizations have found that employees work better when they are comfortable in their workplace, as they are able to focus more on their job, and use their initiatives. When employees are unable to use their initiatives and ideas to promote work effectiveness, there can be a reduced efficiency and productivity, according to research.

In a 21st century workplace that is bracing itself to face the challenges of an emerging future, having employees that are loyal and committed to the goals of organizations can lead to competitiveness, sustainability and innovation. As new organizations emerge everyday to challenge existing organizations for their constantly diminishing market shares, it might augur well for organizations to continually invest in the efficacy, and innovation of their employees. One of the many ways that organizations can do this is by giving employees the opportunity to use their inborn talents and skills to add to the growth and productivity of the organization. This is not saying that employees should be left to do what they like; it simply means that employees should be made to feel as if they are part of the ownership of the organization so that they can treat it as a stakeholder would.

An employee that sees water spilled on the floor and walks by as if it is not his business whether a customer slips and falls will likely not be a loyal employee who is committed to the wellbeing of the organization. But an employee that sees water spilled on the floor and goes to fetch a paper towel to wipe away the water, or calls the janitor or housekeeper to clean the water, will be deemed loyal and committed to the wellbeing of the organization. The latter employee will probably feel that exposing his organization to liabilities that can occur from a customer slipping and falling due to the water that is spilled on the floor, will lead to monetary payout to compensate such a customer. Such a concerned employee will feel the brunt and pinch of any form of monetary payout as the owner of the organization would. An unconcerned employee who is not committed to the goals and objectives of the organization will feel unobligated to protect the interests of the organization.

The most effective way that organizations can promote, protect, and increase employees' commitment and loyalty is to ensure that every employee is treated as significant contributor to the growth and performance of the organization. All employees should feel a sense of fairness in the way their organizations treat them. It does not matter whether one employee is a cleaning lady or the other is a high-tech employee, everyone should feel a sense of fairness. One employee should not be considered to be more important than another employee. It is when employees feel they are just as important as the manager at the desk or the director in the big office, that they will see themselves as part of the ownership or part of the stakeholders of the organization.

In George Orwell's *Animal Farm*, after the animals had seized control of the *Manor Farm* from the drunken and irresponsible Mr. Jones, they would rename the farm *Animal Farm*, to reflect the spirit of the revolution. To promote equality, they had established the principles of animalism as a reflection of their freedom and equality. Though the philosophy of animalism would later be altered to reflect the change of baton in the farm's hierarchy, from Snowball who taught the animals to read and write, to Napoleon who had taken the role to educate young puppies, the animals would still feel a sense of equality that would motivate them to work harder. The new creed that "all animals are equal but some animal are more equal than others," which was meant to portray a sense of equality of some sort, would *hold* to still motivate the animals, even when the feeling of betrayal had pervaded the farm. The animals were motivated by the principle of animalism to contribute their fair shares even as the wind of change started to make them feel as if they were still under the oppressive rules of Mr. Jones, whom they saw as a common enemy: "Whatever goes upon two legs is an enemy."

In a workplace, as in the case with the animals in the satiric *Animal Farm*, the sense of equality motivated the animals to work harder, and the same is true with employees that feel they are part of the decision making process, or part of the management. Even if they may not necessarily be part of management, at least they can think they are by the way they are treated and respected by the higher hierarchy of the organization. Just like the animals in the *Animal Farm* felt justified to work harder to achieve a common goal, so it is with humans or employees if given the freedom and opportunity to contribute their fair shares.

In a bottom-up organizational structure, employees can feel they are part of the decision making process by being allowed to make decisions that pertain to their various departments. In such situations, as bottom-up structure, there is often ample opportunity for employees to use their initiatives to contribute to efficiency and productivity, including creating room for innovation.

The inability of most organizations to create room for bottom-up structure that can increase efficiency and effectiveness makes it impossible for such organizations to have job satisfaction among their employees. Lack of job satisfaction can be a catalyst for disloyalty, and absence of commitment on the part of employees. When there is no commitment and loyalty, employees often become a liability rather than an asset to organizations. Organizations must try to avoid a situation where employees can become a liability. When employees become a liability, it means they no longer represent progress but problems. Problematic employees are counterproductive and do not do organizations any good.

Lack of a bottom-up organizational structure can also pave the way for insubordination and unruly behavior that can jeopardize organizational wellbeing and productivity. Surveys say that unruly and unproductive employees can be a risk to organizational attempt to foster growth and competitiveness. Organizations that do not encourage bottom-up decision-making structures must therefore eliminate unproductive employees who have become liabilities and sources of problems. But the most effective recipe for growth and competiveness is not recognizing and eliminating problematic employees but creating an environment that encourages employees' loyalty and commitment to organizational goals.

Part of the process of rebranding includes creating an atmosphere that fosters inclusiveness of employees in organizational processes. Employees should not at any time feel they are not part of the decision making processes. Like the *Animal Farm*, where the principle of animalism motivated the animals to work harder to achieve the set goals and objectives of the farm, organizations can create an environment that makes employees feel equal even if they are *not* really equal. A sense of belonging, equality and fairness, even if not felt, can still foster employee loyalty and commitment. In the parlance of the Animal Farm, *all animals are equal but some animals are more equal than others*, created a sense of fairness even when it was obvious that fairness was not really prevalent in the farm. This phantom and illusory fairness can create motivation, and drive commitment in the workplace by making employees believe there is fairness even if it doesn't really exist.

The process of a bottom-up decision making in organizations is essentially to create efficiency and effectiveness, and for employees to feel they have the power to contribute to organizational processes. In reality, organizational governance rests at the top hierarchy of the organization than at the bottom. But the ease with which things can move effectively rests on the quickness that decisions are made to get things done. The real essence of a bottom-up organizational structure is to enable processes to move faster without waiting for decisions to be made at the top. Waiting for decisions to trickle down the organizational ladder hampers progress, and slows down processes.

The empowerment of departmental heads to make decisions that affects their departments often allows them to get things down faster and at a much quicker pace than having to wait for top management to decide how each department should execute policies. The process also gives each departmental head the opportunity to enhance their leadership abilities.

And in the spirit of empowerment, where it exists, departmental heads can in turn pass that sense of responsibility and use of initiative to their employees by allowing them to use their ideas in positive ways that will enable the organization to prosper. This is not saying that employees should be allowed to operate without supervision; this process is still subject to supervision. But the method of supervision is often to make sure that procedures are being followed in accordance with the goals of the organization.

Studies have shown that when employees are deprived of the abilities to use their initiatives and ideas that they become like *zombies* and *robots* that do things that are stipulated, machinelike, by organizational policies, regardless of whether such decisions are right or wrong. In a situation where employees can use their initiatives, if the process that is used in creating a product or service is wrong or defective, an employee should be able to stop the process, report the defect to his immediate supervisor to have it corrected. Such a process will not only pave the way for a better quality product but will also give the employee a sense of accomplishment and to a certain degree, a sense of empowerment. An employee that perceives this sense of empowerment, no matter how limited in scope, will more than likely have a better job satisfaction than employees who follow orders without room to use their initiatives.

Rebranding salespeople's mindset can also include the use of empathy whereby salespeople will feel that their organizations understand and share their individual experiences and emotions. This type of rebranding can make salespeople feel they are not alone when they do face personal problems. The feeling that an organization is empathic can change how employees behave in organizations, from negative to positive, according to social psychologists. An employee that feels his organization cares and will be there to help when things don't go right in their personal lives is likely to be loyal and committed to organizational goals and objectives. And such employees can sometimes systemically rebrand themselves to behave in ways that will help their organizations. The sense that to: *whom much is given much is respected,* will subliminally, and mildly seep into the psyche of such employees to where they will begin to think of their organizations first, even in situations that may seem unfavorable to their organizations. In other words, they will become better representatives and ambassadors of their organizations. So, in many ways, empathy can foster employee rebranding in a psychological dimension to where all involved can benefit.

But the use of empathy as a catalyst of change that can foster loyalty and commitment rests with the type of leadership an organization has. Some organizations do not do enough to imbue, and encourage empathy. If an employee feels he is on his own when things go awry in his life, and that his organization will not be there to render assistance, it is highly unlikely that such an employee will be positively poised to go beyond the call of duty to lookout for his organization. Empathy is one of the traits of transformational leadership.

Transformational leaders, by virtue of their characteristics, often help in transforming, not just the organization, but the employees as well, to be better, productive employees. Some of the characteristics of a transformational leader, in this situation, include the ability of a leader to identify the changes that are needed in an organization, and the ability to create a vision that will guide the needed changes, by inspiring the workforce to commit to such objectives.

The process of rebranding, if not psychologically done by employees themselves, should be systemically done by a transformational leadership style that will ensure that employees are able to change from their former attitudes to a new transformative attitude. Such attitudes can sometimes be recreated through the visions generated by a transformational leader. That vision may provide a foreseeable role that the rebranded employee can see as a beneficial role that will inspire him to see himself as a team player in the organizational process.

The theory of transformational leadership involves the type of leadership style that inspires the workforce to work harder, and to become productive. The characteristic traits of transformational leadership can create an atmosphere that can systematically rebrand salespeople's way of doing things to benefit organizational processes. The reason this can be possible is primarily because transformational leadership can create positive changes that can rebrand the workforce in such a way that followers will be able to see and share the benefits that accrue from such leadership behaviors. The positive changes that a transformational leader brings to the workforce often heralds a mindset of understanding that followers will believe in, that their interests will be taken care of, and as a result act in the interest of the organization. With transformational leadership, the opportunity exists to enhance salespeople's motivation, morale, and resultant performance. The transformational leader is, by nature of the traits that are characteristically inherent in the leadership style, able to inspire enthusiasm and loyalty that an employee or salesperson can bring to a task or a job. Such moral principles and teachings that a transformational leadership inspires, can also bring about a new rebranding in the mindset of the salesperson that will translate into a positive work habit.

In a globalized world stage where internet has brought the world much closer than hitherto, the need to have employees who have congruent mental and emotional wellbeing that can be productive is more urgent than ever. As competition has become cutthroat and customers have become more discerning than ever about available products and services, having a workforce that is built on confidence, loyalty, enthusiasm, and a positive mental and emotional state, is pivotal to organizational growth and competitiveness. For organizations to have the right employees or salespeople that they can depend on, an environment must be created for the right leadership to prevail. Transformational leadership is by far the most productive leadership style because of the traits that are inherent in the leadership style. The ability to inspire the loyalty of an individual employee or all the employees in the organization by ensuring that there is a strong and overwhelming belief in the function or tasks at hand is what makes the transformational leadership style a workable solution to the sales-force.

Another trait that the transformational leadership has, that makes it work for organizational processes, is the sense of common purpose that it creates in the workforce. That sense of common purpose often leads to a positive teamwork or esprit de corps that can translate into productivity and profitability. Transformational leadership style also raises the level of individual psychological wellbeing because of the sense of purpose and confidence in the future that it inspires. Salespeople can increase their productivity with the right mental rebrand and the right leadership style, and since the transformational leadership style has been known to inspire loyalty, enthusiasm, commitment, and positive attitude, then it should only make sense that organizations should adopt the style that seems most suitable. Salespeople by the nature of their profession, often needs their morale to be inspired by a leader who understands the needs and onerous functions of a salesperson.

From the outset of the concept that was incubated and developed by James MacGregor Burns in 1978, in his widely acclaimed book: *Leadership,* transformational leadership style has gained acceptance and prominence as it has been widely applied by many organizations. And the results of the workability of the leadership style speak for itself, as many organizations have benefited tremendously from its application. The reason transformational leadership has been a tremendous success can be traced to the following characteristics. The first of the four components of transformational leadership style include (1) the leader's use of charisma or idealized influence; (2) the leader's use of inspirational motivation; (3) the leader's use of intellectual stimulation; and (4) the leader's application of personal and individual attention.

With the first component in which the leader applies charisma and idealized influence to positively lead the workforce and inspire productivity, this trait typically includes the manner the leader inspires positive behavior, by behaving in ways that is admired by followers, and displaying confidence; and by taking positive stands that can cause employees or followers to emulate and identify with the leader. The leader is able to use idealized influence to inspire followers to identify with his clear set of values, and to act as a role model to his followers who admire and emulate his conduct.

The second component is another form of psychological rebranding. This process involves the way a transformational leader is able to inspire motivation in his followers. The process of inspirational motivation enables the leader to articulate ideas clearly and effectively in speech or in writing that followers can easily understand. When the leader is able to clearly articulate his vision it can appeal and inspire his followers with enthusiasm, optimism, future goals, and create significance for the tasks at hand. Inspirational motivation can be pivotal in rebranding salespeople into having enthusiasm and optimism about their jobs, especially those salespeople that have low morale.

Perhaps one of the most significant traits of a transformational leader is *intellectual stimulation*. With intellectual stimulation, the leader often challenges assumptions and stimulates creativity and initiatives in his followers. This process tends to bring out the best in an employee or a follower who is enthused enough to be influenced by its inherent challenges of assumptions. The leader uses intellectual stimulation to encourage followers by establishing a framework that followers can easily understand or relate to, in organizational processes. With intellectual stimulation, an employee can overcome obstacles that may occur in the course of handling a task, as the process invokes creativity and ideas that can lead to solutions to difficult tasks.

The fourth component is the ability of the leader to apply personal and individual attention to ensure that followers' needs are attended to. This process entails the leader's ability to attend to followers' needs and to act as a mentor and coach to followers. The essence of this process is to inspire confidence by ensuring that individual follower's contribution is acknowledged, respected and appreciated. This confidence-building component helps the leader to motivate the employee to believe in himself as a significant contributor to teamwork and organizational processes. In addition to building followers' confidence, it also helps to fulfill and enhance followers' need for self fulfillment and self worth. This component can help to rebrand salespeople's mindset in order to renew their confidence and self-worth, so that they can be inspired to increase their achievement and growth.

Other types of leaderships that can enhance organizational outputs and competitiveness include transactional and situational leadership styles. With the transactional leadership style, employees are motivated by reward and punishment; but followers or employees have to obey the orders of the leader. With this type of leadership, employees are not self-motivated and they have to be micromanaged by often being closely monitored and controlled to get them to perform assigned tasks. This is primarily because the power of the transactional leader comes from his vested authority and responsibility in the organization that allows him to use the power in ways that benefit both the followers and organizational output. While transformational leadership can inspire enthusiasm, morale, and the motivation to work hard, particularly in sales, transactional and situational leadership styles work differently in harnessing and motivating human capital, to induce productivity.

Human capital, according to Gary Becker, an economist from the University of Chicago, and Jacob Mincer, can be properly utilized to achieve organizational objectives when certain factors are at play. Factors such as knowledge, habits, social behaviors, and personality attributes, including the inherent creativity that are embodied in the ability of humans to perform certain tasks to produce economic value, can be better enhanced with the right leadership style.

In sales, for example, transactional leadership can inspire salespeople to achieve greater sales margins because the transactional leader believes in motivating followers through reward and punishment. With this type of leadership, followers are rewarded when they do a good job, and punished for nonperformance. With transactional leadership, a punishment of some sort will occur if followers do not perform tasks as desired. By rewarding achievement and punishing nonperformers, the leader is able to inspire followers to achieve more. This sort of leadership style works where there is formal use of authority and responsibility in achieving organizational objectives. This basic management strategy works best in a top-down management structure, and may even work in some bottom-up organizations, where there is a reward system in place to motivate and inspire productivity. In sales, the reward system can work well as most salespeople are paid commissions and bonuses, when they sell. Salespeople may be inspired to sell more, if there is an incentive like a reward for selling the most products.

In the automobile retail industry, a reward system that challenges salespeople to work harder can inspire greater sales margins and enhanced performance. With the transactional leadership style, followers may need to obey the leader. This is totally different from the transformational leadership where followers are inspired and motivated by enthusiasm, charisma and influence. The transactional leader is more dictatorial in controlling, managing and planning organizational processes, and by the manner he orders followers to do things that he wants done in the organization. While the transactional leader may have an incentivized reward in place as a form of motivation, those that do not obey or follow instructions are punished, which takes away the freewill to do things without fear of punishment for failing.

In the automobile retail organization, salespeople who sell more cars are rewarded with a plaque, a trophy, or even monetary bonuses, while those that don't do well are reprimanded or reproof, which in a transactional leadership style can be the same as rewards and punishment. When Max Weber, a political economist, first came up with the idea of the transactional leadership style in 1947, it was designed as a basic management strategy that would enable managers and supervisors to get the most out of their employees. But in 1981, Bernard Bass would refine the theory to include a process of incentivizing the workforce to perform more in order to enhance organizational output. While the punishment factor was somewhat subliminal, it served to spur nonperforming employees to do better.

The transactional leadership style is mostly comprised of attributes that entails exchanges and dimensions. One of the characteristics of the transactional leadership style is the use of *contingent reward.* The contingent reward system is usually based on mutually agreed objectives where successful performers are rewarded. With this type of leadership style, goals are linked to rewards, with clarity of purpose, and expectations while the leader provides the necessary tools and apparatus to make the process work for mutual benefits. With contingent reward, the transactional leader often sets goals that are essentially specific, measurable, attainable, realistic, and timely, for their followers.

The next characteristic of the transactional leader is *active management by exception*, which is a process whereby the leader actively monitors the performance of the followers by ensuring that there is no deviation from the goals and objectives, including rules and standards established by the organization. This process also allows the organization to take corrective actions to prevent mistakes that could occur in the tasks and work performed by employees, or followers.

Another characteristic trait of the transactional leadership style is that it is often classified as *passive management by exception*, which in essence entails the process whereby the transactional leader can intervene in tasks that deviate from standards or when performance expectations are below standard or are not met. When there is an unmet expectation or poor performance, the transactional leader may resort to punishment as a response to substandard performance.

Laissez-faire trait is one of the characteristics of transactional leadership style that involves a process whereby the leader creates an environment where followers get opportunities to make decisions that impact organizational processes. With this leadership trait, the leader gives the opportunity to make decisions to followers by avoiding the responsibilities for such decisions. In a way, the laissez-faire leader creates a directionless leadership that often puts the future of the organization in the hands of followers. This can be an ineffective form of leadership as there is no direction or real leadership to make processes work to benefit and enhance organizational output.

The implication of the transactional leadership theory is that there is often overemphasis on details, short-term goals, standards and procedures. Followers are not given the opportunity to use their own initiatives, and as a result often lack creativity and innovative ideas. Since followers do not make efforts to enhance their creativity and initiatives, there is often no room for innovation. And another disadvantage is that followers may not be loyal to organizational goals and commitment. But studies have shown that effectiveness may occur in the workplace as goals are clearly defined. And this style of leadership may also be performance oriented because it is based on reward and punishment. But it can also create a situation where leaders ignore ideas that may benefit organizational processes, especially if such ideas do not conform or agree with the current plans and goals of the organization.

Proponents of transactional leadership style have often opined that transactional leaders can be effective in guiding performance and efficiency which are geared toward minimizing costs and enhancing productivity. According to experts, transactional leaders can be directive, goal and action oriented while their relationships with employees and followers are often structured on transactional and emotional bonds. The significance of the transactional leadership style is that employees are motivated by simple reward rather than by intrinsic satisfaction. Since the assumption is that followers are only motivated by rewards, the only link between the leader and followers is the reward that followers receive for their performance and compliance. In retail organizations, the type of leadership that an organization has can make a difference in efficiency, productivity, and effectiveness. When an organization has the type of leadership that creates retention, and empowers the workforce, that organization will oftentimes end up with a workplace that enjoys job satisfaction.

With transformational leadership for instance, the leader inspires intellectual stimulation, uses idealized influence and inspirational motivation to get employees motivated to do their best. While this type of leadership raises employees' morale and enthusiasm, it also creates a vision that employees can believe in, and see as enhancing their future in the organization. Transformational leadership creates room for employees' ideas, initiatives, and innovation. The ability of the leader to intellectually stimulate the workforce allows employees to brainstorm and use their ideas for the benefit of the organization. And the process also creates an inclusive workforce that makes employees believe they are part of the decision making process in the organization.

The difference between the transformational leadership and the transactional leadership styles is that each leadership category contributes differently to organizational processes. The transactional leadership is essentially responsive or quick to react and respond appropriately; while the transformational leadership is more proactive in its characteristics and the way it controls situations by ensuring that things are done efficiently, and also by preparing for likely future problems. With transformational leadership, the leader often uses the inherent traits in the leadership style to prepare the workforce in anticipation of future problems, crucial needs and changes that are likely to occur.

Another crucial characteristic of transactional leadership that differentiates it from transformational leadership is how the process operates within the culture of the organization. Since the leadership style in this category is more directive than by mutual understanding, things tend to work according to strict adherence to established goals rather than the ideas of the individual employees. The transactional leadership ensures that things are done as directed within the organizational culture. This tends to primarily differentiate the leadership style from transformational leadership.

With the transformational leadership style, the leader works to fundamentally change the organizational culture by inculcating and implementing new ideas that usually benefits the organization as well as the followers. This process works by allowing employees' ideas to flourish in ways that they can benefit the future of the organization. Intellectual stimulation is one of the processes that generate new ideas that can flourish among employees within the culture of the transformational leadership style, when adopted. Another avenue that produces new ideas is empowerment which often occurs in transformational leadership. Empowerment allows employees the freedom to use their initiatives and ideas to improve processes in the workforce. And the use of empowerment by itself generates new ideas. In transformational leadership, the leader often works to change the organizational culture by implementing new ideas, and oftentimes these new ideas comes from the employees or followers.

Perhaps one of the most distinctive differences between transactional leadership and transformational leadership is that with transactional leadership, employees are usually compelled to achieve organizational objectives and goals through the reward mechanisms and punishment. In the transactional leadership style, employees have limited choices and it is often to work hard for a reward or face punishment, for nonperformance. This is markedly different from the transformational leadership style where employees work hard to achieve organizational objectives through inspirational motivation, rather than by contingent reward.

One of the ways that transformational leadership style contrasts transactional leadership style is that the leader that practices transformational leadership style motivates and empowers employees to achieve organizational goals and objectives by simply appealing to their higher ideals and moral values. In this process, employees are intellectually challenged to give their all, but not by force but by simple appeals that is based on enhanced morale. The process often appeals to the mental and emotional condition of employees with regard to the function or tasks at hand. Experts say that employees under transformational leadership are creative and innovative because of the idealized influence that they are exposed to, within the framework of the characteristics of the leadership traits.

A transactional leader will likely motivate his followers or employees by seeming to appeal to their self-interests. With this type of leadership style, employees can be motivated to think of the contingent reward that is likely to be the benefit of working hard, or the punishment that is likely to occur for not working hard. The contingent reward can be a beneficial interest to the employee that works hard to achieve it, while those that lack the will to reach for the reward are punished.

While the contingent reward appeal may work well to motivate employees under the transactional leadership style, what essentially motivates employees to work harder is when they are encouraged to transcend their own interests for the group. This is somewhat an unselfish reach for a teamwork paradigm where the goal is not to satisfy individual self-interests but to satisfy the needs of the group. Though the motivation may have the same effect but the lasting and greater productivity comes from being inspired to accomplish not just for individual interests but for the interests of the group or unit.

In all, the transactional leadership can be a good style for the retail industry since it has a contingent reward mechanism. Salespeople by trade often work on commission, and the contingent reward can be an added incentive for them to work harder, even if the punishment for nonperformance can be a psychological drawbacks and downer that can create a reverse effect on productivity.

Transformational leadership can also work well, if not better, for salespeople since it encourages intellectual stimulation, and increases morale. Salespeople tend to often experience a rollercoaster type of mood as sales go up and down. If sales are good, they are likely to experience better moods and when sales are bad, they are likely to experience bad moods. Intellectual stimulation can enable salespeople to challenge their inner drives to generate new ideas that can benefit their sales margins and general behavior. Transformational leadership can also help rebrand salespeople, through intellectual stimulation, especially as they do not often enjoy consumer respects because of the nature of their sales profession.

While transactional and transformational leadership styles have their pluses and minuses, another form of leadership style that benefits organizational processes is the *situational leadership* style. This form of leadership style is essentially based on how a leader adjusts his leadership style to fit the development level of the employees or the workforce he is trying to lead or influence. This type of leadership style is based on adaptability and flexibility and on how a leader can adjusts his style to create and manage effectiveness that can enhance organizational output and efficiency. A transactional leader will unlikely be flexible enough to adapt as a situational leader; as his characteristics are based on established procedures. On the other hand, a transformational leader will likely adjust his style to fit the development level of employees or followers he is trying to influence. The reason why a transformational leader will likely be a change agent that will possibly adjust his ways and be flexible enough to adapt, is because this type of leader believes in using personal interest and attention to ensure that his followers are enthusiastically attuned to work hard enough to contribute to organizational processes. Another reason is that the transformational leader will use idealized influence to motivate his followers, and sometimes, this process may include adjusting certain characteristics to any given situation.

The situational leadership style was first developed by Kenneth Blanchard and Paul Hersey in 1972, when it became apparent that organizational leaders must adjust their styles to meet evolving workforce. Situational leadership essentially stresses the essence of adaption, and how organizations must adapt their leadership styles in conformity with the development level of organizational needs. The situational leadership style works well in a workplace where employees have less inclination to contribute or work hard. This might work well in retail organizations where some salespeople may not work as hard as their colleagues to reach their sales quotas.

Studies have shown that situational leadership works best when leaders are able to identify their priorities or define what matters most in the organization. The leader must be able to identify tasks and priorities, including being able to ascertain the readiness level of employees, and able to match a fitting leadership style to the situation. This works best when leaders can assess the readiness of their employees in order to determine the ability and willingness of each employee. The outcome of assessing the abilities and willingness of employees is what essentially signals the need to adjust to the development level of the workforce.

Blanchard and Hersey identified four categories of situational leadership which include: (1) directing; (2) coaching; (3) supporting; and (4) delegating. *Directing* as a form of situational leadership style enables the leader to use suitable approaches when employees have low willingness and ability to perform their tasks. This process only becomes imperative when employees are unable to perform the tasks at hand, or have less inclination to try because of fear of failure. At this juncture the leader must assume a directive role to make necessary changes. The essence of this process entails directing those in charge to clarify the roles and tasks of employees in order to create room for proper supervision. With this process of directing, decisions are often made by those directly in charge and the process of communication is usually a one-way type, as it is part of the process of directing. The leader must be careful not to confuse employees with the tasks at hand and on what must be done or the options available. Oftentimes, the leader only resorts to directing when there are serious problems that can lead to serious consequences if the process is not successful. The purpose of using the directive option is usually to make sure that necessary actions are accomplished.

The next component of the situational leadership factor is *coaching*. Coaching can become necessary when employees want to work but don't have the ability or have insufficient ability for the task at hand. Coaching is pretty much like directing as it means the leader will need to define tasks and roles in a clear format. But to do this effectively, the leader may need to seek ideas and suggestions from employees on how best to define roles and tasks so that everything will be clearly understood.

In *coaching*, the decisions about the tasks and roles remain the leader's responsibility but unlike directing, communication is a two-way process. Employees that need coaching will generally require the direction and supervision of the leader. The reason for this is that employees or followers are often assumed to be inexperienced and as a result will rely on the leader to build their self-esteem through support and encouragement. Part of the coaching process also entails infusing a sense of commitment on the part of followers by getting them involved in the decision making process. This part is essential as involvement in the decision making process will not only build commitment but self-esteem on the part of followers or employees. And part of the coaching process includes listening, advising, and helping employees to gain significant and necessary skills that will enable them to perform tasks without supervision, in the future.

Supporting is another form of situational leadership whereby the leader applies suitable approach to lead when employees or followers have low willingness but high ability for the task at hand. When employees are qualified to do a job but are refusing because of lack of commitment, and or loyalty, the leader may step in to play a supportive role. Playing a supportive role means that the leader will need to use tact and diplomacy to persuade employees or followers to cooperate and perform the tasks at hand. Supportiveness here does not mean that the leader would give direction about the tasks at hand or show employees what to do, but simply that the leader should be concerned about finding out why employees are refusing to work and to find ways to get these uncommitted employees to work and perform the tasks at hand.

Supportive leadership will generally require the leader to motivate those that can do the job but won't do it because of lack of commitment or low morale. What the leader in this supportive role should do is to motivate and help build confidence in these uncommitted employees so that they can be team players and be ready to perform given tasks or the tasks at hand. When dealing with qualified employees or followers who already know what to do, clarification of details of the process may not be necessary as all the leader needs to do is motivate them to act. The keyword here is *motivation* and how to motivate highly skilled or high ability employees to become committed to performing the tasks at hand. According to experts, the key to motivating highly skilled but uncommitted employees is listening, encouragement, and raising their morale when they show enthusiasm and commitment for success.

Delegating is another key aspect of situational leadership; which is often used in bottom-up organizations to increase effectiveness, efficiency and high productivity. Delegating is crucial when employees or followers have high willingness and high ability. In an organization where employees have high willingness and high ability, the leader may need to delegate tasks without worrying about commitment and ability, and of the job getting done. The leader may rely on delegating tasks when it is obvious employees can do the job with enthusiasms and are as a result, motivated to do so. With employees that have high willingness and high ability, the leader does not need to do much but create an environment where morale and enthusiasm will prevail. These types of employees are significant assets as they represent essential human capital that can enable organizations to meet the demands of an ever growing competiveness and cutthroat competition, for market shares.

In an organization where delegating or empowerment play vital roles in accomplishing the goals and objectives, there is often a significant amount of trust embedded in the employees that they will do well and meet expectations. As often the case with employees with high willingness and high abilities, minimum, if any, supervision or support is required. These employees are generally self-motivated and they are high achievers that do not need to be heavily micromanaged. They know how to do what needs to be done to achieve and accomplish the tasks at hand.

While the act of delegating enables the leader to entrust employees with high willingness and high ability to perform the tasks at hand, the leader will still need to be involved in the decisions and problem-solving; but the real work and performance or execution of the tasks at hand will be left in the capable hands of employees or followers. Since this is typically a bottom-up process where trusted employees are allowed to make decisions and solve problems that pertain to their departments, employees or followers still have the responsibility to communicate information to the leader about the current status of the tasks at hand, and progress report. These categories of high willingness and high ability employees often have less need for frequent encouragement and support as they are self-motivated. But to keep these types of employees inspired and committed, leaders may still need to offer them occasional props as a form of motivation, for them to continue to do the good work they do. It is not that these categories of employees really need to be encouraged but occasional recognition can serve as a form of appreciation for their performance.

Leaders can serve as change agents when they effect changes in the organizations they lead. Effecting changes entails bringing in new ideas that can benefit organizational output or encourage employees with ideas to come forward with their ideas so that such ideas can be vetted and perused for advantages that can benefit organizational processes. In an evolving organizational environment that continually seeks new ways to improve, every idea is crucial and employees with ideas should always be encouraged to bring such ideas to the table. Most organizations often downplay the significance of employees' ideas to the decision making process at their own peril. In the 21st century internet age, the best and most productive ideas can come from the lowest employees in the organization, if organizational

leaders are smart enough to recognize such employees.
Every employee should be important contributor, and in most modern technology-based organizations, especially organizations in Silicon Valley, every employee is seen as a significant contributor to growth and innovation.

The lowest employee in the organization can become the high-tech boss of tomorrow, one never knows! But smart leaders who recognize the significance of every employee will stand a chance to catch that employee that may take his ideas to form a new startup that can become a significant competitor tomorrow. Facebook has done well in ensuring that employees play vital roles in organizational processes by allowing room for every employee to brainstorm ideas that can contribute to growth and processes. And there are several high-tech employees that are already doing this. In today's high-tech environment, it is not just the guys in the geek squad department that knows everything; it could just be the high school dropout mopping the floors that has the newest innovative ideas about a future product. One never knows. After all, the innovative products of today were created mostly by dropouts!

In today's high-tech world, an eight-year old can become a tech wiz or even a hacker who may have ideas for the next best thing. It is never a good idea to underestimate any individual's potential contribution, regardless of that person's position in the organization or in life. It is hard to know what ideas lay in a person's brain that has not even been given the opportunity to prove what he can do! Sometimes, allowing ideas to come forth, regardless of the contributor, can create room for brainstorming and innovation. It is important that organizations realize and understand that ideas are not limited to a chosen few; everyone has ideas; some are lucky enough to have them heard and turn into commercial value, while others often don't get heard.

In organizational context, the most productive and competitive organizations are the ones that don't discriminate against those that may be considered too inferior to contribute. In other words, it is counterproductive to practice elitism in the workplace and as a result cutoff those who are likely to be important contributors. Salespeople have often fallen into the cadre of employees that do not usually get heard because of the nature of their jobs or simply because many organizations do not place enough value on their significance to consider them worth listening to. And several studies have shown that many salespeople think their organizations don't value their contributions to decision making. While many retail organizations cannot survive without the services of salespeople, they seldom see salespeople as meaningful contributors to organizational processes. Many organizations would sooner appoint outsiders to manage salespeople than give salespeople the opportunity to climb the organizational ladder, or hierarchy.

Many organizations can actually contribute to rebranding the mindset of salespeople by simply creating an environment that will enable them to progress beyond just being salespeople. That is not saying that selling is not lucrative to become an essential career objective; but for those less skilled salespeople who do not make enough or have high willingness but low ability to become productive salespeople, it might be a good idea for dealerships to promote these categories of salespeople to management positions, if their loyalties can be counted on.

In other words, automobile dealerships need to learn how to reward loyal employees, especially salespeople who have been with the organization for a long time, but have willingness and low ability to perform. This is not saying that low ability performers should be rewarded over high ability performers, no, the idea is to create a future that salespeople can believe in, and trust, in order to create job satisfaction and retention. This might sound ironic but creating a business culture where salespeople can have a future can actually promote the rebranding of salespeople's mindset in organizations. If a salesperson believes he has a future in the organization, and an opportunity to climb the organizational ladder, he is going to try to often be in his best behavior, and most especially treat customers well.

And in some cases, a salesperson can have high willingness and high ability but has been with the organization for a long time, and has essentially used up all his energy to continue to maintain his high ability in sales. This type of salesperson should be promoted to managerial positions as a form of 'thank-you' for the long service he has given to the organization. The fact that a salesperson with high willingness had had high ability but because of age now has low ability to perform in sales, does not mean such an individual cannot be a high ability manager. The energy might be drained and used up in selling but not in managing! And oftentimes, such an experienced former high ability salesperson can be a productive manager that would benefit the organization.

Many retail organizations often allow the skills of their ageing high willingness and high ability salespeople to waste away. There are however some organizations that will reward their superstar salespeople with a befitting managerial position after they have reached a certain age; where their mobility may not be as agile and as nimble as when they were younger and selling high volumes. But such organizations are rare. Several organizations will allow a former superstar salesperson to waste away until he has nothing left to offer the organization, and at that point, the organization will force him to retire; that is if he doesn't die on the job first! This type of habit does not promote commitment on the part of salespeople who are still young but have high willingness and high ability. Watching the way an organization treats its ageing high ability performers might be a sign to younger high ability performers that when their days come that they will be treated in the same way. This type of perception can lead to a situation where high ability can lead to low willingness or low commitment among salespeople.

Organizations have to be careful not to indirectly promote low morale by not creating an atmosphere or culture that nourishes individualized attention and interests. This is where the type of leadership that an organization has can pay dividends. A transformational leader will be quick to recognize the needs of an employee because of the character traits of his style of leadership. This will be different in a contingent reward culture where reward and punishment are the modus operandi, in the organization. The application of idealized influence, which is a characteristic of a transformational leader, can also foster commitment among high ability employees who lack willingness because of low morale.

In the 21st century workforce, where employees are attuned to changes and trends in the world, organizations that change their ways to meet evolving workplace will be better equipped for the challenges of tomorrow. For the future that is emerging, only organizations that constantly improve their cultures will survive. In the 199 0s, many organizations that did well during the pre-millennial period found out too late that the millennial brought with it a different market challenges that they could not cope with, because of their lack of preparedness. Many of these organizations discovered that the market had changed, right under their nose, with new products and new market values and shares. Had these 1990s organizations embraced changes, they would have remained relevant players in the millennial but they had allowed old traditions, and complacency to rule their processes.

Retail organizations, on the other hand, face different challenges that are mostly employee-related. Since salespeople are the lifeblood of retail organizations, having to manage retention of good salespeople has been a big challenge. The reason why it has continued to be a big challenge for retail organizations to keep good and experienced salespeople is that many retail organizations do not do enough to promote commitment, increase morale, build enthusiasm, and inspire motivation among salespeople. Studies have shown that many salespeople do not feel their organizations show personal interests in them as human beings but as robotized humans who are meant to work until they are no longer useful. According to studies, this perception among salespeople have led to lack of job satisfaction, low willingness, increased mobility from one job to another, and lack of commitment. If dealership organizations will do more to show personal interests and incentivized selling, and increase morale among salespeople, more salespeople will stay longer with one dealership, and contribute to productivity and competiveness, studies say.

Intellectual stimulation is another area where retail organizations have not done well. Salespeople would like to contribute to the decision making processes of their organizations if they are given the opportunity, studies show. But because many organizations do not give them the opportunity, the general consensus among salespeople is that they are not important enough to be considered during decision making processes that may even pertain to their area of expertise, which is selling! And in addition, many salespeople said in a recent study that they are never considered for job promotions, and vacation bonuses like trips and many other perks that they feel they are entitled to, but are never given. Retail organizations shouldn't have to wait for other organizations to lure their best salespeople with perks and incentives that they neglected to offer, before making a move to replicate such perks, oftentimes when it is already too late!

In organizations, having the right leadership is pivotal in

providing an appropriate and effective leadership that will benefit employees and organizational processes. The type of leadership that an organization has can make a big difference in productivity, and in employee satisfaction. For example, a transformational leader will likely provide a more satisfying workplace because of the manner motivation is stimulated and inspired than a transactional leader who believes the only way an employee can be motivated and productive is through contingent reward or punishment. While there are employees that may be motivated by reward, and the potential consequence of punishment, many employees are likely to be influenced by a leader who believes in creating a vision that can benefit them, studies show.

Chapter 16

Leaders as Change Agents

In today's sales-force, the type of leadership that an organization has can make a difference in productivity and profitability. In an evolving technological and globalized world, leaders must be capable of embracing change or risk losing the ability to lead effectively in a 21st century business organization. A leader has to be able to adapt to the situations that are dictated by the pace of market demands in order to survive. According to experts, a workforce that is infused with a top-down hierarchy will be required to change in order to succeed in an internet-age business environment. This pace of change is needed in order to meet the growing needs of a market that is essentially influenced by evolving and discerning consumers. Change is also needed in order to bring effective leadership to a constantly changing workforce that is dealing with employees' subtle nuances and variations. Such emerging change in leadership behavior will entail having patience, poise, positive attitude, optimism, charisma, and the ability to seamlessly create more opportunities for employees as well as for the organization.

Leaders need positive attitudes that can permeate the most conservative workplace where change can sometimes be difficult. Some conservative employees are not likely to accept changes or new ideas that a leader may bring to an organization. This is why a positive attitude and, patience are important in bringing about change. As a change agent, a leader will require the ability to change conservative employees to believe in the needed change that will increase productivity, market shares and competitiveness. Organizations have to change with the times or risk losing substance and the ability to remain relevant in the marketplace. As new products hit the marketplace so do the attitudes and loyalty of consumers. And organizations that fail to follow the dictates of the new market trend will likely lose market shares.

To ensure that their organizations do not miss out in an evolving consumer market, leaders need to change employees' attitude to meet and embrace the new trends in the market. Such new trends can be emerging new products or a general direction of change. It can also entail a new way of behaving and moving along with the new order of change that is developing and becoming ubiquitous. The ability to lead effectively must also include having the vision to know what is currently in vogue and in demand. To do this, leaders have to ensure that their employees are properly trained to sway along with the tide of change. And the leader has to also create an environment that can bring about new innovative products or services that will be in-tune with evolving consumer market, and with the times.

According to Forbes, "The marketplace requirements to compete are evolving so quickly that leadership is struggling to stay ahead of the course." The struggle is often informed by some leaders' inability to embrace change or to envision future changes. Oftentimes, when a leader has the vision to anticipate what product is likely to be popular in the future, that leader is likely to be able to "stay ahead of the course," and be in the forefront of product innovation. A leader like Steve Job for instance, was able to envision a new future market for a different type of smart phone and was able to anticipate the demand, by quickly working towards meeting that future demand. Steve Job was able to stay ahead of the course of the smart phone market, by changing the way smart phones are used. The innovativeness of the iphone that Steve Job introduced to the cellular phone marketplace would forever change the significance of smart phone in individual and business multipurpose usage.

A leader's ability to embrace change or serve as a change agent must be in the characteristic traits of the leader and how he pursues the fundamentals of change. Inability to envision an effective change, or unsuccessful attempts to be proactive and prepare for future change, can be costly. A good organizational leader must be willing and capable of creating and tackling change in an effort to maintain sustainability and competiveness. According to Forbes, "change management is no longer a term that denotes only operational improvements, cost efficiencies and process reengineering," it is also inclusive, and interwoven with the entire processes of the organization. The leader that is serious about bringing an effective change must be able to recognize that leadership has become more complex than ever, and that the overall business essence and productivity are embedded in good and effective leadership.

A leader must be a change agent to be effective, or risk losing the overall business fabric of what makes organizations succeed. The role of organizational leaders in the 21st century has gradually and rapidly evolved to encompass a workplace that needs to be motivated to change with the times, or risk complacency and poor quality product and services. The 21st century leader must be ready and capable of nourishing attitudes that will stimulate innovation, and good customer service. In addition, the employee must be inspired to believe in, and commit to the goals and objectives of the organization which should include bringing about change that will benefit output and create sustainability.

Leaders must be able to reinvent themselves in order to be relevant in the new millennial. And to reinvent, organizational leaders must have a strategy to reinvigorate their primary roles and responsibilities that are constantly evolving in an ever demanding consumer marketplace. To reclaim their significance and relevance, many leaders have had to adapt to the changes that are occurring in their organizations and in the market. As organizations strive to follow market dictates and consumer changing demands, leaders have to constantly evolve or become obsolete in their roles and responsibilities. Oftentimes it is the organization that could become obsolete if it does not change. For example, Sony had to quickly adapt when cassette tapes gave way to disks. And as new technology introduces streaming and digital downloads, CDs may also soon become a thing of the past. Consumers change with new technologies, and organizations that fail to change with the changing demands, will find out that their products are no longer in demand. It happened to turntables or LPs and then to cassette tapes, and now it is happening to CDs. When it was in vogue and in use, turntables or phonographic record designed to play at 33⅓ revolutions per minute, were exceedingly popular and in demand, and then cassette tapes had arrived and became just as popular as had phonographic records and turntables.

Change in the organizational spectrum can sometimes be overdue and organizations may not know it until it is too late. But if an organization has the right type of leadership, it may be easy to quickly embrace changes taking place. And it may be easy for organizations to work hard at the same time to meet or exceed the change. An organization can exceed change by coming out with its own future products in anticipation of the future that is emerging. Oftentimes when a product has peaked in its popularity, it is an indication that change is in the offing.

Leaders have to be able to create strategies for change in order to reclaim their relevance, and reinforce accountability and influence. According to Forbes, "if leaders don't feel comfortable with renewal and reinvention, they will begin to lose their impact and influence." This is especially mandatory as change has become the new norm in leadership relevance, effectiveness, efficiency, and success. And leaders that want to succeed must come to grip with the new normal or lose their relevance.

As change agents in organizational processes and functions, leaders in the millennial and in the 21st century will have to be able to continuously improve their ability to manage crisis and change in order to lead from the future. The ability to lead from the future as it emerges, according to Otto Scharmer, means that organizational leaders cannot be blind to emerging complexities that are often characterized by unexpected opportunities and disruptive change. The leader has to be able to envision and anticipate the products and services of the future so that likely unexpected opportunities can be explored to benefit organizational processes. In that sense, the leader as change agent has to be steps ahead to know what occurs in the business environment, and beyond, in order to anticipate the unexpected.

To become an effective change agent, certain characteristic factors are proposed, which according to Forbes, include multigenerational influence or the leader's ability to harness available talents, garner productive perspectives, and explore adaptive experiences that can bring needed changes to organizational processes. To maintain adequate multigenerational influence, a leader must be flexible as a change agent. In addition, the leader must have the right attitude or be willing to change his attitude, approach, and method in order to be effective in meeting the needs of the organization, and in seizing available opportunities that exist within multigenerational orbit.

The essence of multigenerational influence is that leaders have to transcend their own generations to embrace other generations in order to tap into the opportunities that exist in other generations, and to take their organizations beyond the confines of the needs of their own generations. Gravitating to the needs of the generation one belongs to as a leader can be counterproductive and can no longer be sufficient to meet competitiveness and the challenges presented by multigenerational influence. To reach a "broader multigenerational reach," organizational leaders have to move beyond the comfort zones that they are often familiar with, and explore the opportunities that abound in other generations. By transcending one's own generation, a leader can increase the opportunities that exist for growth, and innovation, to meet the demands o f multigenerational needs. This will also enable organizations to gain insights and understanding of multigenerational talent pool that exist within this reach, and be able to tap such talents and skills, including new market shares in the form of customers in this category. Transcending one's own comfort zones as a leader has numerous advantages which can include taping into new talent pool and acquiring new customers that will benefit organizational processes through market shares and inherent innovation. Reaching beyond one's own generation into multigenerational orbit can strengthen core competencies, efficiencies, and increased productivity.

Another factor that can effectively add to the leader's effort as a change agent is cultural intelligence, or the various opportunities that abound in demographic shift. *Cultural intelligence* is the leader's ability to understand the basic fundamentals of other cultures and the opportunities that abound therein. Leaders have to be able to transcend their own culture to tap into other cultures; and explore the talent, skills and markets, in multigenerational culture, in order to broaden their reach in market shares and innovation. According to Forbes, "lack of cultural intelligence is making it difficult for leaders to understand the new business models and best practice requirements that lie within reach." In today's globalized market, leaders can only succeed when they are able to explore the talents and market opportunities that exist in other cultural landscapes. Understanding the markets and how transcending culture and generations can add to innovation and consumer market, can enable organizations to enhance their productivity and competitiveness.

The keyword here is *diversity*, and about being culturally intelligent regarding other races and cultures. The value of demographic shift lies in exploring the advantages in other cultures. According to Forbes, "culture is the new currency for growth and leaders must change their perspective about diversity," or risk losing their competitive edge and possibly the innovation that can occur from exploring the talent pool in other cultures. Most innovative organizations today have cultural influence. According to experts, diversity can enable organizations to acquire new knowledge and talent that can boost their growth, and enhance productivity. Leaders must be culturally intelligent and attuned to others' culture, so that they can be able to explore the opportunities that exist in demographic shift. The way to do this is to change the way leaders perceive diversity as a cost center rather than as profit center where innovative new products and solutions to organizational problems abound, and can prevail.

The 21st century marketplace is reinventing a focus on knowledge and talent acquisition and consumer engagement that transcends cultures, and creates diversity that can enable the proliferation of significant strategic planning. Leaders that have the ability to develop cultural intelligence and to traverse obstacles that often occurs due to inhibitions of generational limitations, and who can explore the advantages of multigenerational influence or orbit, can be able to see opportunities that not only abound in other cultures but the innovation that can occur in diversity.

According to experts, "growth requires hyper-market segmentation and the ability to have deep and rich conversations with target consumers." Cultural intelligence enables organizations and their leaders to focus on the markets that exist in other cultures. Cultural intelligence can also help leaders to create and enhance values that can lead to solutions to problems that can occur in organizational processes. As information has become ubiquitous and as consumers now have unlimited access to information about products and services, leaders have to be able to see beyond their own cultures and be able to tap into the opportunities that exist in other cultures. But to do this, leaders have to be intelligent about other cultures by learning about the dos and don'ts, in other cultures. To effectively transcend cultures, leaders have to be able to respect others' cultures in order to explore the opportunities therein. Most cultures have their established dos and don'ts and for organizational leaders to tap into the opportunities that exist in such cultures, they have to not only respect the traditions of the cultures but abide by the rules and regulations that exist in such cultures. Being able to understand, respect, and learn about other cultures can form a core part of cultural intelligence.

For leaders to effectively operate as change agents, they have to understand how to bring about the forces of change in their organizations. Doing this requires the ability to understand the workforce and the employees that can help bring about change in the organization. Leaders that wish to become effective change agents must also be flexible and attentive to the needs of their employees so that they can be able to motivate them to believe in the proposed change. Now, this process is not just proposing a change but changing the mindset of employees to believe in the goals and objectives, and or direction of the organization. If the organization is refocusing on a new direction that will create new markets, employees have to be influenced in a positive way to adhere to the new order of change. New attitudes or change of attitudes on the part of the leader can also help bring about this change. Here flexibility will play a significant role. Oftentimes, the leader that has the most flexibility and is able to inspire the workforce with idealized influence can stand a better chance of being a change agent.

Some employees can be resistant to change if the leadership of the organization tries to force a change by adopting a transactional type of leadership in which the leader uses a contingent reward mechanism or the attendant consequence of punishment for nonperformance, or low willingness and low ability to perform. To inspire high willingness and high ability to contribute to change in the organization, leadership must first change its attitude so that stakeholders can become active participants in the change process. According to experts, transformational and situational leaders can adaptively become effective change agents because of their ability to influence the workforce with flexibility, and to intellectually stimulate employees to believe in the values of change.

In today's competitive global market environment where organizations are attuned to priorities that can produce results, and where the needs of consumers have become paramount, organizations that can keep pace with evolving and rising market demands will stand a better chance to benefit from market shares. But organizations have to be willing to overcome the human desire to maintain a sense of equilibrium, in order to bring about viability and sustenance.

As organizations are constantly being forced to change with the times, and with new market and consumer demands, the need to change as the market environment dictates has never been more urgent and crucial. In the 21st century internet age, consumers have access to information that can enable them to make decisions about their purchases. If a product is advertised on the internet at a certain price, they can compare that product with other products on the internet to see which one is better with a lower price. Consumer preference will be determined by the quality, appearance, and price of the product. If the price is right but the product is rough and of low quality, the consumer is likely to keep shopping until he finds the right product that matches his desired price. Leaders have to be able to recognize how consumers have changed and are no longer willing to settle for less than what they want.

In the pre-internet age, consumers had to drive from one place of business to another to shop for products, services and prices. And back then they would look through the yellow pages and newspapers for the best prices and products and then visit businesses to compare products and prices. But with internet, it is now possible to sit in the comfort of one's living room to compare products and prices. And leaders have to recognize the new paradigm shift that has put consumers in the driver's seat. The market has shifted to be coming a consumer market where organizations have to abide by the demands of the consumers or risk losing out.

As a change agent, the leader has to be able to recognize, and prioritize what matters most to the organization in order to effectively strive to meet goals and objectives. Some consumers are worth fighting for if their intentions are noble and will contribute to the output of the organization. There are consumers that will cost the organization money rather than contribute to it, and as a change agent, a leader has to recognize the intentions of such consumers and be able to discern the good and the bad consumer. As a change agent, the leader has to be able to have a workforce that can discern between consumers with good intentions and consumers with bad intentions. While it may be sometimes hard to peruse these different categories of consumers, being consumer-smart can often help. And a good leader will often know that having the right type of consumers will enable his organization to accomplish its goals; while the wrong consumers will be counterproductive in organizational efforts to meet and achieve objectives.

In a globalized economy, it may not be wise to unjustifiably be selective of what type of consumers to aim for, as the cutthroat competition for good consumers have never been so keenly crucial and competitive. But leaders have to be careful not to mistake good customers for bad customers, and then lose the edge in competitiveness. Just like in organizational processes, there are disruptive consumers while there are productive consumers. The disruptive consumers are the professional time-wasters who will come into your establishment under the pretext of buying your goods and end up costing you money and time. The productive consumers are the serious consumers that will come into your establishment, ready to buy if the price is right, without causing headaches and trouble. Oftentimes, good and bad consumers are differentiated by buying power and whether each consumer in each category has the wherewithal or creditworthiness to buy, or does not. With a consumer that is ready to buy and that is creditworthy, there is always the tendency of the organization to compete for such customers. But for the subprime or less creditworthy consumers that can barely buy, but want to buy, the leader might need to often work extra hard to earn such business, but not because the consumer is reluctant to buy but because of the limited financing available to finance such consumers. But these categories of consumers cannot be classified as time-wasters because of their creditworthiness or lack of it, but if in each category it becomes impossible to effect a transaction, then a diminishing return of some sort can occur, which may render the process less productive.

The leader that eventually serves as a change agent will enjoy multiple benefits if he is able to effectively maintain flexibility. Flexibility is crucial as a characteristic trait in a leader that wishes to help his organization grow, and perform in meeting set goals and objectives. In the production sector, flexibility is needed to make sure there are defects-free and quality products in the production line so that the need for future recalls can be minimized if not totally eliminated.

As a change agent, the leader must be ready to follow the dictates of the demands of the markets, and of consumers so that an organization is able to prepare itself for the challenges of tomorrow. Meeting the challenges of tomorrow will depend on the effectiveness of the leader, and the sacrifice he is willing to make to ensure that employees and all stakeholders believe in the same objective as he does. Many employees may not be committed and loyal to the goals of the organization, if the leader refuses to be a flexible change agent. According to experts, inflexibility breeds inefficiency and ineffectiveness that can ruin or handicap the future of an organization. A leader cannot allow his personal agenda to overshadow the objectives of the organization. Any leader that cannot function as a change agent must allow those that can do so to assume the mantle of leadership. Organizations must be aware of those leaders that will put their personal agenda before organizational objectives and as a result will not allow necessary changes to prevail. The needs, goals and objectives of the organization must supersede all other needs, including the needs of upper management executives. The only needs that matter in organizations are consumer needs, employee needs, and adherence to goals and objectives. The needs of a select few at the top of the hierarchy should always be secondary to the crucial primary needs of the organization especially the needs of a few overpaid executives that do not essentially help in creating growth, sustainability and competitiveness.

Most organizational leaders, in Asia, especially in Japan, receive less bonuses and salaries than their counterparts in the United States, and still, *sometimes*, over-perform, such over-paid top executives. High salaries and huge bonuses do not necessarily lead or translate to increased productivity and high willingness to commit to the goals and objectives of an organization. Organizational experts believe executives in Japan are often more inclined to adapt to situational changes and as a result often become more effective change agents than their counterparts in the U.S. who are often paid more.

In terms of quality performance and the drive to attain excellence in quality production of goods and services, executives in Japan are more likely to commit to such goals as their U.S. counterparts who often get paid more salaries and higher bonuses, according to studies. Organizational leaders in Europe are just as quickly and more inclined to adjust to situational changes than their counterparts in the U.S., even though they may not receive nearly as much salaries and bonuses.

The question is whether higher incentives create efficiency and effectiveness in the top hierarchy of an organization, and whether being paid more equates to being more efficient in leadership. While there are exponential organizational icons who have championed effective changes in their organizations in the U.S., like Lee Iacocca who gave up most of the perks of leadership in 1979 to ensure that Chrysler survives, and Steve Job, who innovatively changed Apple Inc., upon his return to the organization he had created, after he had been unconscionably removed from the organization; and Jack Welch who brought innovative changes to General Electric, there are thos e leaders who do not commit as much to change as Iacocca, Job, Welch, and many others.

Organizational leaders like Kenneth Lay who led Enron to bankruptcy in 2001, and Bernie Madoff who essentially stole billions of dollars from investors, and Allen Stan ford, who like Madoff, brought ruins to investors who had invested their hard -earned monies in their organizations, the culture of change or of becoming a change agent who puts the needs of their stakeholders first, was clearly absent in the characteristic traits of such leaders.

The role of leaders as change agents should include, but not limited, to the following. The leader should be capable of adapting to the situations that are often heralded by global market demands, and be able to motivate employees in the workplace to work towards meeting the challenges of such market demands. This can often be done by creating a workplace where job satisfaction and employee commitment are interwoven. Experts believe job satisfaction often lead to commitments. And as a result, leaders should always make sure they create a workplace that promotes employees' job satisfaction so that employees can be able to have high willingness to commit to the goals and objectives of the organization. Another significant role of leaders as change agents also includes creating a vision that employees in the organization can believe in. Creating a vision entails allowing a workplace environment where employees can perceive there is a future for them, and that they are part of the organization instead of just contract labors that are dispensable. What most organizations have started doing to create some form of vision of a future for employees is to create, and allocate shares/stocks to employees so that employees will know they have a stake in the organization.

Many organizations have started building this form of incentivized trust and vision that will make employees believe that the survivability and sustainability of the organization is as much in their hands as it is in the hands of top executives. This type of incentivized vision encourages employees' contribution to organizational growth, productivity, and competitiveness. Another role of leaders as change agents include ensuring that employees are intellectually stimulated so that they are able to understand their significance, and contributions to organizational processes. Intellectual stimulation is another form of leadership characteristic trait that can lead to change in the organization. This can occur when a leader encourages innovation and creativity as well as critical thinking and problem solving environment in the workplace. Employees can increase their self-worth, self-esteem, with intellectual stimulation, and as a result become a believer in a change catalyst that can lead to effectiveness and high performance.

Intellectual stimulation can enable the leader to inspire employees' thought processes, imagination, ideas, and the ability to look at a problem in multiple ways, before coming up with a solution. This process also allows employees to become significant contributors to the decision making process of an organization. The characteristic of a leader as a change agent is perhaps one of the most inspiring traits a leader can have in motivating a workplace to believe in a change that the leader can bring to employees in the workforce. And employees are often ready to adapt to whatever change is necessary to enhance growth, and create sustainability in the organization. But what can help a leader more than anything in serving as a change agent, is to allow flexibility in the workforce so that employees will be able to function as change agents in order to ensure that change becomes part of the productive apparatus.

Change takes time but the amount of time it takes in organizational processes can be expedited if a leader is willing to make the sacrifice that will result in a change. Change can also happen when a leader puts all the factors of change in motion, to bring about change. In an organization where effectiveness can only occur when a leader applies effective measures, change is often easier to put in place than in an organization where lukewarm attitude and ineffectiveness become part of the modus operandi of organizational processes.

Studies have shown that for leaders to become progressive change agent that they must have a workforce that is quick to adaptation. Such adaptation must be initiated by the leader which he must systemically allow to permeate the workforce in a gradual process. Since change takes time, the measures to make it happen must be in place and constantly improved so that its presence will be felt by all employees. In some organizational settings, some employees may become resistant to change because they have gotten accustomed to certain ways of doing things. This should not be allowed as employees have to abide by the change that the leader proposes and introduces, whether they like it or not. This is not saying that change should be forced on the workforce but in order for an organization to move ahead and remain sustainable, change has to take place and everyone *must* be a part of that change.

The process of change shouldn't have to be a choice that an employee must make; it should be systemic and gradual so that it can permeate potential resistance in the organization. Organizations cannot survive without changing its processes to agree with the changing pace of the times. If organizational processes lag behind, so will its products and services. In an age where things are quickly evolving and where products are changing on a constant basis to meet consumer demands, organizations have to be able to move with the times, or be ahead of the times, in order to satisfy the demands of the present and of the future. The future is emerging and will happen, whether an organization is prepared or not, to partake in it. That future may introduce new products and services, and even new ways of living, but those that cannot be part of it, will be sidelined as has happened with many organizations that ignored the clarion call of the future!

In the 21st century, and since the onset of the new millennial, many organizations that were once the pacesetters in innovative new gadgets and current products, and services, failed because they became complacent and satisfied with how things were in their organizations, without wanting to change. The result of such complacency was that these organizations were quickly overtaken by organizations that envisioned the future and were ready for it. Organizations like Apple saw a different future for smart phones than Blackberry and Nokia saw, when they came up with smart phones that changed the way smart phones have ever been used in our daily lives. Experts believe that lack of constant innovation, and or greed often makes it impossible for many organizations to invest in the future. Though Apple has been an agent of change that brought the iphone, ipad, ipod, and many pioneering products into the marketplace, the successes of these gadgets should be a springboard to move ahead to embrace new innovation, or it can be a decimating factor that can create complacency and derail progress and sustainability, for the organization.

In order for organizations and their leaders to embrace change, they have to be ready for it, experts say. And organizations have to be ready to invest in the future by way of research and development in order to create innovation. And employees in such organizations have to be inspired to believe in the change. Organizations can do this by ensuring that all employees are part of that change. Some organizations have departments that are devoted to research and development, and as a result invest only in such departments. This should not be the case. Organizations should also make sure that employees in other departments of the organization are also part of the change in the organization. All employees should be trained to embrace the change that an organization is investing in, not just the employees in the research and development department. If all employees are trained to embrace change, change can then become a catalyst for future growth.

Chapter 17

Conclusion

Many organizations often engage in one form of selling or the other and in a way, the processes of selling is the same, whether one is selling intangible, or virtual services, or selling insurance, jewelries, stocks, computers, clothes, shoes, automobiles, parts, and even paraphernalia, appurtenances, and virtual products, the process is the same. Selling is an all encompassing process that tends to embrace all facets of life. In some cases, selling can even entails selling one's personality, talent, skills, or image, as often occurs with models, newscasters, and politicians, etcetera. Selling is not effective until the end result is positive or produces results. In other words, a sale is made when it is consummated, and the end result becomes a dividend of some sort.

But not everyone is gifted with accomplishing the science or art of selling, to achieve positive results. But like with most professions, many may be called but only few will actually achieve success in sales. Just like in music where talented musicians abound, only few will actually enjoy the lucre of success. Many colleges and universities have curriculums that are devoted to programs in sales and in music, where students are taught the art of selling, and where musicians are taught music and how to play instruments, but even with such expensive trainings, success only has room for a chosen few. And those that will be successful will be, not because they were trained better, but because they were gifted to achieve commercial success in such ventures.

In sales, no academic training is required or needed to achieve success, just as no academic knowledge is needed for a musician to achieve success. Most successful musicians of the current era, and of the era before, did not even take college courses in music, and yet they became international superstars and icons who achieved renown in those fields. In a broader sense, it is the same with sports, even though most colleges and universities devote lots of resources to developing many sports. In sales, success will only come when a salesperson does what he is gifted to do. A true salesperson does not need pretenses as his craft will come natural to him at all times. The same is true with those lucky enough to be gifted with talents and skills, in other professions. Though schools teach skills, they essentially only nurture what is already there.

Result oriented salespeople cannot actually achieve success until they have a mentor of some sort to guide them in the right direction. As great as the Greek leader, Odysseus, was, he still believed in the essence and power of mentorship, that he would entrust his son, Telemachus, with a mentor to educate him. Mentoring can help in providing former education, but it cannot help with what is not there. Unlike Odysseus's son, Telemachus whose need was education, salespeople who are gifted only need to be guided in the most appropriate form and behavior so that they can be able to tap into the enormous wells of talent that they have been lucky enough to have.

Though selling is a talent that is sometimes lucrative, it has not always been accorded the respect that is due the profession. Though the word, sales, is broad and includes all facets of selling, which can be intangible, virtual, abstract and concrete, the category of sales that has suffered poor perception, disrespect, and indignity, from members of the public, has been frontline selling. Frontline salespeople can be car salespeople, door-to-door salespeople, and many other cadres of salespeople who engage in frontline selling. While some salespeople have been tainted with notoriety that includes deception, trickery, thievery, sleaziness, and all sorts of societal misgivings, they have also been an essential part of the business community that connects consumers with the products of their choices. Without salespeople, buying will even be more cumbersome and difficult for the consumer, as he would have to endure extra hardship in the buying process. Imagine if there were no salespeople in the automobile retail industry and how consumers would buy their vehicles and take delivery of the vehicles! It would be difficult, especially with regards to making selections, and helping to make the purchase process comfortable. If there were no salespeople, buying a vehicle would be akin to eating in a restaurant, in a buffet without waiters to serve the food!

Society needs salespeople to help them with their purchases and to make the process smooth and easy. But oftentimes, salespeople are treated as if they are not needed, according to studies. The reason for this is that over the years, many salespeople systematically created a systemic state of not being respected or trusted, and as time passes, this notion of disrepute permeated the profession to where traditional sleaziness became synonymous with salespeople.

Retail organizations have not helped in providing a better understanding about the roles of salespeople in their businesses, even though salespeople provide the bulk of their productivity and sustenance. Critics say that dealership organizations have helped fuel the bad image that has permeated the automobile sales profession by treating salespeople as inconsequential and dispensable employees who are of lower class, without any significance to outputs and sustainability. Though dealership organizations have often downplayed the significance of salespeople to their productivity, they actually cannot *function* without salespeople. Over the years, many dealership organizations have sprung up with a *no haggle, no hassle* policy, in order to make consumers feel comfortable, to make purchase without having to go through salespeople. But such dealerships have often ended up needing salespeople to even make the *no haggle, no hassle* process possible. The only difference has been that customers can no longer be able to negotiate prices as the prices are set.

While many consumers have appreciated the no haggle, no hassle price tags, some consumers see the process as another tactics to manipulate them into paying more than they should. Some customers have even gone as far as saying that they prefer the haggling process where they could negotiate price with a salesperson, instead of not being able to negotiate prices. And studies have shown that dealerships that promote no haggle, no hassle prices, often sell lesser vehicles than dealerships where customers can negotiate prices.

The obvious attempts to avoid, and do away with salespeople have been futile as dealerships have often ended up hiring more salespeople to make the no haggle, no hassle processes possible. The only difference has been that salespeople do not get as much commissions as they would, in the traditional negotiating process. Experts say many dealerships that adopted this method use it as a ploy to pay salespeople less, while at the same time making customers pay more. In traditional dealerships where prices can be negotiated, some customers would even pay less than at dealerships where prices are not negotiated, studies have shown.

The way dealership organizations promote their businesses and treat salespeople have mostly contributed to how sales people have been perceived by members of the public, according to research. Some dealerships believe salespeople are a dime a dozen, and as a result have no need to provide job satisfaction to ensure that salespeople in turn behave appropriately in the process of doing their jobs. And on their part, salespeople do not feel they have to kowtow to their bosses since they do not always get the respect they feel they deserve. The situation has been dicey and unpredictable that there have been personality conflicts between salespeople and their managers that have often ended fatally. But the relationships between salespeople and their management shouldn't be built on unpredictability and mutual distrust. Instead it should be based on mutual trusts on the basis of shared interests. As partners working towards achieving the same objective, there should be shared and mutual respects. And there should be a core understanding, and improved strive, on the part of management to portray salespeople as significant factors in productivity rather than as dispensable and inconsequential employees.

The type of leadership that most dealerships have often plays a role in the way salespeople are treated. Most retail organizations are structured in a top-down hierarchical structure that puts salespeople at the bottom of the strata or ladder. And because of the unfavorable positions that salespeople occupy in the dealerships' hierarchical structure or organizational chart, it sometimes becomes difficult for salespeople to be seen as significant and indispensable part of the organizational processes. One of the major reasons salespeople often get treated the way they do is partly because of the poor training that managers and management have about human capital, and on how to treat essential human capital in the workplace. But since dealerships are not in essence considered traditional business organizations where decorum is adhered to, many ethical behaviors are often not abided by.

The key to having an equitably placed workforce, with regards to salespeople and how they are treated, is having the type of leader that understands salespeople and what they need, to be good employees. One of the characteristics of transformational leadership is the ability to inspire motivation, apply idealized influence, identify needed change, create a vision to guide the workforce, and to use intellectual stimulation, personal interests and attention, to guide employees to where they can be loyal, and committed to the goals and objectives of the organization. Most dealerships appear to have adopted the transactional leadership style where contingent reward, and punishment for non-performance rule as the modus operandi of organizational processes. Studies show that organizations with leaders that can inspire employees with high willingness and high ability to work towards achieving set goals and objectives often achieve higher productivity and profitability, than leaders that believe in using contingent reward as a form of motivation. The difference is that one form of leadership creates intrinsic satisfaction that often yields ideas and initiatives, while the other form of leadership creates lack of commitment that does not allow room for employees to use their initiatives.

References/Index

Abrahamson, E. (1996). "Management fashion". The Academy of Management Review, 21, 1, 254-285

Abraham H. Maslow. A. H. (1966). The Psychology of Science: *a reconnaissance. New York. Harper & Row.*

A brief history of ISO 9000: Where did we go wrong? The case against ISO 9000 (2nd ed.). Taylorville, Illinois. Oak Tree Press.

Aguayo, R. (1990). Dr. Deming: The American who taught the Japanese about quality. Whitby, Ontario. Fireside Publishing House.

Aguayo, R. (1991). Dr. Deming: The American who taught the Japanese about quality. New York. Simon & Schuster.

Airbag recall widens to 34 million cars as Takata admits defects. Retrieved May 20, 2015, from http://www.nytimes.com/2015/05/20/business/takata-airbag-recall.html?_r=0

Alcorn, J. E. (2008). A collection of papers presented at the 55th conference on glass problems: Ceramic engineering and science proceedings, Volume 16, Issue 2". Ceramic Engineering and Science Proceedings

Allinson, G. D. (1997).. Japan's postwar history. New York. Cornell University Press.

American society for training and development. (ASTD) (April, 2008). *Sales competency project*. Retrieved June 5, 2016, from www.russorights.com.

Apple ordered to stop selling iPhone 6, iPhone 6 Plus in Beijing. eWeek. Retrieved June 20, 2016, from: http://www.eweek.com/video/apple-ordered-to-stop-selling-iphone-6-iphone-6-plus-in-beijing.html

Apple is now worth over $700 Billion: First American company ever to pass that milestone. Time.com. Retrieved February 10, 2015, from: http://time.com/3704014/apple-700-billion/

Apple supplier halts China factory after violence. Yahoo! Finance. Retrieved September 27, 2012, from: http://finance.yahoo.com/news/apple-supplier-halts-china-factory-violence-055718608.html

Articles of association of nokia corporation. Retrieved 26 June 2015, from http://company.nokia.com/sites/default/files/downloads/nokia-articles-of-association-may-2014..

Arthur, C. (29 September 2014). Ten things to know about BlackBerry -- and how much trouble it is (or isn't) in. *Retrieved February 15, 2015, from TheGuardian.com.*

Bailine, A. & Dall, M. (2004). Service this! Winning the war against customer disservice (1st ed.). P.A. Plymouth Meeting.

Bamford, R. & Deibler, W. (2003). ISO 9001: 2000 for software and systems providers: An Engineering Approach (1st ed.). Bacon Raton, Florida. CRC-Press

Beattie, K. R. & Sohal, A. S. (1999). Implementing ISO 9000: A study of its benefits among Australian organizations. Total Quality Management. Routledge, part of the Taylor & Francis Group.

Becoming Steve Jobs: The evolution of a reckless upstart into a visionary Leader. Crown (ebook

How Steve Wozniak's breakout defined Apple's future". *Gameinformer. June 27, 2013 archived from the original on November 1, 2013.* Retrieved February 13, 2014.

Becker, S. B. (1964, 1993, 3rd Ed.) Human capital: A theoretical and empirical analysis, with Special Reference to Education. Chicago. University of Chicago Press

Berger, K. S. (1983). The developing person through the life span. Duffield, United Kingdom. Worth Publishers.

Biography of Michael Dell. The Associated Press. Retrieved May 6, 2016 from http://www.bloomberg.com/news/articles/2007-01-31/biography-of-michael-dellbusinessweek-business-news-stock-market-and-financial-advice

BlackBerry to be sold to group led by Fairfax Financial". *CBC News. (September 24, 2013).* Retrieved March 5, 2014, from http://www.cbc.ca/news/business/blackberry-to-be-sold-to-group-led-by-fairfax-financial-1.1864922

Bowling, A. (1997). *Research methods in health*. Buckingham: Open University Press

Brooks, F. P. (1986). No silver bullet — essence and accident in software engineering, proceedings of the IFIP tenth world computing Conference.

BSI group annual report and financial Statements. Retrieved April 25, 2010, from www.BSI.com.

BSI strengthens position in Australia with acquisition of NCS international. Retrieved June 4, 2016, from www.BSI.com

Buchanan, L. (March 1, 2011). A customer service makeover". Inc. magazine. Retrieved 29 Oct 2, from www.Inc.com

Bunkley, N. (March, 2008). Joseph Juran 103: Pioneer in quality control dies. Retrieved July 5, 2014 from http://www.nytimes.com/2008/03/03/business/03juran.html?_r=0

Burns, J.M. (1978). Leadership. New York. Harper & Row.

Burns, N., & Grove, S. K. (1997). *The practice of nursing research conduct, critique, & utilization.* Philadelphia. W.B. Saunders and Co.

Burns M. (July 8, 2014). BlackBerry is one of the hottest stocks of 2014, seriously. *TechCrunch. AOL Inc.* Retrieved July 12, 2014 *from Aol.com/business.*

Car Salesman arrested in shooting of boss. (November 30, 2012). Retrieved from http://www.chron.com/news/houston-texas/houston/article/Car-salesman-arrested-in-shooting-of-boss

Cardone, G. (2014). Sell or be sold: How to get your way in business and in life. Austin. Greenleaf Book Group Press

Choi, D. H., Kim, C.M., Kim,S. & Kim, S. H. Customer loyalty and disloyalty in internet retail stores: Its antecedents and its effect on customer price sensitivity. International Journal of Management. Retrieved June 10, 2016, from https://www.questia.com/library/journal/1P3-

1197221341/customer-loyalty-and-disloyalty-in-internet-retail

Christensen, R. (2002). Plain answers to complex questions: The theory of linear models (Third ed.). New York. Springer

Collins, R., (1997). An Asian route to capitalism: Religious economy and the origins of self-transforming growth in Japan. American Sociological Review, Vol. 62, No. 6. Retrieved June 10, 2014, from https://www.researchgate.net/publication/271689261_An_Asian_Route_to_Capitalism_Religious_Economy_and_the_Origins_of_Self-Transforming_Growth_in_Japan

Collisson, N. (1996). Examination of the influence of Japanese culture and the failures of economic reforms proposed by Supreme Command Allied Powers (SCAP). Economic missions from 1947 to 1949, on high rates of personal savings in Japan by Nancy Collisson / EALC MA Thesis. University of Kansas Library.

Consumer advisory: Vehicle owners with defective airbags urged to take immediate action. Retrieved October 30, 2014, from http://www.nhtsa.gov/About+NHTSA/Press+Releases/Vehicle-owners-with-defective-airbags-urged-to-take-immediate-action

Compendium of professional selling. *United Professional Sales Association. n.d.*

Corbett, C. J., Montes-Sancho, M. J., & Kirsch, D. A. (2005). The financial impact of ISO 9000 certification in the United States: An Empirical Analysis. Management Science.

Cord, D. J. (April 2014). The decline and fall of Nokia. *Schildts & Söderströms*

Creech B. *(1994). The five pillars of TQM: How to make total quality management work for you. New York. Truman Talley Books/Dutton*

Cunningham, S & Turner, G. (2006). Media and communications. Australia. Southwood Press Pty Ltd.

Deming, W. E. (1950). Edwards lectures on statistical control of quality. Nippon Kagaku Gijutsu Remmei.

Deming, W. E. (1993). The new economics for industry, government, and education. Boston, Ma: MIT Press.

Deming, W. E. (2000). Out of the crisis (1. MIT Press ed.). Cambridge, Mass.: MIT Press.

Deming, W. E. (1993). The new economics for industry, government, education. Second edition. Boston. MIT Press.

Deming, W. E. (1986). Out of the crisis. Boston. MIT Press

Deming, W. E. (1994), Out of the crisis. Boston. The MIT Press

Dell, M. & Fredman, C. (1999). Direct from Dell: Strategies that revolutionized an industry. New York. HarperBusiness

Drucker, P. The practice of management. Harper, New York, 1954; Heinemann, London, 1955; revised edn, Butterworth-Heinemann, 2007

Drucker, P. (1954). The practice of management. New York. Harper Heinemann,

Drucker, P. (1973). Management tasks, responsibilities, practices. New York. Harper & Row,

Dunn, P. (January 1997). "James Lind (1716-94) of Edinburgh and the treatment of scurvy". *Archive of disease in childhood fetal and neonatal edition. United Kingdom. British Medical Journal Publishing Group*

Dusharme, D. (1995). Federal quality institute set to close. Quality Digest. Red Bluff, California. QCI International.

From dorm room to board room: Michael S. Dell. Academy of Achievement. Retrieved January 4, 2013, from http://www.achievement.org/autodoc/page/del0bio-1

Ending the war between sales and marketing. *Harvard Business Review.* Retrieved 16 August 2014 *from hbr.org.*

Enron ethics and today's corporate values. Forbes Business. Retrieved May 14, 2014, from http://www.forbes.com/sites/kensilverstein/2013/05/14/enron-ethics-and-todays-corporate-values/

Freedman, D. A. (2005). Statistical models: Theory and practice. Cambridge. Cambridge University Press

Foremski, T. The Steve Jobs way: Exploring the intersection of psychedelics and technology | ZDNet". *ZDNet.*

Retrieved 2016-02-24.

Forsberg, A. (2000). America and the Japanese miracle. Chapel Hill. University of North Carolina Press

Four U.S. organizations honored with the 2014 Baldrige National Quality Award. Retrieved June 2, 2016, from Baldrigenationalqualityaward.com

Galton, F. (1989). Kinship and correlation (reprinted 1989). Statistical science (Institute of mathematical statistics) ***4*** *(2): 80–86.*

Giddens, A. (1971). Capitalism and modern social theory: An analysis of the writings of Max, Durkheim and Max Weber. Cambridge. Cambridge University Press.

Gilbert, D. (2006). Stumbling on happiness. New York. Knopf Doubleday Publishing – Penguin Random House LLC.

Gilbert, D. (2006). Stumbling on happiness. Toronto. Ontario: Random House

Global 500 2013. *Fortune. 2013. Retrieved 16 August 2013 from http://www.huffingtonpost.com/2013/05/06/fortune-500-2013_n_3222779.html*

Goud, N, N. (2008). Abraham Maslow: A personal statement. Journal of Humanistic Psychology.

Greening, J. (1993). Selling without confrontation. Binghamton. Taylor & Francis, Inc.: Imprint: The Haworth Press, Inc.

Hacking, I. (September 1988). Telepathy: Origins of randomization in experimental design. Retrieved August 22, 2016 from www.journals.uchicago.edu/doi/10.1086/354775

Hankins, J. (2001). Infusion therapy in clinical practice. Philadelphia. W.B. Saunders.

Harkinson, J. (March–April 2011). American magnate: Michael Dell: how a homegrown geek outsourced, downsized, and tax-break his way to the top. Mother Jones. Retrieved March 10, 2011 from http://www.motherjones.com/toc/2011/03

Harlow, L. L., Stanley A., Mulaik, J. & Steiger, H. eds. (1997). What if there were no significance tests? Mahwah, New Jersey. Lawrence Erlbaum Associates.

Hersey, P. & Blanchard, K. H. (1969). Life cycle theory of leadership. Training Development, 23, 26-34.

Hersey, P. & Blanchard, K. H. (1977). Management of organizational behavior 3rd edition. Utilizing Human Resources. New Jersey. Prentice Hall.

Hersey, P. (1985). The situational leader. New York. NY: Warner Books.

Hindo, B. (June 6, 2007). At 3M a struggle between efficiency and creativity. Business Week.

Hindle, T. (2008). Guide to management ideas and gurus. New York. Bloomberg Press,

Hoffman, E. (1999), Abraham Maslow: A brief reminiscence. Journal of Humanistic Psychology Fall 2008 vol. 48 no. 4 443-444. New York. McGraw-Hill

Holmes, K. (1992). Total quality management. Leatherhead. United Kingdom*: Pira International, Ltd*

House of Commons Welsh affairs committee - first report cross-border provision of public services for Wales: further and higher education. Retrieved June 5, 2016, from www.houseofcommons.com.

How to organize your marketing department in the digital age". *Retrieved January 27, 2016, from www.cmo.com.*

Hoyle, D. (2007). Quality management essentials. Oxford, United Kingdom. Butterworth-Heinemann

Huber, T. (1994). Strategic economy in Japan. Boulder: Westview Press.

Hutchins, D. C. (September 2008). Hoshin Kanri : the strategic approach to continuous improvement. Burlington, Vermont: Gower.

Hutchins, D. C. (1985). The quality circles handbook. New York: Pitman Press.

Iacocca, L. (30 May 1994). I couldn't just play golf all day'. *Interview with Alex Taylor. Fortune*. Retrieved 2012-04-16.

Iaccoca, L. (1984). Iacocca: An autobiography. New York: Batam Bookes.

Imai, M. *(1986). Kaizen (Ky'zen), the Key to Japan's Competitive Success (1 ed.). New York. Random House.*

Ishikawa, K. (1985). *What is total quality control? The Japanese Way (1 ed.). Englewood Cliffs, New Jersey. Prentice Hall.*

Ishikawa, K. (1968). Guide to quality control. Tokyo. JUSE.

Ishikawa, K. (1976). Guide to quality control. Asian Productivity Organization. ISBN 92-833-1036-5.

Itzkoff, S. W. (2003). Intellectual capital in 21st century politics. Ashfield, MA. Paideia.

Ivan. F. (2014). Applied problem solving. Method applications root causes countermeasures Poka-Yoke and A3: How to make things happen to solve problems. Milan, Italy. Createspace, an Amazon company

Jeffrey S. (1987). Steve Jobs: The journey is the reward.. Amazon Digital Services, 2011 ebook edition (originally Scott Foresman*).*

Johnson, C. (1982). MIT and the Japanese miracle: The Growth of Industrial Policy, 1925-1975. Stanford. Stanford University Press, 1982

Juran, J. M. (2004). Architect of quality: The autobiography of Dr. Joseph M. Juran (1 ed.). New York city. McGraw Hill.

Juran, J. M. (1992). *Juran on quality by design: the new steps for planning quality into goods and services. New York. Free Press*

Kahle, D. ()How to spot a potential star salesperson: "Six qualities of superstar salespeople". Retrieved May 29, 2016, from http://www.presentation-pointers.com/showarticle/articleid/558/

Kaiser health tracking poll. Retrieved August 20, 2015, from: http://kff.org/health-costs/poll-finding/kaiser-health-tracking-poll-august-2015/

Kasler D. (1988). Max Weber: an introduction to his life and work. University of Chicago. Press.

Kitagawa, H. & Tsuchida, B. T. (1975). The tale of the Heike. Tokyo. University of Tokyo Press.

Kotler, P. (1980). Principles of marketin. New York. Prentice –Hall.

Ladendorf, K. (2011). Dell remembers his beginning while looking toward the future. Austin American-Statesman. November 27, 2011.

LaFollette, W. R.; & Fleming, R. J. (1977-08-01). The Historical Antecedents of Management by Objective. *Academy of Management Proceedings.*

Lee Iacocca Joins Board of Koo Koo Roo restaurants.. *Los Angeles Times. 14 August 1995*. Retrieved 2012-04-16

Leadership: Every leader must be a change agent or face extinction. Retrieved July 20, 2016, from: http://www.forbes.com/sites/glennllopis/2014/03/24/every-leader-must-be-a-change-agent-or-face-extinction

Levinson, P .(2004). Cellphone. New York. Routledge.

Liker, J. (2004). The Toyota way. New York. McGraw-Hill

Likert, R. (1932). A technique for the measurement of attitudes. *Archives of Psychology*.

Markoff, J. (October 5, 2011). Steven P. Jobs, 1955–2011: Apple's Visionary Redefined Digital Age. The New York Times.

Machinery of government. (July, 2009). Creation of the Department for Business, Innovation and Skills. Cabinet Office.

Management by objectives. *The Economist.* ISSN 0013-0613.

Martin, S. W. (June 27, 2011). Seven personality traits of top salespeople. Harvard Business Review. Retrieved May 30, 2016, from: https://hbr.org/2011/06/the-seven-personality-traits-o/

Maslow, A. H. (1943). A theory of human motivation. Psychological Review.

Maslow, A. H. (1967). A theory of metamotivation: The biological rooting of the value-life. Journal of Humanistic Psychology.

Maslow, A. (1998). Towards a psychology of being. Wiley. 3 edition. PBS

McBurney, S. (2013). Steve Jobs 1994 uncut Interview with English subtitles (Video). Menlo Park, California: Silicon Valley Historical Association.

McCloskey, D. N., & Ziliak, S. T. (2008). The cult of statistical significance: How the standard error costs us jobs, justice, and lives. Chicago. University of Michigan Press

McLeod, S. (2007). Maslow's hierarchy of needs. Simple psychology. Retrieved July 10, 2016, from http://www.simplypsychology.org/maslow.html

Micah, S. (4 March 2010). Seven keys to building customer loyalty--and company profits. Fast Company. Retrieved 29 Oct 2012.

Microsoft buys Nokia's devices and services unit, unites windows phone 8 and its hardware maker. *The Verge. Vox Media.* Retrieved 3 September 2013.

Microsoft closes Nokia deal, pays more than expected. *CNET. CBS Interactive,*

Mogull, R. G. (2004). Second-semester applied statistics. New York. Kendall/ Hunt Publishing Company.

Morris, I. (1964). The world of the shining Prince: Court life in ancient Japan. Oxford. Oxford University Press.

Motivation and cognitive abilities: An integrative/aptitude-treatment interaction approach to skill acquisition. Journal of Applied Psychology.

Muelaner, . J. E (2014). Gage repeatability and reproducibility (Gage R&R) in an excel spreadsheet.

Nayak, P., & Ranganath, J. K. (1994). Breakthroughs! How the vision and drive of innovators in sixteen companies created commercial breakthroughs that Swept the world. Rawson Associates

Naveh, E. & Marcus, A. (2007). Financial performance, ISO 9000 standard and safe driving practices effects on accident rate in the U.S. Motor carrier industry. Accident Analysis & Prevention

Naveh, E.; Marcus, A. (2004). When does the ISO 9000 quality assurance standard lead to performance improvement? Assimilation and going beyond. IEEE Transactions on Engineering Management

Nelson, R. T. (1991-01-10). Coast guard total quality management (TQM). Generic Organization. Washington DC. United States Coast Guard.

Neave, H. R. (1992). A brief history of Dr. W. Edwards Deming. Knoxville, Tennessee. SPC Press.

Nokia Corporation. Archived from the original *on 8 February 2009*. Retrieved 16 March 2009.

Nokia celebrates first day of combined operations with Alcatel-Lucent. *Nokia.*

Orwell, G. (1946). Animal Farm. London. Penguin Group.

Ovide, Shira. Microsoft in $7.17 Billion Deal for Nokia Cellphone Business". *Wall Street Journal.* Retrieved 3 September 2013.

Petersen, G. S. (2008). The profit maximization paradox: Cracking the marketing/ sales alignment code. Booksurge in 1221. p. 176.

Palmer, B. (2011-10-06). Did Dropping Acid Make Steve Jobs More Creative? . *Slate.* ISSN 1091-2339. Retrieved 2016-02-24.

Paulhus, D. L. (1984). Two-component models of socially desirable responding. *Journal of personality and social psychology,*

Pfeifer, T. (2002). Quality management: Strategies, methods, techniques. Munich, Germany: Carl Hanser Verlag.

Phillips-Donaldson, D. (May 2004). 100 years of Juran. Quality Progress. Milwaukee, Wisconsin. American Society for Quality.

Poksinska, B, Dahlgaard, J. J., & Antoni, M. (2002). The st ate of ISO 9000 certification: A study of Swedish organizations. The TQM Magazine

Press release: BSI reports highest profits and revenue in 114 year history. Retrieved August 4, 2016, from www.BSI.*com.*

Pyle, K. (1996). The making of modern Japan. 2nd ed. Lexington: D.C. Heath and Company

Rajan, M., Tamimi, N. (2003). Payoff to ISO 9000 registration. The Journal of Investing

Rainford, Paul (20 April 2016). Eurobites: Nokia Sales to Hit $26.5B in 2016 – Analyst. *Eurobites.* Retrieved 28 April 2016.

Rawlings, J. O., Pantula, S. G., Dickey, D. A., eds. (1998). Applied regression analysis. Springer Texts in Statistics.

Rennie, D. (2008). Two thoughts on Abraham Maslow. Journal of Humanistic Psychology.
Retrieved July 12, 2015.

Research in motion reports fourth quarter and year-end results for fiscal 2005

Rheingold, H. (2002). Smart mobs: the Next social revolution. Cambridge, Massachusetts. Perseus.

Rosen, S. (1987). Human capital. The New Palgrave. Retrieved from the New Palgrave dictionary of economics online.

Rother, M. (2010). "6". Toyota Kata. New York: MGraw-Hill

Salacinski, T. (2015). SPC - statistical process control. Warsaw. The Warsaw University of Technology Publishing House.

Samsung becomes the world's largest smar tphone maker as Apple's market share hits a three-low. Daily Mail. Retrieved September 3, 2016, from http: / / www.dailymail.co.uk.

Scott, A. J. (2012). Illusions in regression analysis. International Journal of Forecasting (forthcoming).

Selden, P. H. (1997). Sales process engineering: A personal workshop. Milwaukee, WI: ASQ Quality Press.

Selden, P. H. (December 1998). Sales Process Engineering: An Emerging Quality Application Quality Progress: 59–63.

Shakespeare, W. (1610). Julius Caesar: The Fault is not In Our Stars. London, England.

Shakespeare, W. (1611) Macbeth. London. England.

Scharmer, C. O. (2009) Theory U: Leading from the future as it emerges. San Francisco. Berrett-Koehler Publishers.

Shewhart, W. A. (1980). *Economic control of quality of manufactured product/ 50th anniversary commemorative issue. American Society for Quality*

Shewhart, W. A. *(1939). Statistical method from the viewpoint of quality control. New York. Dover.*

Shively, D. H. & McCullough W. H. (1999). Introduction in D. H. Shively and W. H. McCullough, (eds.). The Cambridge History of Modern Japan; Volume 2, Heian Japan, (Cambridge: Cambridge University Press

Shigeto, T. (1993). Japan's capitalism: Creative defeat and beyond. Cambridge, England. Cambridge University Press.

Smith, A. (1776): The Wealth of Nations. New York. Bantam Classic.

Sommers, C. H. & Satel, S. (2006). One nation under therapy: How the helping culture is eroding self-reliance. New York. McMillian.

Special Reports: Timeline: The career of Lee Iacocca. - Detroit News. - March 17, 2002.

Strategies for managing change: Transformational leadership theory Leadership with values, meaning and a higher purpose. Retrieved July 10, 2016, from http://www.strategies-for-managing-change.com/transformational-leadership-theory.html

Swartz, T. & Iacobucci, D. O. Handbook of services marketing and management. California. Thousand Oaks.

Sweeny, A. (2009). BlackBerry planet: the story of Research in Motion and the little device that took the world by storm. *Canada. John Wiley & Sons*

Tague, N. R. (2004). Seven basic quality tools. The Quality Toolbox. Milwaukee, Wisconsin. American Society for Quality.

Tang, T. L. P., Tollison, P. S., & Whiteside, H. D. (1991). Managers attendance and the effectiveness of small groups: The case of quality circles. Journal of Social Psychology,

Tang, T. L. P., & Butler, E. A. (1997). Attributions of quality circles' problem-solving failure: Differences among management, supporting staff, and quality circle members. Public Personnel Management

The PC is born. Joomla. Archived *from the original on June 24, 2012.* Retrieved March 27, 2012.

The GM recall scandal: Who knew what and when? Congress and the Department of Justice want to know whether General Motors knew of a dangerous ignition problem years before it issued a recall. Retrieved March 21, 2014, from http://www.popularmechanics.com/cars/a10261/the-gm-recall-scandal-who-knew-what-and-when.

The thinking production system: TPS as a winning strategy for developing people in the global manufacturing environment. Retrieved February 19, 2014, from www.TPS.com

The seven basic tools of quality. (2007). Improvement and innovation. London.

The personal meaning of social values in the work of Abraham Maslow by John H. Morgan interpersonal. An International Journal on Personal Relationships. The Steve Jobs nobody knew. *Rolling Stone*. Retrieved 2016-02-24.

The lost interview: Steve jobs tells us what really matters. *Forbes. November 17, 2011.*

This is the new Nokia. *The Verge*. Retrieved 23 November 2014.

Tsim, Y.C., Yeung, V.W.S, Leung, & Edgar T.C. (2002). An adaptation to ISO 9001:2000 for certified organizations. Managerial Auditing Journal

United States Department of Defense (1989). Total quality management: A Guide for implementation. Springfield, Virginia. National Technical Information Service.

Vokurka, R. J., Stading, G. L. & Brazeal, J. (August 2000). A comparative analysis of national and regional quality awards. *Quality Progress*. Milwaukee, Wisconsin. American Society for Quality.

Walton, M. (1986). The Deming management method. New York. Penguin Group.

Weber, M. (1905). The protestant ethic and the spirit of capitalism. Translated by Stephen Kalberg (2002). Roxbury Publishing Company.

Webber, L. & Wallace, M. (15 December 2006). Quality control for dummies.

Wheeler, D. J. (2000). Normality and the process-behavior chart. ISBN 0-945320-56-6.

Wheeler, D. J. & Chambers, D. S. (1992). Understanding statistical process control. ISBN 0-945320-13-2.

Wheeler, D. J. (1999). Understanding variation: The key to managing chaos (2nd ed.). SPC Press. ISBN 0-945320-53-1

Why honesty is the best policy: Corporate deceit is a slippery slope. The Economist. Retrieved January 10, 2016, from Economist.com.

Why management by objective is unsustainable. (February 6, 2015). Forbes leadership. Retrieved June 17, 2016, from http://www.forbes.com/sites/georgebradt/2013/02/06/why-management-by-objective-is-unsustainable

Wichura, M. J. (2006). The coordinate-free approach to linear models. Cambridge series in statistical and probabilistic mathematics. Cambridge. Cambridge University Press

Wilson, B. (2014). Five-by-five whys. Retrieved October 7, 2014, from http://www.Bill-Wilson.net.

Wise, S. A. & Fair, D. C. (1998). Innovative control charting: Practical SPC solutions for today's manufacturing environment. ASQ Quality Press.

Wojdyla, B. (). The top automotive engineering failures: The Ford pinto fuel tanks. *Popular Mechanics.*

.Wolferen, V. (1990). The enigma of Japanese power. New York. Vintage.

Yoshikawa, E. (1956). The Heike story: A Modern translation of the classic tale of love and war. New York. Alfred A Knopf.

1.

About the Author

Adrian Davieson, PhD, is the author of 10 bestselling books: *Management in Troubled Times; Ebola: Stigma and Western Conspiracy; Nemesis; Identity Thieves and Swindlers; Twisted Intentions; Buhari's Way; Boko Haram and Its Suicide Squad; Deadly Odyssey; A Poetry of Contemporary Times; The Hunt for a Notorious Terrorist*; among others. Dr. Davieson is a scholar, and a businessman cum salesman of international repute, who combines charisma and in-depth knowledge of world affairs, in the pursuit of his esteem goals. With more than 10 bestselling books and counting, he is probably one of the most prolific writers of all time. As a writer, he shows versatility in his writings, covering topics ranging from terrorism, social misadventures, global economies, political dichotomy, to everyday living. His versatility and profound knowledge of world affairs has earned him numerous accolades and renown, worldwide.

Married with four adoring children, Dr. Adrian Davieson lives in his adopted state of Texas, where he has lived his entire adult life.

For inquiries and feedback, please contact the author at: adavieson@yahoo.com; adavieson@aol.com, or at 281-250-2480, or follow him on twitter, facebook, and instalgram.

www.ingramcontent.com/pod-product-compliance
Lightning Source LLC
Chambersburg PA
CBHW070225190526
45169CB00001B/85